# Amazing Bible Facts

## A Great Way To Test Your Knowledge

Wanda Reed

WestBow
Press
A Division of Thomas Nelson

*WestBow Press books may be ordered through booksellers or by contacting:*

*WestBow Press*
*A Division of Thomas Nelson*
*1663 Liberty Drive*
*Bloomington, IN 47403*
*www.westbowpress.com*
*1-(866) 928-1240*



*ISBN: 978-1-4497-1344-7 (sc)*
*ISBN: 978-1-4497-1345-4 (e)*

*Library of Congress Control Number: 2011924749*

*All quoted scripture is from King James Version of the Bible*



*WestBow Press rev. date: 3/25/2011*

# Preface

I want to thank my husband David, and my two daughters, Stacie Wilson and Crystle Reed for their love, help, patience, understanding and prayers in helping me get this project put together that the Lord placed upon my heart.

This book was designed to help us get a deeper understanding of God and His Word. To help us get back to where we used to be when we first got saved, when we got excited about everything we read in the Bible. It is to help us want to go deeper in our walk with Him, and as we read to take and just pause and think about what He is doing or saying, or what actually is taking place in that particular verse.

God is calling His people to come back to the holy and righteous living that He has instructed us to live in His Word, to be full of faith and excitement for Him and about Him. Everything we read in the Bible about His relationship with different ones, and the things He did in their lives, He will do in each and every ones' life today that truly believes in Him.

Expect Him to be the God of the Bible in your life and watch things begin to happen.

* Enoch and Elijah are the only 2 people in the Bible who never died. (Gen. 5:24, 2 Kings 2:11)

* Jubal is Cain's great, great, great, great grandson, and he was the 1st musician. He created the harp and flute. (Gen. 4:21)

* There are "6" different men in the Bible named "Ishmael," but only "1" named "Isaac."

* Deborah was a prophetess, the only female judge of Israel, a singer, and a courageous military leader. (Judges 4-5)

* Miriam was Praise and Worship leader, and the 1st woman mentioned in the Bible as a prophetess. (Ex. 15:20)

**Adam lived to be**
**________years old.**

* Ishmael's family grew into what are now the people of Arabia.

* "God" is mentioned approximately 4,379 times in the Bible.

* God made the 1st set of clothing. He made it out of animal skins. (Gen. 3:21)

* In the beginning God made water come up out of the ground to water all of the land, because He had not yet sent rain. (Gen. 2:5-6)

* God Himself breathed life into man's nostrils. (Gen. 2:7)

* Adam was the only man to ever name his wife.

* Adam named his wife Eve. (Gen. 3:20)

* Adam and Eve's first-born child, Cain, committed the 1st murder. (Gen. 4:1, 8)

* Adam lived to be 930 years old. (Gen. 5:5)

* Methuselah was the oldest person whom ever lived. He died at the age of 969 years old. (Gen. 5:27)

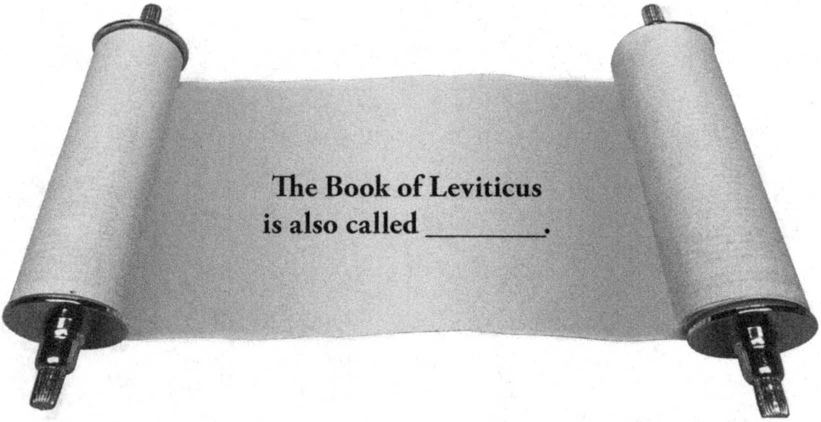
The Book of Leviticus
is also called ________.

* Arphaxed was the third son born to Shem, Noah's son. He was born 2 years after the Flood. (Gen. 11:10)

* Noah's son Shem, was 98 years old when he was in the Ark during the Flood. (Gen. 11:10)

* Shem lived to be 600 years old. (Gen. 11:12)

* Noah lived to be 950 years old. (Gen. 9:29)

* When God called Abram to leave his country and relatives, to go to a land that He would show him, he was 75 years old. (Gen. 12:4)

* The Year of Jubilee took place every 50 years.

* During this time all debts were cancelled, slaves were freed, all land that had been taken away to pay a debt went back to the original owners.

* The purpose of this was to give everyone the opportunity to start over, economically and socially. (Lev. 25:8-55)

* Aaron, Moses' older brother, was the 1st priest of Israel.

* The 3rd book in the Old Testament is Leviticus; it means "Book of the Levites." It is also called, "The Priests' Manual."

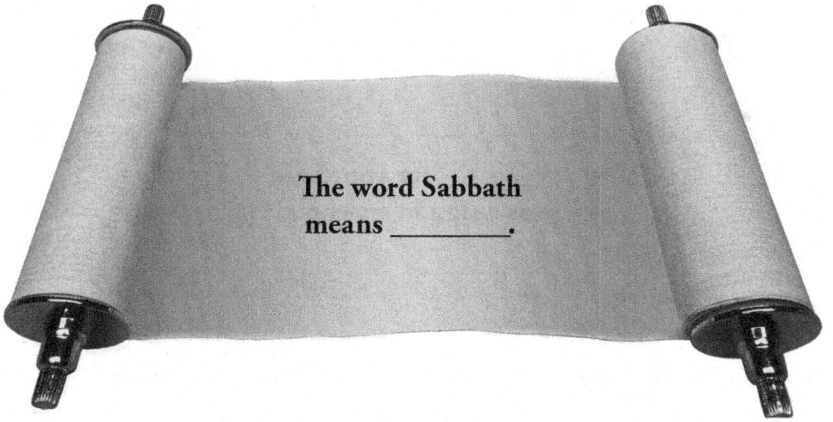


* In the great city of Babylon, the walls surrounding the city were so wide that 6 chariots could drive side by side along the tops of the walls.

* In 1947, in the Qumran Caves, the Dead Sea Scrolls were discovered.

* They were found stored in clay jars.

* In Biblical times, clay storage jars were used to store foods, wine, oil and valuable scrolls.

* In Biblical times, most houses were small and had outdoor kitchens.

* A lot of houses were so small they didn't have much room for furniture, so everyone slept on mats, and then they would roll them up in the morning.

* It was cooler in the evenings so the roof was a favorite place to sleep in warm weather.

* In the ruins of Capernaum, historians believe that the house they found was the home of the Apostle Peter and his family. This house was later enlarged and used as a church.

* At harvest time, God had the Israelites deliberately leave behind some of the crops for the poor and travelers passing through.

* They would search through the orchards and fields and take all of the leftover produce they could find. This part of the harvest was called "gleaning."

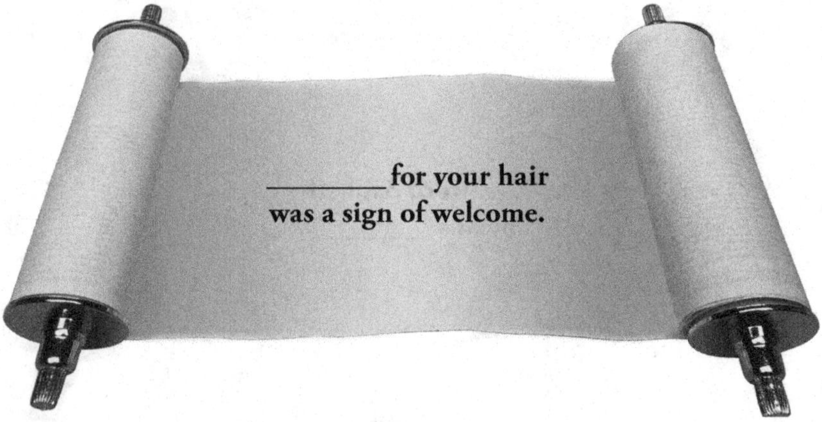
________for your hair
was a sign of welcome.

* Ruth, in the Book of Ruth, was a gleaner.

* She was a poor widow in the fields of Boaz.

* Boaz ordered his men to leave extra grain for her to take home.

* The word Sabbath is from the Hebrew word meaning "Stop."

* A beautiful head of hair was a sign of great beauty to the Israelites. Men and women both wore their hair long.

* People would put oil on their hair for festivals, because anointing your hair with oil was a sign of joy and good fortune.

* They would also have extra oil for their guests, and would offer it to them as a sign of welcome.

* A timbrel is similar to a tambourine and was mainly played by women while they sang and danced.

* To the Israelites, names were believed to describe a person's character and purpose that God had planned for them.

* When a person experienced a spiritual change, or when God chose a special purpose for them, sometimes God Himself would change their name.

Sarah lived to be
________years old.

* Esther and Ruth are the only 2 books in the Bible named after women.

* Hebrew physicians only treated minor ailments, set broken bones and bandaged wounds.

* The people believed going to the doctor was a waste of time; they just trusted God to heal them.

* The most important and dangerous job in the royal court was that of a cupbearer.

* It was the job of the cupbearer to taste the King or Queen's drink, to make sure no one had put any kind of poison in it.

* The Book of Mark records more miracles that Jesus performed than any other of the 4 Gospels.

* Asaph wrote 12 of the Psalms. He was not only a Priest, but he was also Praise and Worship leader.

* God told Abraham that his descendants would be oppressed as slaves in a foreign land for 400 years.

* Later after the death of Abraham the Israelites were enslaved in Egypt for 400 years.

* God also told Abraham that He would deliver them and that they would leave with a lot of wealth.

Isaac lived to be
________years old.

* God used Moses to deliver them out of Egypt. (Ex. 3-14)

* As they were leaving God also had the Egyptians look favorably on the Israelites and give them clothing, silver and gold. (Ex. 12:35-36)

* God told Abraham about this over 250 years before it happened. (Gen. 15:12-14)

* Sarah, Abraham's wife, lived to be 127 years old. (Gen. 23:1)

* Abraham lived to be 175 years old. (Gen. 25:7)

* In Abraham's day there were no undertakers or funeral homes, the friends and relatives would prepare the body for burial.

* Burial would take place the same day because of the warm climate.

* In Genesis 18, it tells how one day around noon time, 2 angels and the Lord came in bodily form to sit and talk with Abraham.

* They were there for several hours, because Abraham had Sarah and his servant prepare food for them, then they sat and ate.

* Abraham's servant, Eliezer and his 10 camels, had been traveling for a week when he met Rebekah, Isaac's future wife.

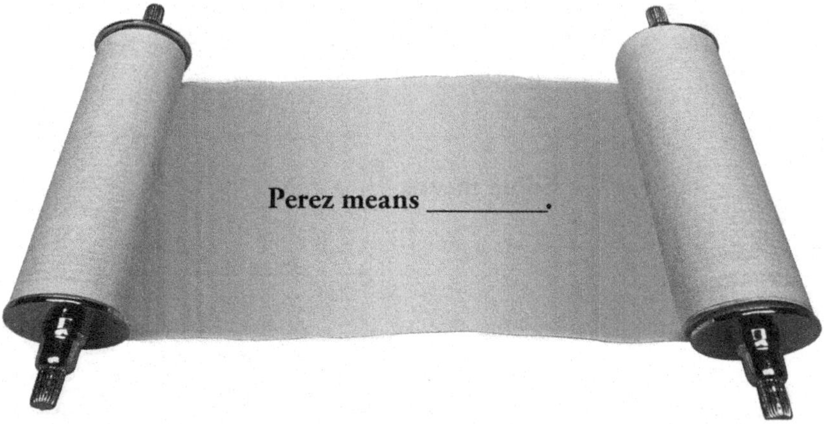


* So when Rebekah offered to give Eliezer's camels water she was taking on a huge job; it takes about 25 gallons of water to quench the thirst of one camel and he had 10, so that's 250 gallons of water. (Gen. 24:18-21)

* Isaac was approximately 37 years old when his mother, Sarah died.

* Isaac and Rebekah were married for 20 years before they were able to have children.

* After 20 years Isaac and Rebekah gave birth to twins, Esau and Jacob.

* Isaac lived to be 180 years old. (Gen. 35:28)

* Esau, Isaac's 1st born, had 2 wives with the same name, Basemath, which means "fragrant." (Gen. 26:34)

* Leah had the honor of being the mother of Levi and Judah.

* The Tribe of Levi and the Tribe of Judah came from Levi and Judah.

* These 2 Tribes played the most significant role in the history of Israel.

* The priesthood came from the Tribe of Levi.

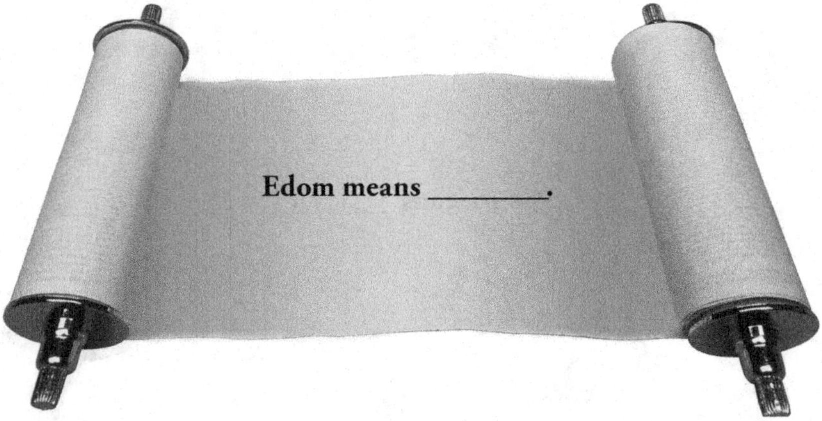


* Jesus Christ the Messiah came from the Tribe of Judah.

* Jacob's son, Levi, lived to be 137 years old. (Ex. 6:16)

* Kohath, Levi's son, lived to be 133 years old. (Ex. 6:18)

* Er, Judah's son was a wicked man in the Lord's sight, so the Lord took his life. (Gen. 38:7)

* Perez means "breaking out."

* During birth his twin brother, Zerah stuck his hand out 1st, so one of the midwives tied a scarlet ribbon on it thinking he was going to be the 1st one born.

* Instead, Zerah pulled his hand back in and Perez was born 1st. (Gen. 38:28-30)

* Esau was also known as Edom meaning "red" because he gave his birthright to his brother for a bowl of red stew. (Gen. 25:30)

* Esau was also very red and hairy when he was born. (Gen. 25:25)

* Within a 13 year period in Joseph's life he was thrown in a pit, sold into slavery by his brothers, put in prison and became 2nd in command in Egypt.

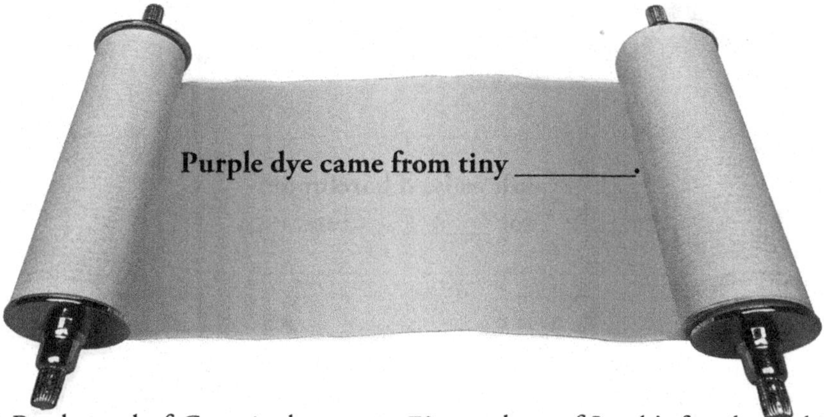
Purple dye came from tiny ________.

* By the end of Genesis there were 70 members of Jacob's family in the land of Egypt. (Gen. 46:27)

* There were different levels of slavery in Egypt.

* Some slaves worked long hot hours in the mud pits; others were skilled carpenters, jewelers and craftsmen.

* But they were all watched by ruthless slave drivers at all times.

* Amram, Moses' father, lived to be 137 years old. (Ex. 6:20)

* Built in 232 A.D., in the Syrian Desert at Dura-Europas, is the oldest surviving Christian meeting house.

* It has a baptismal basin and paintings of Jesus' life.

* The word "baptism" comes from a Greek word meaning "immerse" or "dip."

* The word "baptism" 1st appears in Matthew 3:7.

* In Biblical times cloth in the color purple was a symbol of power and wealth.

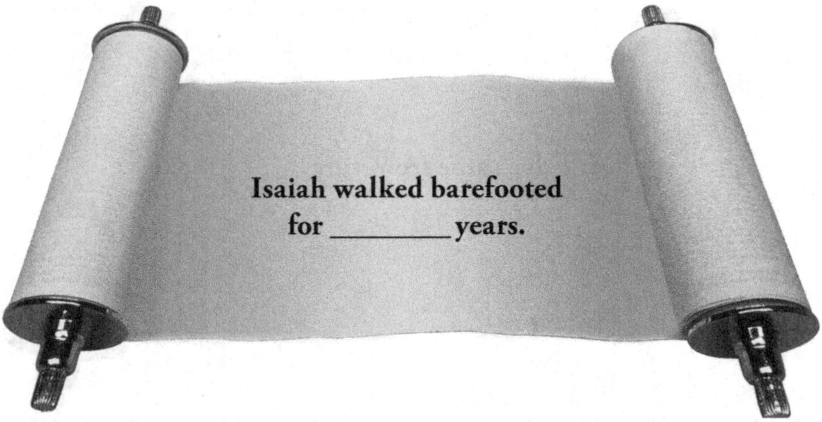
Isaiah walked barefooted
for ________ years.

* Paul's first convert in Europe, Lydia, sold purple cloth for a living. (Acts 16:14)

* Purple dye was made from tiny sea snails found in the Mediterranean Sea.

* Purple cloth was expensive; it would take the dye from 10,000 snails to get enough dye to color one robe, because each snail only yielded only a drop or so of dye.

* In Biblical times most people wore sandals.

* Shoes or boots were worn only by the very rich and the Romans.

* Only the very poor or those that were very active in worship and prayer went barefooted.

* The Prophet Isaiah walked naked and barefooted for 3 years.

* God had him do this to symbolize the humiliation, enslavement and poverty that God was going to bring upon Egypt and Ethiopia. (Isaiah 20:3)

* Some sandals were made of wood, some of fiber, like reeds woven together, but the majority of them were made with leather soles.

* In Biblical times children's toys were made from materials that were readily available, such as clay, wood, stone or pieces of cloth.

* The earliest rattles were made of dried, hollow gourds with loose, dried seeds moving around inside.

* Older children helped their families with housework, farming or watching over the younger brothers and sisters, but they still found time to play.

* The older children played catch with nuts, stones, pieces of fruit or balls.

* The timbrel is a small hand-held instrument much like the tambourine. They were 1st made by stretching 2 thin layers of animal skin over a round or triangular wooden frame.

* Warriors were welcomed home with the playing of timbrels.

* Women played the timbrels and danced in wedding processions and at banquets.

* When an honored guest or relative was going on a journey, the women of the household sent them on their way while dancing to the beat of the timbrels.

* The timbrel was one of the instruments that prophets listened to when they were seeking a Word from God.

* A tunic was an undergarment made from woven linen or wool.

* To make a tunic they would take a rectangular piece of cloth fold it widthwise, and then sew it up the sides.

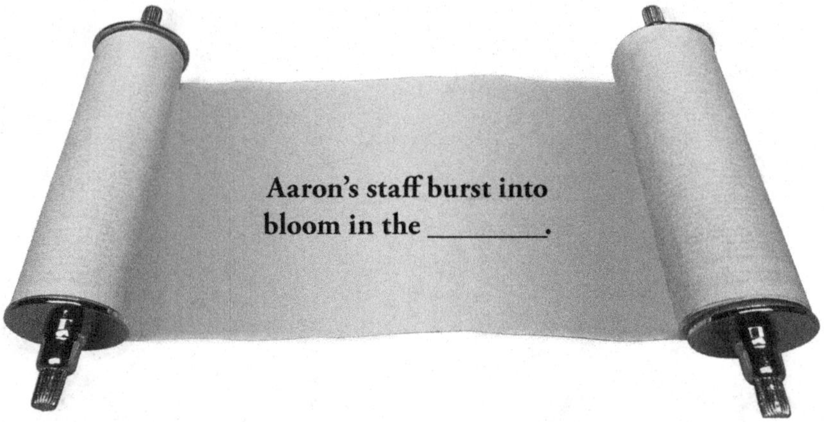
**Aaron's staff burst into bloom in the ________.**

* There were holes for the arms and a slit for the head.

* A man's tunic was only calf length and was off white with red, yellow or black stripes.

* A woman's tunic came to her ankles and was sometimes dyed blue with a village pattern embroidered around the neck.

* When a man pulled up his tunic and tucked it in his belt, it was called "girding up his loins," which meant he was getting ready to work, run or fight.

* Cloaks were worn over tunics and were usually made of thick wool.

* Cloaks were made by sewing strips of brown material together and then sewing it at the shoulders.

* Slits were cut in the sides for the arms and the hem was often fringed. A part of the cloak could also be pulled up to cover the head.

* A rod or staff was a branch that was cut from a tree. In the Bible they were often a symbol of Kingly authority or divine power.

* Rods are branches that are shorter and thicker than staffs.

* When all 12 Tribes of Israel placed their staffs in the Tabernacle Aaron's staff was the only one that miraculously burst into bloom.

_______ was served
at almost every meal.

* By his staff doing this God was showing them that Aaron was His choice as High Priest.

* The 1st person after the Flood to plant a vineyard, make wine and get drunk was Noah. (Gen. 9:20)

* As grapes ripened on the vines in July, August and September, the farmers in ancient Israel built small huts made of woven branches or a stone tower in their vineyards and temporarily moved in to guard their crops against hungry animals and thieves.

* Scattered throughout Israel ruins of these towers can still be found today.

* Some grapes were left on the vine for fresh fruit.

* Some grapes were spread out on the rocks to dry into raisins.

* Most grapes were used to make wine.

* Wine was served at almost every meal.

* Harvesting the grapes was hard work. But it was also a time of rejoicing with friends and families who gathered together to help with the harvest.

* They would all share the latest news and stories, and have outdoor feasts with singing and dancing.

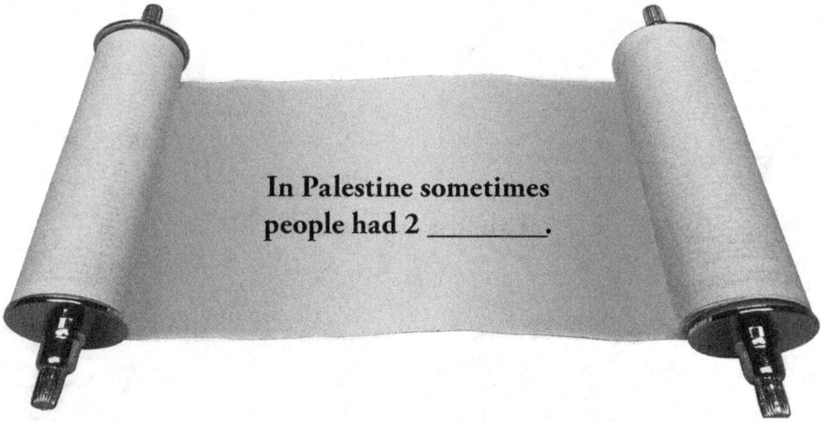
In Palestine sometimes
people had 2 ________.

* At every meal bread was served as the basic food.

* Food in general was described as "bread."

* In daily life breaking or sharing bread with others was very important.

* People sealed agreements, contracts and even marriages with the breaking of bread with one another.

* Bread also had religious significance, 12 fresh loaves of bread were brought to the Temple on the Sabbath and placed on a table in the Most Sacred part of the sanctuary where only priests could enter.

* At the Last Supper, Jesus and His disciples also shared bread together. (Matthew 26:26)

* Jesus also referred to Himself as "The Bread of Life." (John 6:48)

* Bread and milk sometimes was all a family had for a meal.

* Starting around Jesus' time it was customary in Palestine when a family had a burial cave they would also have a "second burial."

* The 1st burial occurred as soon as someone died. They would first place the body in a burial cave, usually on a shelf that was cut into a rock wall.

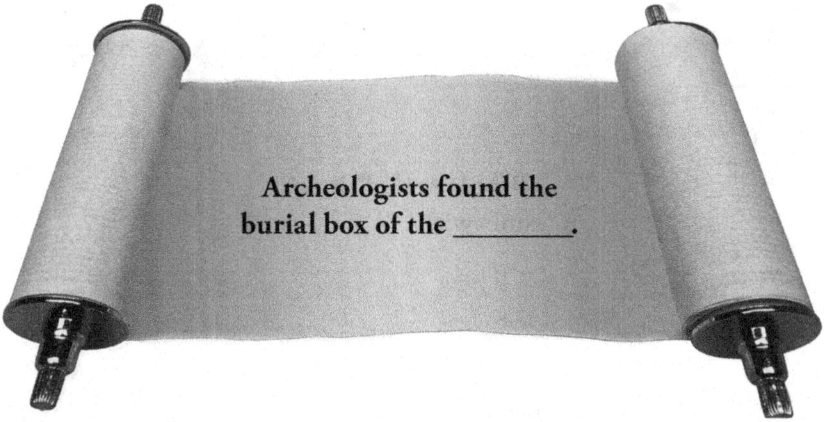
**Archeologists found the burial box of the ________.**

* The 2nd burial would take place later when only the skeleton remained. The bones were then collected and buried a 2nd time in a box, which also contained the remains of other ancestors.

* This box was known as an "ossuary." It was left in the cave either on the floor or in a small niche.

* These burial boxes were small and usually made from limestone.

* They would usually have elaborate carvings on them and the family name carved into it.

* These burial boxes measured only about 20 to 30 inches long and 10 to 20 inches high and wide.

* In 1990, archeologists unearthed the tomb of the Caiaphas family.

* Inside there was a burial box bearing the name of the High Priest Caiaphas who presided over the High Court that tried Jesus.

* In the days of the Old Testament, Inns had no roofs. Some were fenced in but they were more like campgrounds positioned around a well.

* Inns did not serve food, so travelers brought their own food and slept on the ground under the stars.

* In Jesus' day, Inns near or in towns were crude buildings with small rooms.

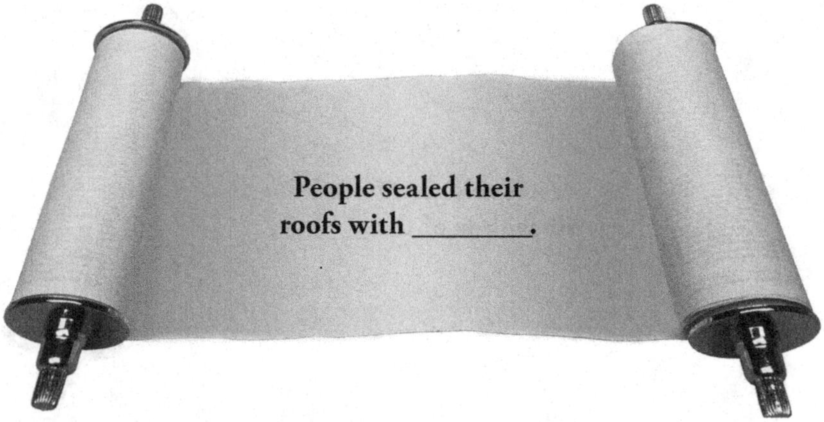
**People sealed their**
**roofs with ________.**

* Most of them served food and many had courtyards where the guests' animals could be tied up for the night.

* Other Inns were just local villagers' houses with spare rooms for rent.

* An Inn is where "The Good Samaritan" took the beaten Traveler to recover, located somewhere between Jerusalem and Jericho. (Luke 10:33-36)

* On an old road between Jerusalem and Jericho still stand today the ruins of a large Inn from Jesus' time.

* Professional carpenters and masons worked only on public buildings or homes for the wealthy.

* With friends helping them most families built their own homes, mostly single story houses with open courtyards.

* First the family would lay a foundation from stones gathered in the fields.

* Next, most people outside the city would use mud bricks to build their walls.

* People in the cities in Jesus' day generally used square stones to build their walls.

* But most all of them used a mortar of wet mud to hold the bricks or stones together.

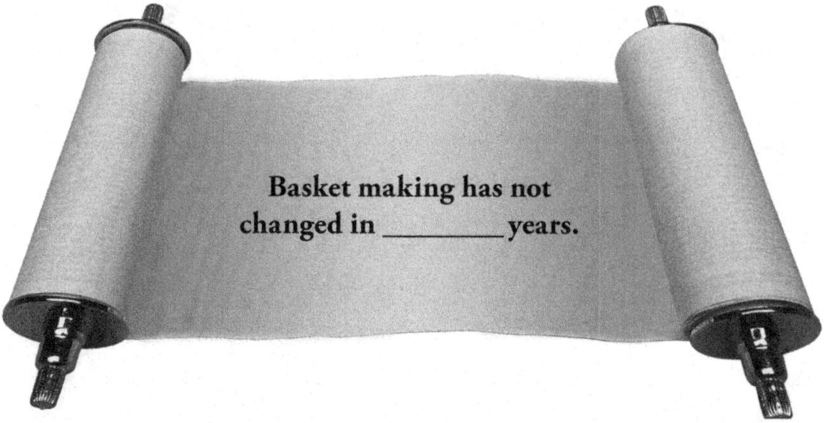
**Basket making has not changed in ________ years.**

* To create a roof they would lay large wooden beams across the tops of the walls to support a flat roof.

* They would then weave reeds or brushwood into panels and place them across the beams. To seal the roof they would then spread mud over the panels. (Deut. 22:8)

* To seal the walls they would plaster the outside walls with lime.

* To create a floor most people would just smooth and pack the ground into a solid surface.

* Sometimes a family might pave it with tiny stones or cover it with a layer of plaster.

* Most houses had to be repaired every year because during the rainy season the mud-plaster walls and roof would crumble.

* Ancient records show that Ramses II had his name stamped on each brick made for that city. He was possibly the Pharaoh during Moses' time.

* People in the Middle East are well known for their basket-making they can make baskets in a lot of different sizes and shapes. To this day basket-making techniques are the same as they were 5,000 years ago.

* There are 2 basic types of baskets, coiled and woven.

* Some of the coiled baskets are so tightly made they are almost waterproof.

In jail Peter was chained
to ________ guards.

* In Egypt the baker would carry his baked goods in baskets. (Gen. 40:16)

* The Apostles gathered up leftovers in 12 baskets, after Jesus fed over 5,000 people with 5 loaves of bread and 2 fish. (Matthew 14:20)

* When Moses was a baby his mother placed him in a basket and sent him down the Nile River to save his life. (Ex. 2:3)

* In Damascus, Paul was put into a large basket and was lowered from a window to escape his would-be killers.

* Basket makers did not just make baskets; they made mats, room partitions, fish traps and sandals as well.

* In Biblical times carpenters would grow their own trees for the building projects because there were no lumber yards.

* They would choose the right size and kind of tree for the job, cut it down, and then they would trim it to the correct size and shape they needed.

* Carpenters made a variety of items such as: beds, tables, footstools, chairs, bowls, spoons, storage boxes, roof beams, doors, window frames and supports, wooden plows, yokes for oxen, tools for processing grain and chariots in times of battle.

* Some carpenters who lived by the sea became shipbuilders.

* King Solomon hired 1,000's of carpenters to build the Temple.

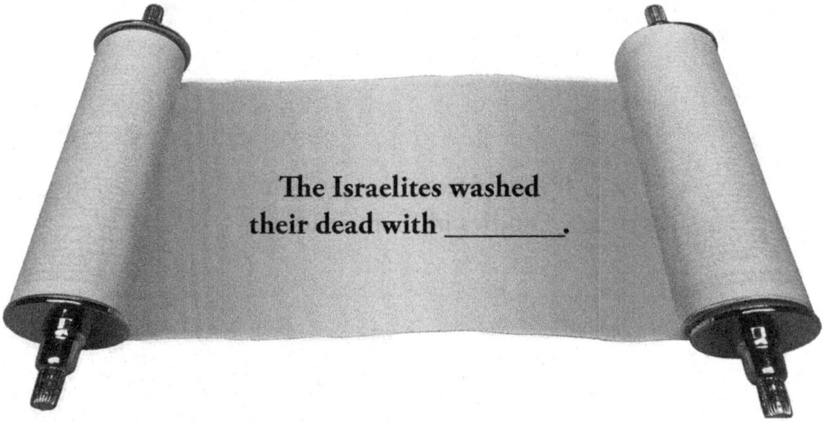
The Israelites washed
their dead with ________.

* Ancient prisons were mainly used like holding cells for people who were awaiting trial, execution or some other form of punishment.

* Some prisoners were also bound in chains.

* When Peter was in a jail in Jerusalem he was chained to 2 guards while other guards guarded the iron gates leading to the room.

* But late one night an Angel suddenly appeared in Peter's cell and his chains miraculously fell off.

* Without the guards even realizing Peter was gone the Angel led Peter to safety. (Acts 12:5-10)

* Some prisoners were bound in stocks.

* Stocks were wooden frames with holes that pulled and held the prisoner's legs painfully apart.

* Burying the dead was an important and serious responsibility that was not taken lightly.

* It was important to bury a relative immediately; failure to do so was showing disrespect for the dead.

* The Israelites would wash their dead with oil.

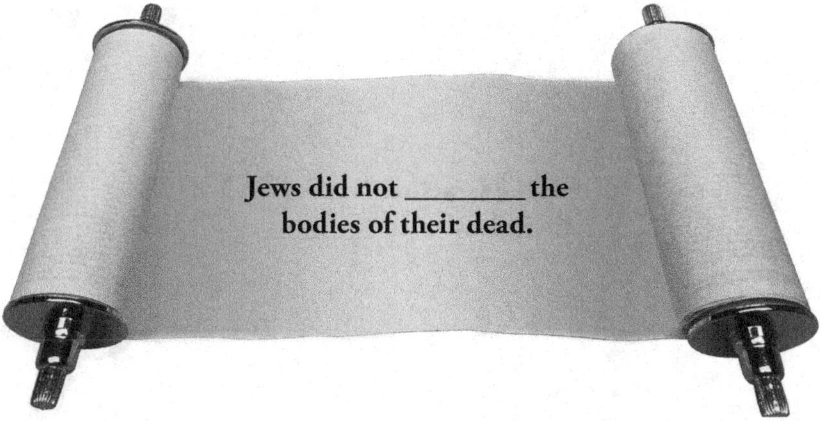

Jews did not ________ the
bodies of their dead.


* They would then anoint them with spices and perfumes, wrap the body in stripes of cloth and then place a linen cloth over their face.

* Nicodemus a Pharisee who was a follower of Jesus spread aloe and myrrh over Jesus' body in the tomb.

* In a funeral procession the mourners would carry the wrapped body to the family tomb.

* Musicians would be hired to play sad tunes on flutes. They would also pay women to wail for the deceased.

* If a stranger passed a funeral procession he was expected to join the procession and also wail for the deceased.

* Jews did not use wooden coffins or embalm the bodies of their dead. They believed the body should go out of this world the same way it came in.

* Luke, who wrote the 3rd Gospel, was a "beloved physician." (Colossians 4:14)

* When the Pharaoh of Egypt wanted someone to interpret his dreams, his cupbearer introduced him to Jacob's son Joseph.

* Through God Joseph interpreted the dream and saved Egypt and his family from famine.

* One of the most beautiful places on earth was the Garden of Eden.

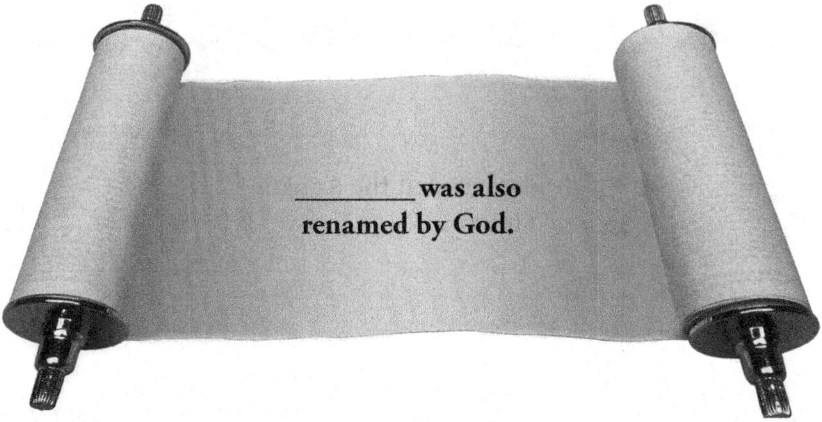


* Animals of every kind lived peacefully side-by-side with one another.

* There was no pain, sorrow or sadness there until sin entered the picture.

* God gave Adam the job of "Caretaker" of the Garden; one of Adam's responsibilities was to name all the animals.

* The main rivers of Mesopotamia are the Tigris River and the Euphrates, which originally flowed from the river in the Garden of Eden. (Gen. 2:10-14)

* According to scholars, somewhere in Mesopotamia, which is now Iraq, is where the Garden of Eden was originally located.

* Abram's parents gave him a name that meant, "The Father is exalted."

* But when God chose Abram as the 1st patriarch he became Abraham, "The Father of Many Nations." (Gen. 17:5-15)

* Sarai, his wife, became Sarah, "A Mother of Nations." (Gen. 17:16)

* Another person who was renamed by God was Jacob.

* The name Jacob may be translated as "he takes by the heel."

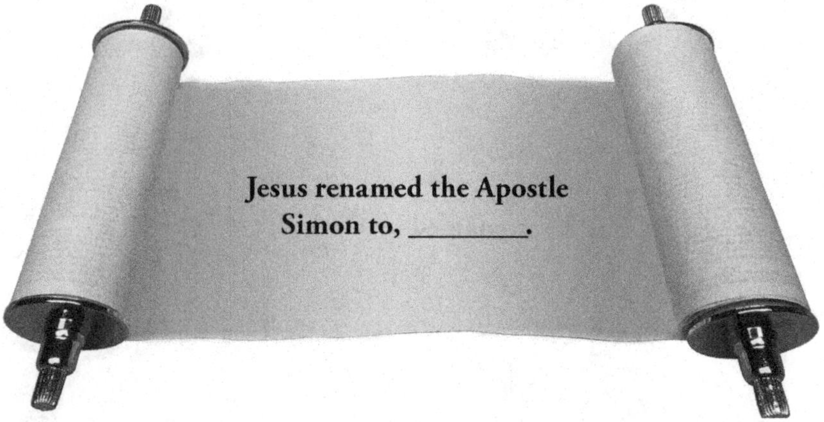
Jesus renamed the Apostle
Simon to, ________.

* Jacob was actually born holding the heel of his twin brother, Esau.

* The name Jacob also has a second more negative meaning, "deceiver."

* Jacob deceived his father to steal his brother Esau's birthright.

* Later, God sent an angel to Jacob and Jacob wrestled with him all night until dawn.

* At daybreak God gave Jacob the new name of "Israel," meaning "he strives with God." (Gen. 32:28)

* Just like God, His Father, Jesus also changed people's names.

* In the New Testament Jesus changed the name of the Apostle Simon, to "Peter."

* Peter means "Rock," because he was the Rock on which Jesus was to build His church upon. (Matthew 16:18)

* Paul was in a different situation, he was a Jew but he was also a Roman citizen.

* Paul's Jewish name was Saul.

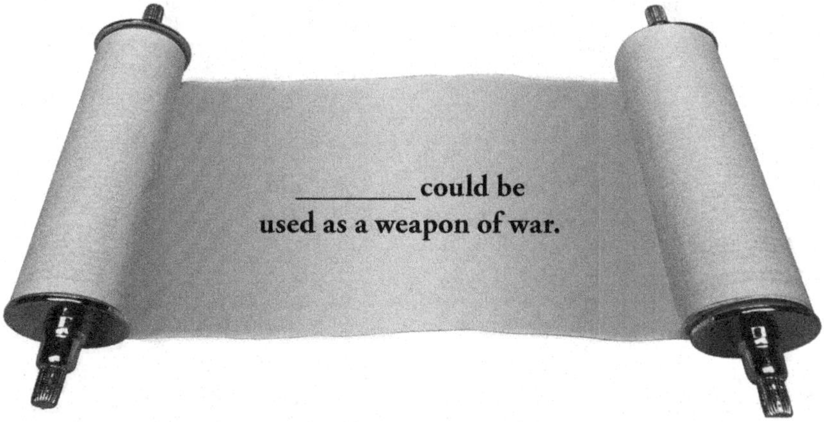
_______ could be
used as a weapon of war.

* His Roman name was Paul.

* After Saul was converted and became a follower of Jesus he went by his Roman name Paul.

* On the south side of the Dead Seas there were strange formations on the surface of the water where salt had collected.

* Ancient Israel had an abundance of salt because of this.

* The Israelites would get their salt by mining these salt formations.

* The outer layer was removed and the usable salt would be washed and pounded into fine granules.

* Salt was needed to keep food from spoiling and to add flavor to food as well.

* Salt was an important symbol as well as an everyday item.

* Sharing a meal seasoned with salt was one of the ancient customs used to seal an agreement.

* When 2 nations entered into a peace treaty salt was often given as a gift.

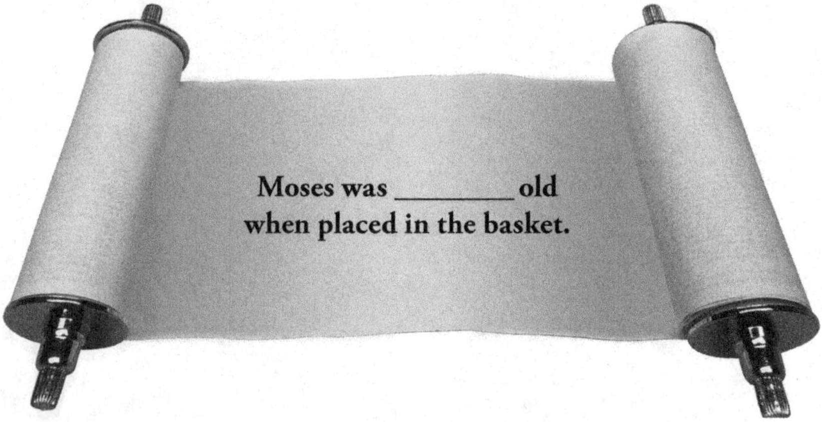

Moses was ________ old
when placed in the basket.


* Meat offerings to God were seasoned with salt.

* This was done as a reminder of God's covenant with His chosen people; a covenant that would last forever. (Lev. 2:13)

* In the Bible salt represents loyalty and trustworthiness.

* Salt could also be used as a weapon of war.

* Sometimes nations would throw salt onto their enemies' fields to kill their crops, turning it into a wasteland.

* Jesus said we are "the salt of the earth."

* But when we stop trying to affect others around us in a positive way we are worthless to God's Kingdom.

* We become like salt that has lost its flavor, "It will be thrown out and trampled underfoot as worthless." (Matthew 5:13)

* Unlike the Israelites, other people in Biblical times could only produce salt by evaporating seawater in great shallow pools.

* Miriam watched over her little brother Moses when their Mother hid him in the reeds in the Nile River.

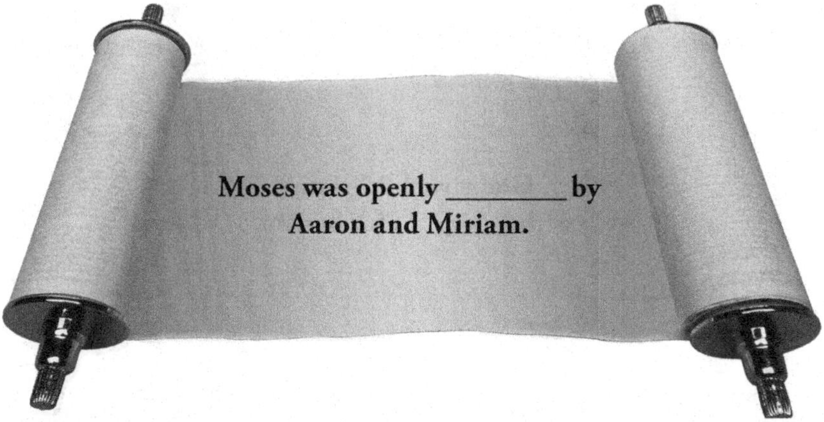
Moses was openly ________ by
Aaron and Miriam.

* When Pharaoh's daughter came to bathe at the Nile River she saw the basket and had her maid go and fetch it.

* When Pharaoh's daughter opened the basket Moses cried and she had compassion on him and she realized that he was one of the Hebrews' children.

* Miriam boldly stepped forward and asked the Pharaoh's daughter if she would like her to go and get her a Hebrew nurse to take care of the child.

* So Miriam went and got Moses' Mother to take care of him. (Ex. 2:4-8)

* Moses was 3 months old when his Mother put him in a basket and placed in the Nile River to save his life. (Ex. 2:2)

* Since Moses' Mother, Jochebed loved her son and God, and was obedient to save his life; God reunited her with her son.

* Moses' Mother was able to take care of him, her own child, for awhile and get paid for it. (Ex. 2:9)

* Moses' life was also saved by Miriam's quick thinking of approaching Pharaoh's daughter.

* Miriam became one of the spiritual leaders of her people when God led them out of Egypt, along with her brothers, Moses and Aaron.

* Miriam was not only a prophetess, but she was a Praise and Worship leader as well.

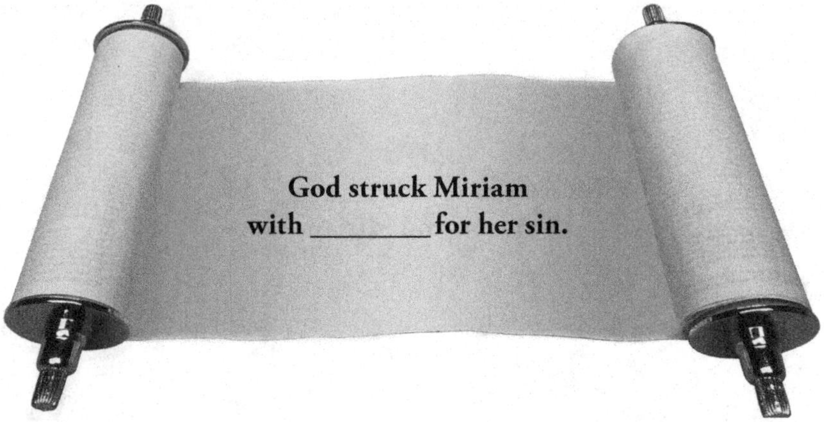
God struck Miriam
with ________ for her sin.

* She led the women in a victory dance to praise God for their new freedom, when God miraculously parted the Red Sea and led them across on "dry" land. (Ex. 15:20)

* Moses was a Praise and Worship leader as well.

* Moses led the people in song, also, after crossing the Red Sea.

* When the Israelites were in the wilderness, Aaron and Miriam openly criticized Moses for marrying an Ethiopian woman.

* They also openly expressed their jealousy of his authority as the Leader of the Israelites.

* They thought since they were spiritual leaders as well that they should be on the same level as Moses.

* This angered God and He told them, "There is no other one that I speak face to face with like I do Moses."

* So God struck Miriam with leprosy for her sin.

* She had to stay outside of the camp for 7 days until she was healed. (Numbers 12:1-15)

* The Hebrews thought education was very important.

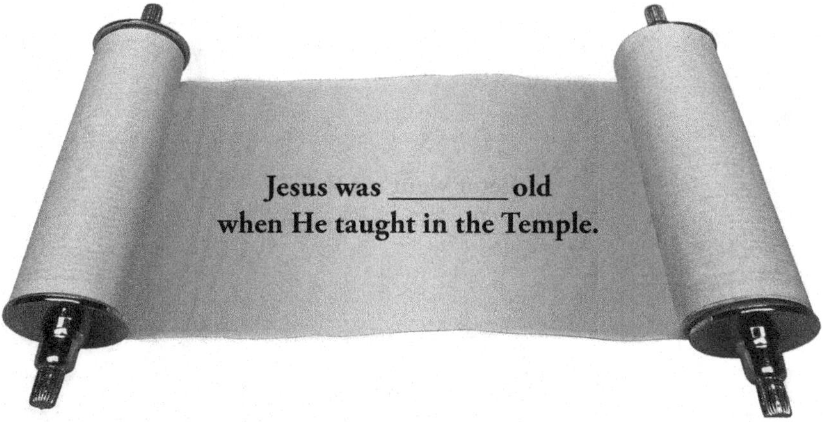

Jesus was ________ old
when He taught in the Temple.


* But in earlier times there were no formal schools.

* So the parents taught the boys a craft or trade.

* They would teach the girls household skills.

* It was up to the parents to teach their children about God's laws and the history of the Israelites.

* The local synagogues began serving as schools around the 6th century B.C., but only boys and men attended.

* They would go to the synagogues to study the Law; which are the teachings found in the first 5 books of the Old Testament.

* The 1st elementary schools came a few centuries later. Boys from 6 to 16 were required to attend, but it was optional for girls.

* "Scribe" was another name for teacher, later they were called "rabbis."

* There were no desks or chairs so the students would gather around the teacher and sit on the floor.

* The teacher would teach them the Hebrew alphabet and passages from the Law.

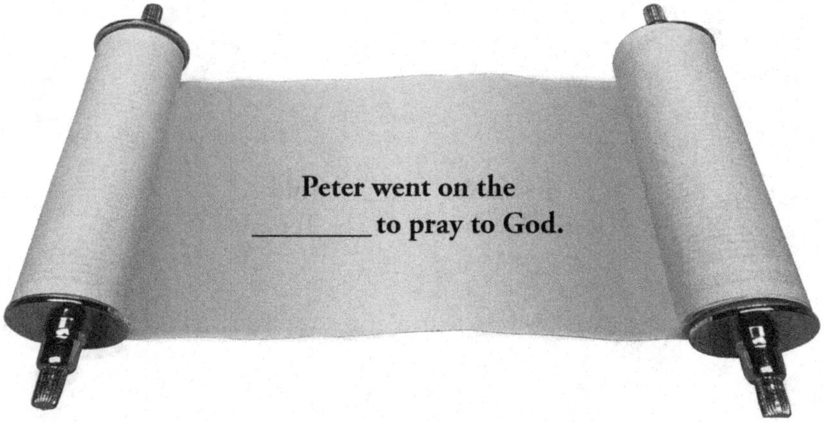
Peter went on the
________ to pray to God.

* He would also have them memorize the passages and recite them out loud.

* Scholars interpretations of the Law, as well as the Law itself were studied by older students.

* The teacher would sometimes engage the older students in a debate over the meaning of certain passages.

* Elders at the Temple in Jerusalem were amazed with the deep understanding of God's Word by the 12 year old Jesus. (Luke 2:46-47)

* Just enough mathematics, science and geography were studied by Jewish boys to better understand the Law that's in the first 5 books of the Old Testament.

* In Biblical times a roof was not just protection from the weather; it was an important part of the home.

* People would entertain guests, work and sometimes sleep on the roof on hot summer nights.

* Jewish Law required that a parapet, a low wall, to be built on edges of roofs to keep people from falling off or rolling off in their sleep. (Deut. 22:8)

* Sometimes women would dry and grind grain for their bread, prepare simple meals, or weave cloth on their rooftops.

* Putting up tents on the roof gave people guest rooms.

The 1st Roman road was
over ________ miles long.


* From his rooftop is where King David first saw the beautiful Bathsheba. (2 Samuel 11:2)

* The Apostle Peter prayed to God from a rooftop. (Acts 10:9)

* Jesus told His disciples, "What I whisper in your ears, shout from the housetops for all to hear." (Matthew 10:27)

* When Jesus was teaching in a crowded house, 4 men made a hole in the roof and lowered a man sick with palsy down through the hole.

* They knew if they could just get their friend in front of Jesus that he would get healed, and he did. (Mark 2:3-5)

* The Roman Empire fell in the 5th century A.D., leaving behind a network of 50,000 miles of roads that reached every part of the empire.

* In 312 B.C. the Romans began building their 1st road.

* This road went more than 350 miles south. It went from Rome to Brindisi.

* It was named "The Appian Way" after its builder Appius Claudius Caecus.

* Paul walked on the Appian Way when he walked to Rome from the Bay of Naples. (Acts 28:15)

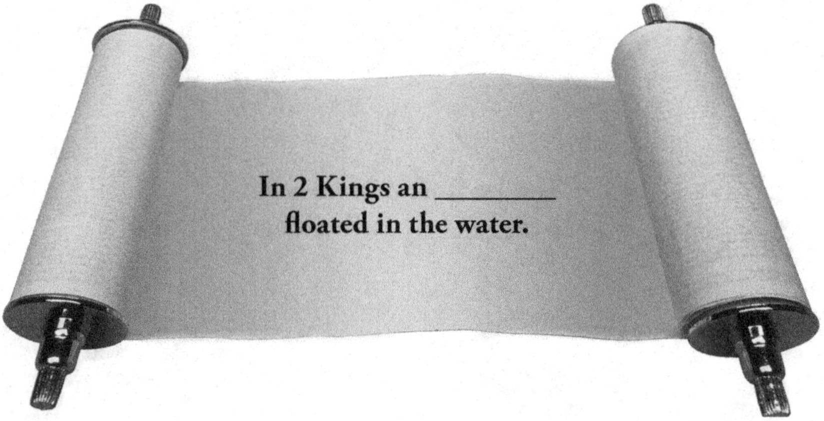
In 2 Kings an ________
floated in the water.

* The main Roman roads were often more than 20 feet wide.

* They would make them by cutting a trench in the ground and then they would fill it with slabs of local rock and clay.

* They would make the center slope downward slightly to let rain water drain off.

* Cars today still travel on some of these roads with foundations that are more than 2000 years old.

* The word "praise" is mentioned approximately 240 times in the Bible.

* Israelites would offer sacrifices, or gifts of their best animals or crops in worshipping God.

* Sacrifices were made to "praise or thank God."

* Sacrifices were made to "atone for sin."

* Sacrifices were made to "celebrate a special occasion."

* The first mention in the Bible of the offering of sacrifices was with Cain and Abel in Genesis 4:3-5.

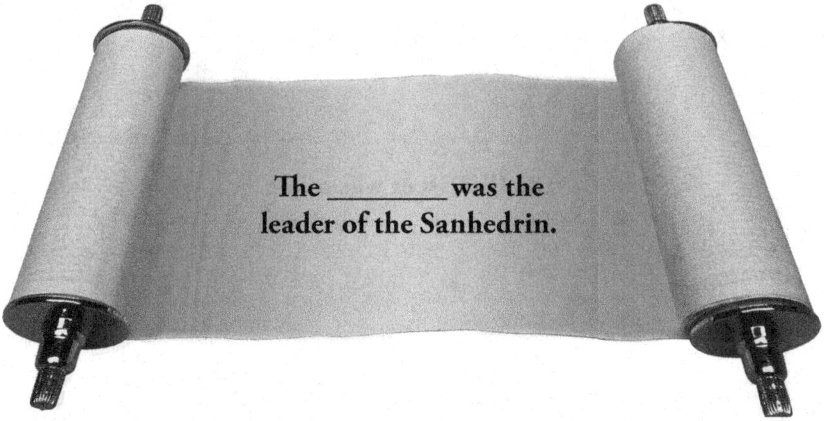
The ________ was the
leader of the Sanhedrin.

* Today, because of Jesus' death, no further sacrifices are needed because Jesus was the perfect, sinless sacrifice. (Hebrews 9:11-14)

* Where an "ax head floated" in the water is in 2 Kings 6:1-6.

* The Romans ruled Palestine in Jesus' time.

* For the most part, the Jewish people governed themselves in things that did not concern Rome.

* The local government was a council called the "Sanhedrin."

* The Sanhedrin was made up of 71 Jewish priests, scribes and political leaders.

* The Sanhedrin had the power to arrest and try people in both civil and criminal cases. (Acts 4:1-7)

* The Sanhedrin had to get the approval of the Roman Governor to condemn a prisoner to death, because they did not have the power to do so. (Mark 15:1-15)

* Like the U.S. Supreme Court of today, disputes over interpretations of the Jewish Law were settled by the Sanhedrin.

* The High Priest was the leader of the Sanhedrin.

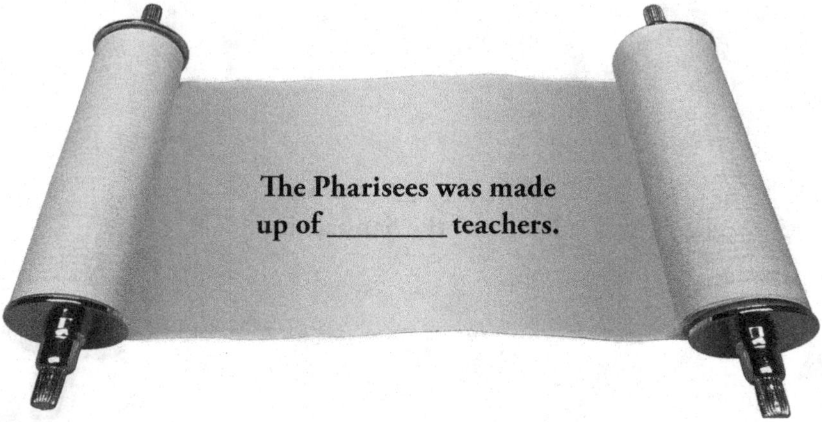
The Pharisees was made
up of ________ teachers.

* When holding a trial, the High Priest sat in the middle with the members of the Sanhedrin in a semi-circle around him.

* They did this while several rows of students faced them and observed the procedures.

* When it was time to decide the guilt or innocence of someone the members of the Sanhedrin voted by standing up.

* They would start with the youngest member of the Sanhedrin standing first then each one followed until they reached the oldest member.

* While they were doing this 2 scribes recorded each and every vote.

* Guilty votes were recorded by one scribe.

* While innocent votes were recorded by the other scribe.

* Because the Sanhedrin could not sentence anyone to death, they had to send Jesus to be questioned by Pontius Pilate.

* They knew that was the only way they could get Jesus to be sentenced to be crucified. (Matthew 26:59)

* The Sanhedrin were not mentioned by name in the Bible when the Gospels talk about the High Priest and others putting Jesus on trial. (Mark 14:55)

Paul was a ________
when he met Jesus.

* The Sanhedrin, Israel's most important court, had some Judges that were Pharisees as well. (John 3:1-2)

* The "Pharisees" main priority was the obeying of Jewish "Law."

* 6,000 teachers in Jesus' time made up the group called the Pharisees.

* The name Pharisees means "separated from others."

* The strict way they observed Jewish Laws may have led to this name.

* Certain kinds of people such as, all non-Jewish people, anyone with a disease and tax collectors were all avoided by the Pharisees. (Luke 18:9-14)

* The Apostle Paul was a Pharisees when he met Jesus on the road to Damascus. (Acts 9:3-7)

* Most Jews agreed they should obey the Laws, God gave Moses.

* But the Pharisees had a lot of extra laws, called the "Oral Laws."

* No work is to be done on the Sabbath. This is clearly and simply stated by the Ten Commandments. (Ex. 20:9-11)

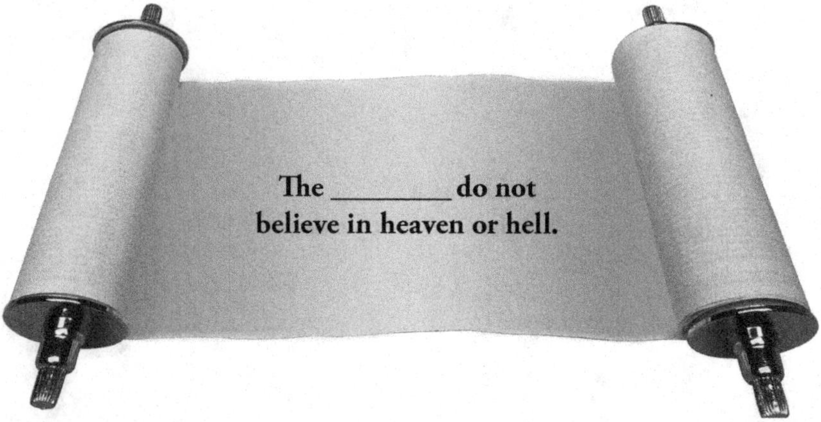

The ________ do not
believe in heaven or hell.


* But not being allowed to carry something more than a couple of yards on the Sabbath, was one example of many where the Pharisees added some of their own "Oral Laws." (Mark 3:1-6)

* They tried to say that Jesus disregarded the "Laws."

* Some of these laws, Jesus argued, were "manmade" and ignored the more important Laws of God.

* Laws such as those calling for fairness, mercy and faith. (Matthew 23:23)

* That statement angered them even more, which made them even more determined in their plot to kill Jesus. (Matthew 12:14)

* The "Pharisees" believed in the power of God and a bodily resurrection after death and eternal life.

* The "Sadducees" did not believe in the resurrection or life after death.

* The Sadducees believe that your soul dies with your body.

* The Sadducees also believe that everything that happens to you is the result of the good or evil that we do in life.

* The Sadducees also do not believe in heaven or hell.

* The word "earth" is first mentioned in the Bible in Genesis 1:1.

* The word "planets" is first mentioned in the Bible in 2 Kings 23:5.

* The word "kiss" is first mentioned in the Bible in Genesis 27:26.

* The word "kiss" is mentioned approximately "20 times" in the Bible.

* It is mentioned "9" times in the Old Testament and "11" times in the New Testament.

* The Bible has "1189" chapters.

* The Old Testament has "929" chapters.

* The New Testament has "260" chapters.

* The "middle" chapter in the Old Testament is Job 29.

* The "middle" chapter in the New Testament is Romans 13.

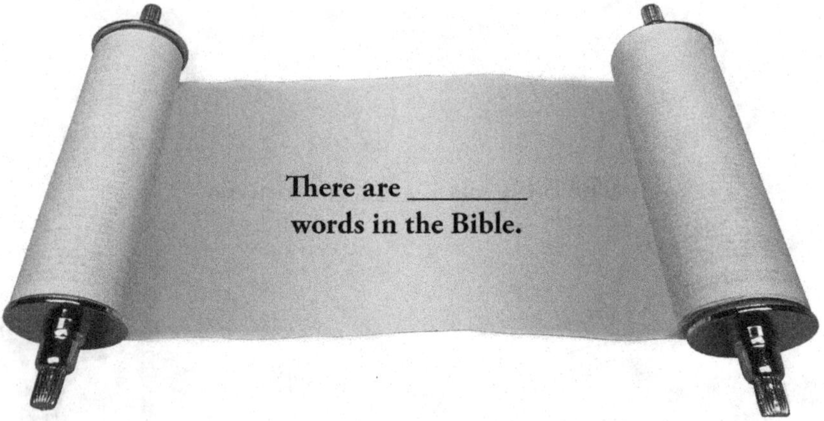
There are ________
words in the Bible.

* The "shortest" chapter in the Bible is Psalm 117.

* The "longest" chapter in the Bible is Psalm 119.

* There are "2" chapters that are "alike" in the Bible they are 2 Kings 19 and Isaiah 37.

* The Old Testament has "23,214" verses.

* The New Testament has "7,959" verses.

* The "middle" verse in the entire Bible is Psalm 118:8.

* The "middle" verse in the Old Testament is 2 Chronicles 20:17.

* The "middle" verse in the New Testament is Acts 17:17.

* The "shortest" verse in the Old Testament is 1 Chronicles 1:25.

* The "shortest" verse in the New Testament is John 11:35.

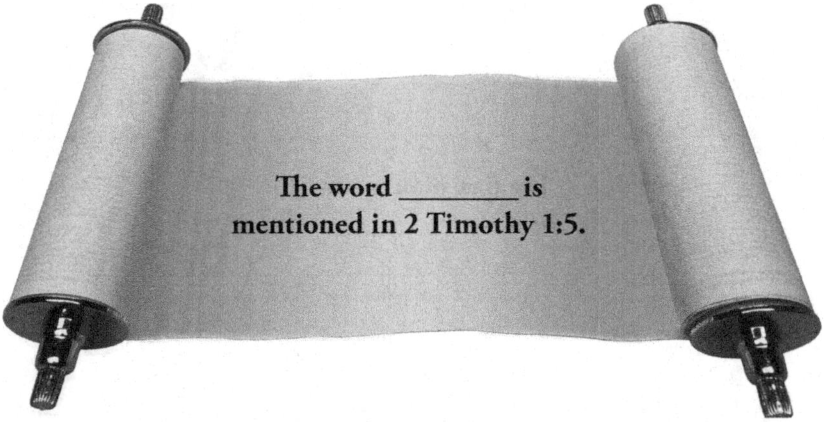
The word ________ is
mentioned in 2 Timothy 1:5.

* The "longest" verse in the Bible is Esther 8:9.

* There are "773,692" words in the Bible.

* There are "592,439" words in the Old Testament.

* There are "181,253" words in the New Testament.

* The "longest" word in the Bible is Maher-shalal-hash-bas in Isaiah 8:1, it has 18 letters.

* The word "eternity" is only mentioned "1" time in the Bible in Isaiah 57:15.

* The word "reverend" is only mentioned "1" time in the Bible in Psalm 111:9.

* The word "grandmother" is only mentioned "1" time in the Bible in 2 Timothy 1:5.

* The word "gnat" is only mentioned "1" time in the Bible in Matthew 23:24.

* The word "planets" is only mentioned "1" time in the Bible in 2 Kings 23:5.

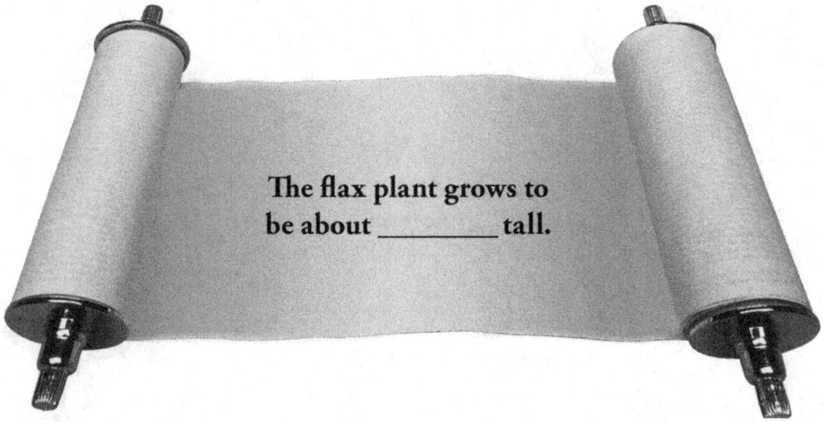

The flax plant grows to
be about _______ tall.


* The word "Lord" is mentioned "7,738" times in the Bible.

* The phrase that says "God helps those who help themselves," is not even in the Bible.

* The "1st words God spoke to man" are in Genesis 1:28.

* The word "angel" is mentioned "188" times in the Bible.

* The word "angel's" is only mentioned "2" times in the Bible and both are in Revelation, chapters 8:4 and 10:10.

* The word “angels” is mentioned “93” times in the Bible.

* The word “angels’ “ is only mentioned “1” time in the Bible in Psalm 78:25.

* The word “archangel” is only mentioned “2” times in the Bible in 1 Thessalonians 4:16 and Jude 1:9.

* A woman in Biblical times had many chores and among them was making clothes for her family.

* But before she could make the clothes she first had to make the thread.

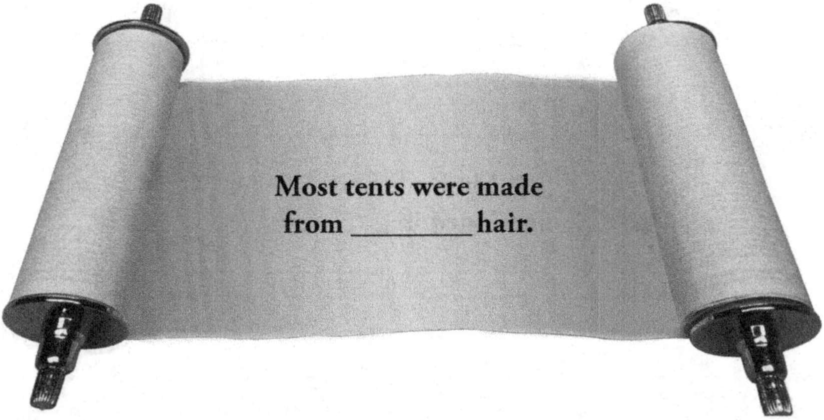
**Most tents were made from ________ hair.**

* They would get thread from two different sources such as, sheep’s wool or plant fibers, such as flax to make linen.

* Flax is a slender upright plant; the stem of the plant is used to make linen.

* The flax plant has small narrow leaves, blue flowers and slender stems that grow to be about 2 feet tall.

* Linseed oil is also made from flax seeds.

* To spin enough thread to make one robe it would take working 8 hours a day for more than a month.

* “Plying” or twisting 2 or 3 strands of fiber together was used to make thread stronger.
* The curtains in the Tent Sanctuary, the Tabernacle, where the Israelites worshipped God were woven of plied linen.
* In Biblical times the most popular choice for thread was wool or linen.
* Goat hair was stronger and water resistant, but it was very itchy.
* Mostly tents were made from goat hair.

Shofar is first
mentioned in ________.

* Shofars are holy trumpets made from rams’ horns.
* The Jewish New Year is still ushered in today with the blowing of shofars near Jerusalem’s western wall.
* The Bible mentions many instruments used in the Temple, but only the shofar is still part of Jewish worship today.
* The shofar can be used as a “call to arms.”
* The shofar can be used as a “call to worship.”

* The shofar can be used as a "command to assemble for an important event."

* The shofar can be so loud that one long blast from it can be heard for miles.

* "To signal the start of the Sabbath" the priest would blow the shofar each Friday during sunset.

* The priests would also blow the shofar at the "end of the Day of Atonement (Yom Kippur)."

* The shofar was also played with other musical instruments in the Temple.

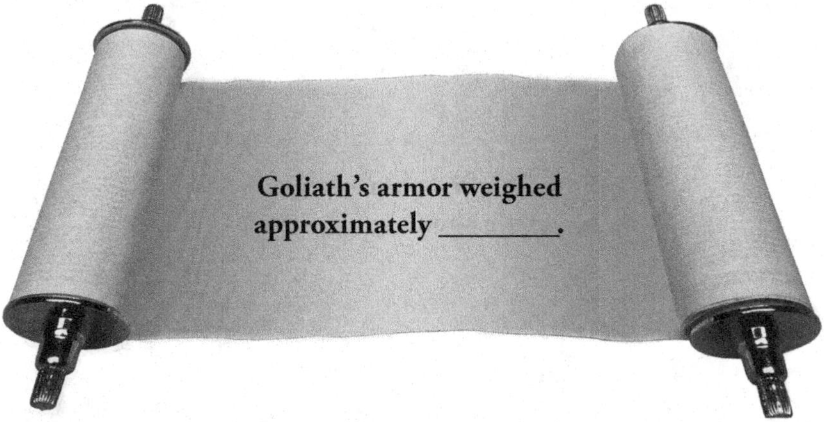
Goliath's armor weighed
approximately ________.

* The first time the Bible mentions the shofar is in the book of Exodus in chapter 19:13 then again in verse 16.

* At Mount Sinai as the Israelites were getting ready to assemble before God they heard a long loud blast from a ram's horn, and all the people trembled. (Ex. 19:16)

* The city of Jericho was surrounded by Joshua's army, 7 priests blew shofars as the people gave a battle shout.

* As a result "the wall fell down flat." (Joshua 6:20)

* The Prophet Isaiah promised that a shofar would sound when the Messiah comes to gather the faithful.

* "And it shall come to pass in that day, that the great trumpet shall be blown." (Isaiah 27:13)

* In Jesus' time gold and silver coins were the currency used.

* No image of a ruler or any other person was stamped on any Jewish coin.

* The Israelites believed that it was breaking the 2nd Commandment that forbids the worship of idols. (Ex. 20:4)

* Like a pound is today, in Old Testament times a "shekel" was a measure of weight.

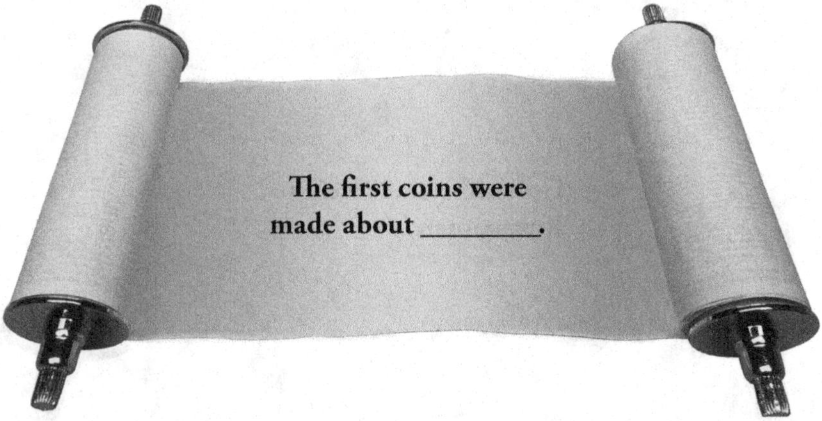
The first coins were
made about ________.

* By the time of the New Testament the term shekel also referred to a gold or silver coin of that weight, but it varied by country and time period.

* The shekel usually weighed about half an ounce or the weight of 4 quarters.

* The term shekel was also used to describe how much something weighed or what it was worth.

* When David killed Goliath, the Philistine giant, Goliath's armor weighed 5,000 shekels.

* In pounds that would be approximately "125" pounds.

* "2 shekels" would buy you a sheep.

* "1 gold shekel" or "15 silver shekels" would buy you an ox.

* "1 gold shekel" or "15 silver shekels" would buy you 2 tons of grain.

* Chunks of silver and gold were weighed and used prior to coins being made.

* Balance scales with stones that weighed a shekel were used to compare the chunks.

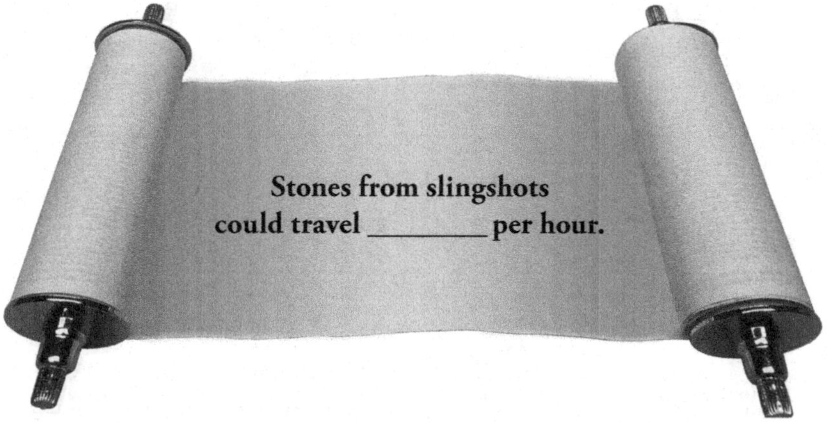
Stones from slingshots
could travel ________ per hour.

* About 650 B.C. the first coins were made.

* Workers began receiving coins for their pay.

* About "1 silver shekel" was a day's pay.

* Today a slingshot is considered a child's toy.

* But it was a serious weapon in Biblical times.

* Shepherds would use a slingshot to drive off wild animals.

* Stones coming from a skilled stone slinger's slingshot could reach 150 miles per hour.

* In battle soldiers would use the slingshot as a long range weapon.

* In the battle between the Israelites and the Tribe of Benjamin, Benjamin had 700 warriors who were left-handed, each of whom could sling a rock and hit a target within a hairsbreadth, without missing. (Judges 20:16)

* The slingshot that David used as a teenager is the most famous slingshot in the Bible.

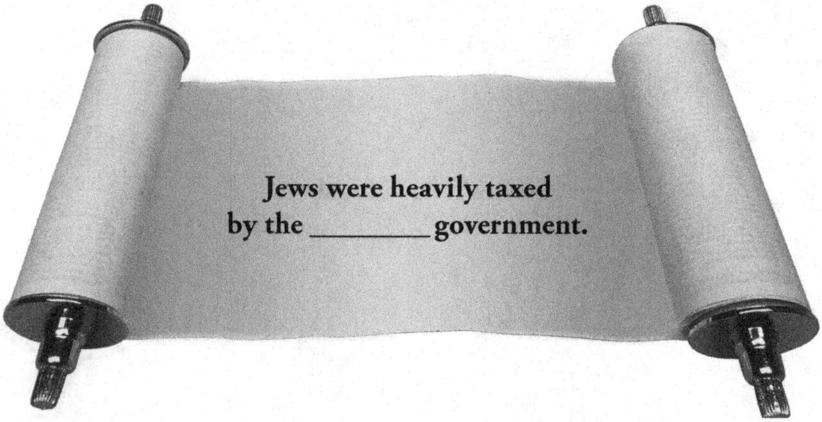
Jews were heavily taxed
by the ________ government.

* The young David used the slingshot to kill the over 9 foot tall Philistine, Goliath. (1 Samuel 17:32-51)

* At many of the Biblical sites that they have found today they have discovered round "sling stones" located there.

* But at some of the sites they have also found sling stones that were oval-shaped like "lead bullets."

* These stones had pointed tips on both ends and they had the name of the city, ruler or commander responsible for them inscribed on them.

* Even throughout the Bible people had to pay taxes.

* King Solomon had tax collectors in his kingdom.

* People paid their taxes in the form of goods like oil, wine or crops.

* Records were kept of the collections and everything was stored in the King's storehouses.

* The Roman government heavily taxed the Jews in Jesus' time.

* The Roman government allowed the tax collector to keep part of the money collected as payment for their work.

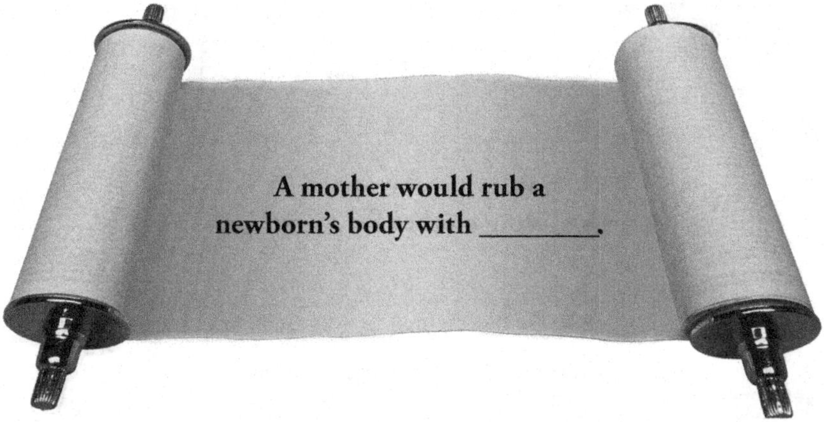
A mother would rub a
newborn's body with ________.

* The most hated people in the Holy Land in Jesus' time were the tax collectors.

* They hated tax collectors as much as they did thieves, murderers and traitors.

* Because they would overcharge the people so they could get rich.

* Zacchaeus in the New Testament was the chief tax collector of Jericho.

* He was one of those tax collectors that overcharged people.

* But when he met Jesus, Zacchaeus repented and gave the people their money back.

* The Apostle Matthew was a tax collector.

* In Biblical times the first thing a mother or mid-wife would do as soon as a baby was born was rub its tiny body with salt and olive oil.

* By doing this it would prevent the baby from getting any kind of skin infections that could make the baby sick.

* The next thing she would do is wrap the baby in "swaddling clothes" which are long narrow strips of cloth.

Babies were wrapped in
swaddling clothes for ________.

* Swaddling clothes are similar to bandages that we have today.

* The baby would be bound so tight in them it would look like an Egyptian mummy.

* They believed that binding the baby's legs straight and its arms at its side would make the baby's arms and legs grow straight and strong.

* The mother or nurse would unwrap the baby several times a day to change the cloth.

* Before rewrapping the baby she would rub it all over with oil, then powder it with powder made from myrtle leaves.

* They would do this process for approximately 6 months or more.

* In rural areas of the Middle East and in parts of Russia, they still wrap babies in swaddling clothes to this day.

* Nothing in the book of Genesis was written down until many years later.

* Up until then, the tradition of "storytelling" is what the Israelites used to pass down to the next generation all the events that had taken place in earlier times.

* Most of the time an elder would repeat the stories about Creation, Noah, the great Flood, Abraham and Isaac, and Jacob and his encounter with the angel.

King Herod built sports
arenas to honor ________.

* Preserving the history of the Israelites and their relationship with God was the responsibility of the "Professional Storyteller."

* They didn't begin writing these events down until about 1300 B.C.

* Moses was the first one to write these events down.

* They didn't have paper as we know it today so they wrote them on papyrus or leather scrolls.

* In the New Testament the early Christians also thought storytelling was very important.

* By word of mouth is how the Christians spread the news of Jesus' life and ministry.

* The Old Testament mentions the sport of wrestling.

* Jacob wrestled all night with what appeared to be a man "gripping him in a hold." Then the angel "strikes Jacob's hip" throwing it out of joint. (Gen. 32:24-25)

* "Hip and thigh" is an actual wrestling throw.

* Samson used this against his Philistine enemies. (Judges 15:8)

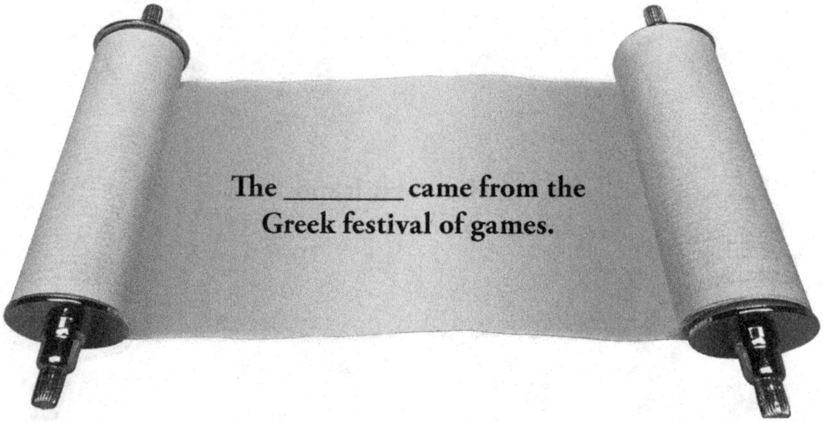
The ________ came from the
Greek festival of games.

* Playing sports while not wearing any clothing was introduced by the Greeks after they began settling in the Holy Land.

* King Herod the Great started a festival of games around 27 B.C. similar to those in Rome.

* Sports arenas to honor the new Roman patron Augustus Caesar were built by King Herod.

* Weight lifting, boxing, foot races and discus throwing were some of the events included in the games.

* Some Jews participated in the games but the devout Jews were angered by them and were opposed to them.

* One reason they were opposed was because the participants did not wear any clothing.

* The main reason was that they believed that it drew young Jews away from God and drew them to the pagan gods of the Greek culture.

* In referring to sports in 1 Corinthians 9:24-27, Paul said, "Just like runners do to win a race, we must also discipline ourselves in our walk and faith with God."

* Paul went on to say, "I have fought a good fight, I have finished my course, I have kept the faith." (2 Timothy 4:7)

* The first Greek festival of games was held in the 13th century B.C., in Olympia, Greece.

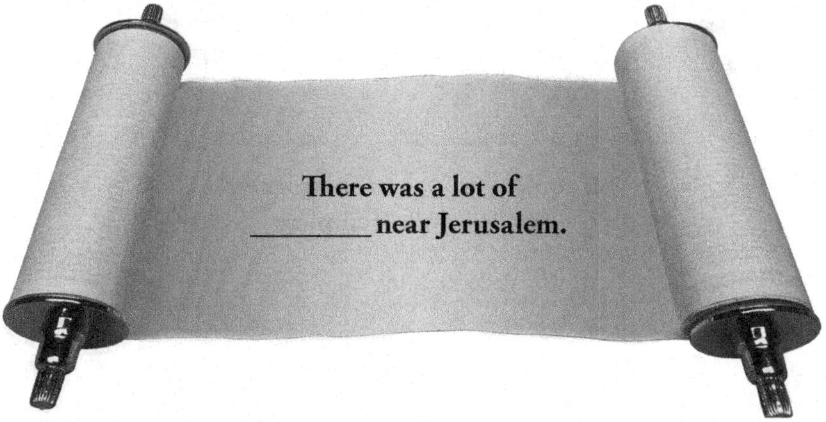
There was a lot of
________ near Jerusalem.

* This was about the time of the "Exodus."

* These games were the start of what is now called the "Olympic Games."

* Just like today, in Biblical times being a stoneworker was a very important occupation.

* Strength and precision were needed to do their difficult work.

* Sometimes no mortar was used on the walls so stones had to be precisely cut.

* A poorly squared stone would cause uneven layers and the wall could become unstable.

* If a wall were to collapse the heavy stones could crush the people below.

* There were not many skilled stoneworkers in Israel until late into the 10th century B.C.

* The Bible called stoneworkers "masons or hewers of stones."

* King Hiram of Tyre's experienced masons helped with all of King David and King Solomon's building projects in Jerusalem.

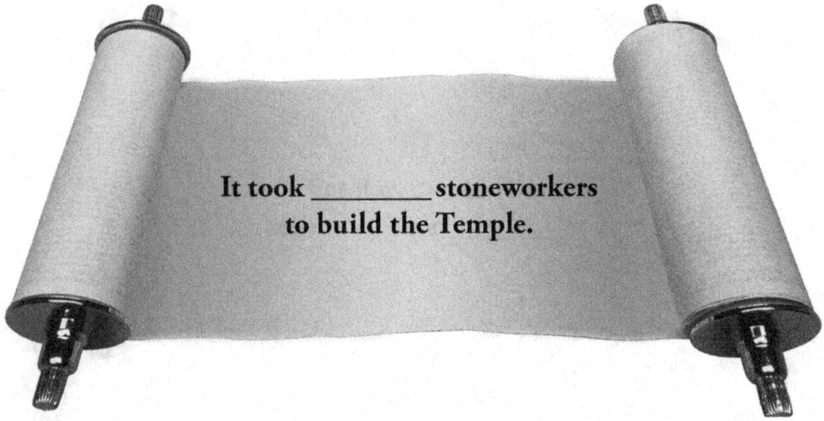
It took ________ stoneworkers
to build the Temple.

* For large structures the most used material was limestone.

* Limestone was easy to quarry and there was a lot of it near Jerusalem.

* Stoneworkers would split away stones in large irregular blocks.

* By looking for a natural crack in the stone they would then drive a wedge in to it until it broke off.

* Then they would break these large pieces down into the size they needed.

* Next they would take them to the building site and there they would finish shaping them and then put them in place.

* When they were building the Temple they had to do things in a different way.

* The Lord gave King Solomon specific instructions concerning the Temple.

* "And the house, when it was in building, was built of stone made ready before it was brought thither:"

* "So that there was neither hammer nor axe nor any tool of iron heard in the house, while it was in building." (1 Kings 6:7)

* In building the Temple in Jerusalem, King Solomon employed 80,000 stoneworkers to do the job. (1 Kings 5:15)

* Interpreting Biblical scrolls was the responsibility of highly educated men called scribes.

* Scribes taught gifted boys that went past the primary education.

* These boys would then be "ordained" as scribes or scholars upon completing their studies.

* Teachers sometimes lived and traveled with ordained scholars if they were considered experts in the Law.

* When they weren't teaching and working together to help the needy they were discussing scholarly matters with one another.

* Although Jesus lived like these scholars, His students, called disciples may not have been ordained scholars.

* Gamaliel was a respected Pharisee and scholar.

* He also is the one who stood up for the Apostles Peter and John, and advised the Jewish court not to persecute them. (Acts 5:33-39)

* Paul was also a student of his.

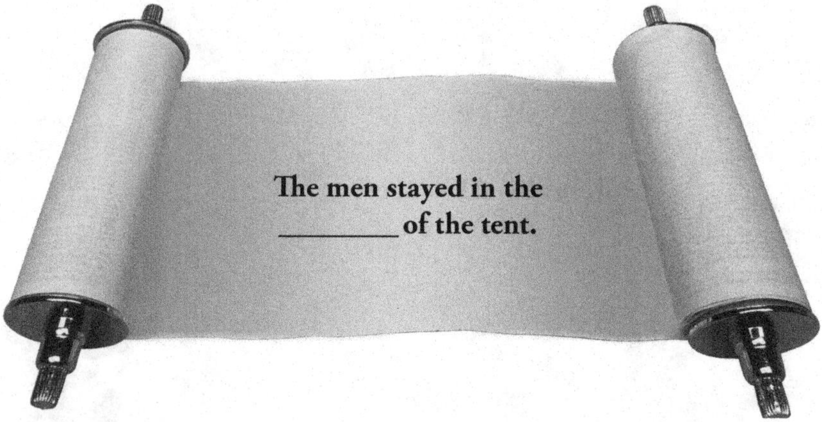
**The men stayed in the**
**_________ of the tent.**

* The Hebrews rarely lived in one place for very long during the time of Abraham, Isaac and Jacob.

* Hebrews lived in tents similar to the tents of today.

* Stretching cloth over vertical poles and driving pegs into the ground is how they made their tents.

* The tents were taller in the middle so that they sloped for the rain to run off.

* Before camel or goat hair was used to make tents animal skins were used.

* The tents of the wealthy had more poles.

* The tent was divided in half on the inside by a curtain.

* The women and children stayed in the back half of the tent.

* The men stayed in the front of the tent.

* In the past the Israelites lived in tents so much that even once they arrived in the Promised Land they would use the word "tents" in describing things in their conversations.

* In Jeremiah 10:20, for example the captives cry out, "My tabernacle is spoiled, and all my cords are broken:"

* "My children are gone forth of me, and they are not: there is none to stretch forth my tent any more, and to set up my curtains."

* While in the wilderness God would speak to Moses and anyone else that wanted to consult with Him in a "special Tent."

* This special Tent Moses called the "Tabernacle of the congregation" or "Tent of Meeting." (Ex. 33:7)

* Many nomadic herders in the Holy Land live in tents today.

* Even when the Israelites lived in permanent homes in the Promised Land, some of them would move into tents in the summer, because the tents were cooler.

* Shepherds slept in tents to protect their sheep in the fields.

* Hundreds of tents were used when armies went to war.

* In Biblical times making tents was a profitable profession.

* In the Holy Land tent making is still profitable today, because many still live in these types of homes today.

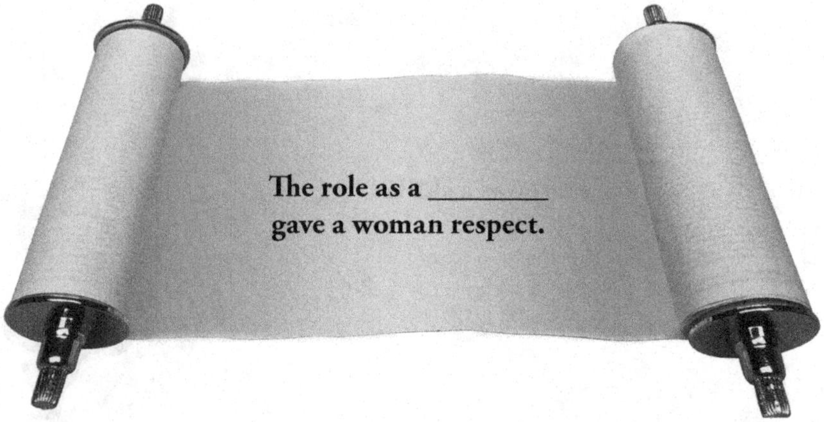
**The role as a ________**
**gave a woman respect.**

* Paul was a skilled tentmaker he used that to help support his ministry.

* Tents were usually dark in color as we read in the Song of Solomon: "I am black, but comely, O ye daughters of Jerusalem, as the tents of Kedar…" (Solomon 1:5)

* Most women stayed at home to take care of the house, their family and the animals in Biblical times.

* Grinding the grain and baking the bread was the woman's responsibility.

* Doing the spinning and weaving were also her responsibility.

* A woman's responsibility also was to do the cleaning and the washing.

* To prepare the meals everyday she would have to fetch water from the stream or from the village well.

* She couldn't sit down and eat her own dinner until her husband, all of his guests and everyone else had eaten.

* The women also had to work in the fields with the men in poorer families.

* The cooking and baking in wealthy families was done by servants.

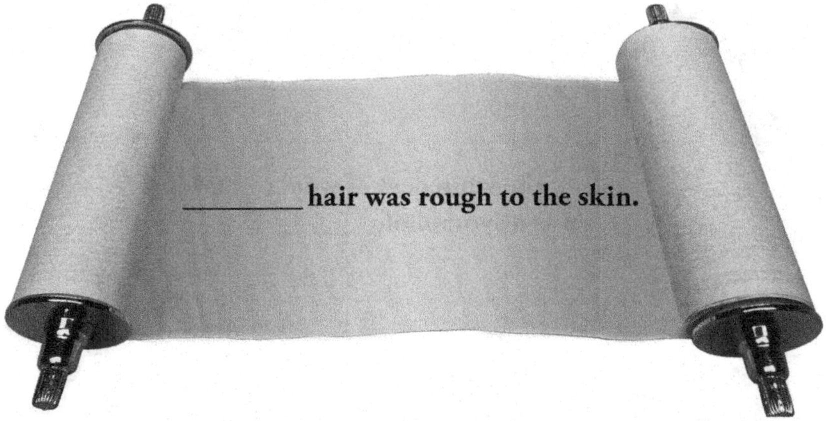
________ hair was rough to the skin.

* The woman of the house could then spend more time with her children.

* The role as a mother gained a woman respect.

* The 5th Commandment requires children to honor their father and mother.

* Equal authority over the family is given to the woman and the man by this Commandment.

* The woman had little power outside the home.

* Women were responsible for seeing that religious observances were kept in the home, but they were not allowed to enter the Temple for services.

* They were responsible for celebrating the Sabbath and keeping a Kosher home, according to the Law.

* Later when women were allowed to attend synagogue services they had to sit apart from the men.

* Many of Jesus' followers were women.

* Mary Magdalene was the most famous of these women.

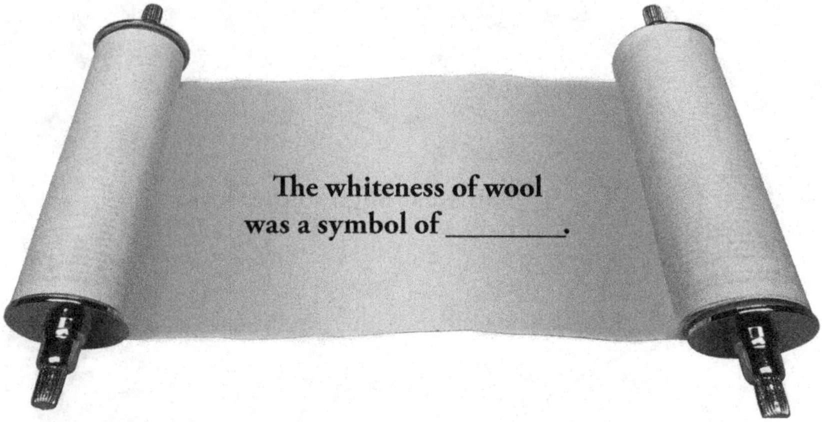
The whiteness of wool
was a symbol of ________.

* Although the warm material wool mostly comes from sheep, it can also be made from goat hair.

* Camel's hair was rough feeling to the skin.

* Linen was very expensive.

* Because of this most people wore wool clothing even though it was very hot.

* So wool became a valuable commodity.

* King Mesha of Moab and his people were sheep breeders.

* They used to pay King Ahab, the King of Israel, an annual tribute of 100,000 lambs and the wool of 100,000 rams. (2 Kings 3:4)

* In the Holy Land one of the main occupations was raising sheep.

* The wool was sheared from the sheep in the spring of each year.

* Shearing time was a time of rejoicing.

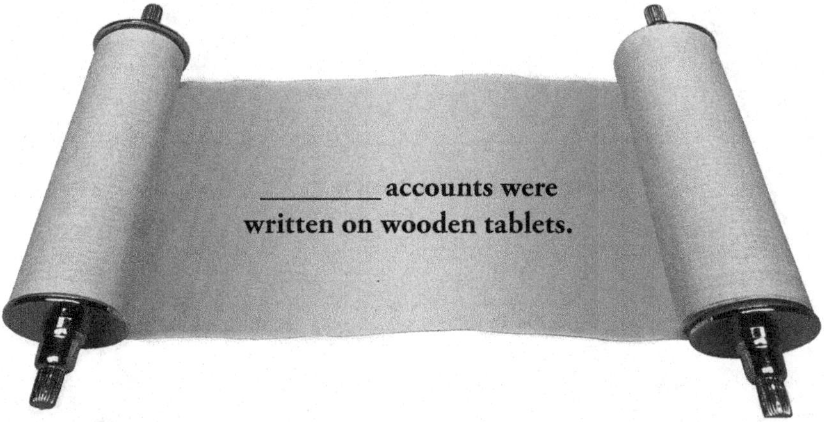
________ accounts were
written on wooden tablets.

* At this time a feast was prepared for shepherds and sheepshearers by wealthy sheep owners.

* One symbol of "purity" was the whiteness of un-dyed wool. (Isaiah 1:18)

* There were several different writing surfaces in Biblical times.

* The Ten Commandments were engraved on stone tablets.

* Some kings would chisel their decrees into the faces of cliffs so that everyone could see them.

* Broken pieces of pottery were sometimes used by school children to write on.
* Wax-coated wooden tablets were usually used to write business accounts on.
* Sometimes wood or soft metals were used to write upon.
* The Scriptures and other important documents were written on treated animal skins or "papyrus" during this time period.
* Papyrus is a tall water plant; it has stems 3 to 10 feet high.

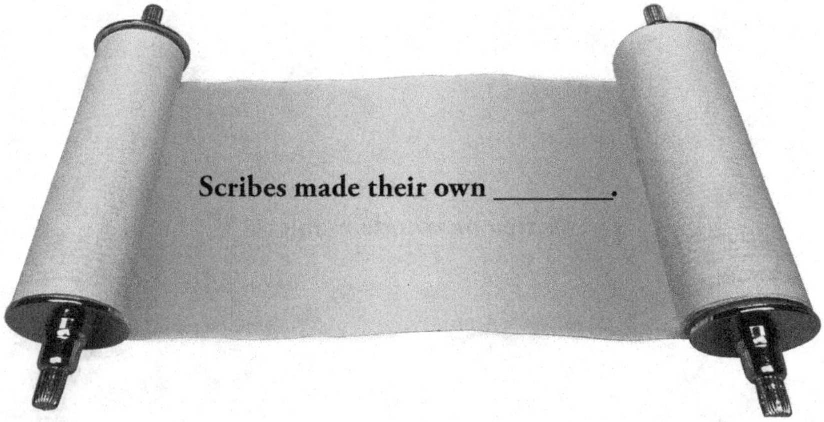


* To make writing paper they would take the pitch (the spongy tissue) from the stem and branches.
* Thin slices of it were taken and laid side by side.
* The whole thing was then soaked, pressed and dried.
* One side of a cured animal skin could be scraped smooth or the leather could be further refined into "parchment."
* "Scribes," professional writers, used ink to write on papyrus or parchment.

* Even though papyrus is rare today it can still be found in Egypt.

* Scribes would use pens they made themselves to write with.

* They would use a knife to split the end of a thin reed, and then they would shape it into a sharp point to make a pen.

* They would re-sharpen their pens to keep the writing clear.

* Scribes would make black ink by taking soot from a lamp and mix it with vegetable gum and then let it dry.

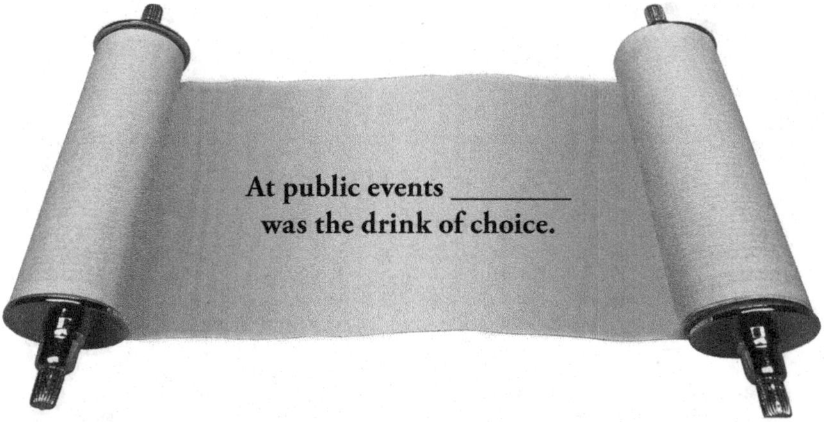
At public events ________
was the drink of choice.

* To make red ink they would use iron oxide instead of soot.

* Before writing they would have to add water to the dry ink and then they would dip the tip of their pen into it.

* Mistakes in writing were erased by scraping the ink off with a knife and then they would just start over.

* Because papyrus was so expensive the same sheet of papyrus was used many times by washing off one message and writing another one.

* An old message hidden under the new one could still be read sometimes by scholars.

* Wine was as common as daily bread for the Israelites.

* At feasts and many public events wine was the drink of choice.

* The Israelites believed that wine eased sadness and physical pain so they believed it was one of God's blessings.

* To make wine, ripe grapes were put into a large stone vat and then stomped on by foot.

* Through a trough the juice would then flow down into a smaller vat.

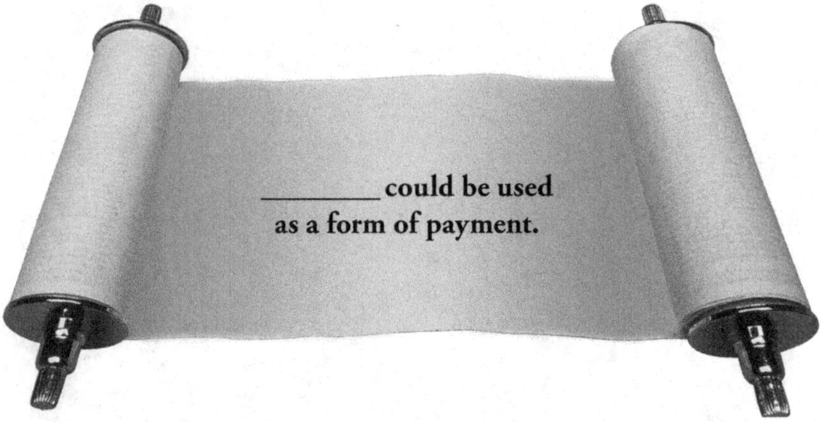
________ could be used
as a form of payment.

* It would begin to ferment, gradually changing from grape juice to wine while it was in the smaller vat.

* "Ferment" means: to undergo a natural chemical change in which substances, especially bacteria or yeast change sugar into alcohol and produce carbon dioxide.

* Next, containers made of animal skins or jars were used to store the partially fermented juice.

* They would then place them in cool storage cellars that were usually places carved into caves.

* There at a constant temperature the fermentation continued.

* Singing while they were harvesting the grapes and making wine was common by the workers.

* There was a special celebration with feasting and dancing after the wine was mixed with water and ready to drink.

* Wine was very important when it came to trading between countries.

* Payments could be made with wine as well.

* In exchange for building materials and craftsmen to construct God's great Temple in Jerusalem, King Hiram of Tyre received wine and other goods from King Solomon.

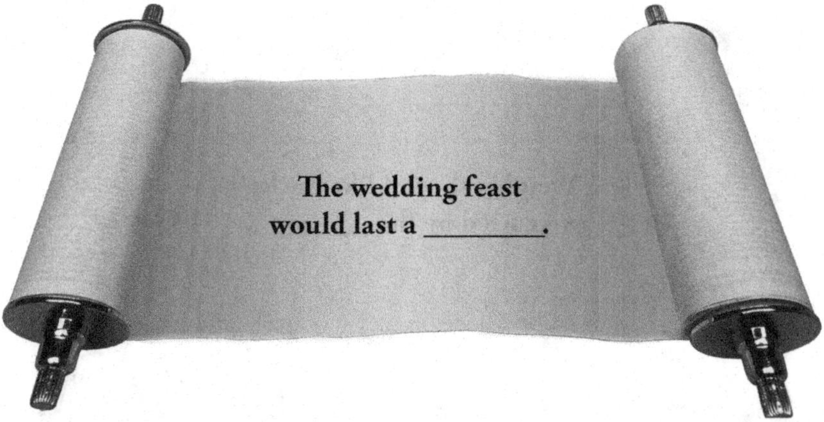
The wedding feast
would last a ________.

* In Gibeon, near Jerusalem, archeologists have recently found and dug up a winemaking center that has 63 stone cellars that would hold 25,000 gallons of wine.

* They discovered that these wine cellars were built 7 centuries before Jesus was born.

* In ancient Israel weddings were always joyous occasions.

* Most weddings were held in the evening.

* The groom would dress in beautiful colorful clothing and would sometimes wear a garland of flowers around his neck.

* After getting dressed the groom and his friends would then go over to the bride's house.

* The bride would be dressed in beautiful robes and jewelry.

* Then the bride, the groom, and the bride's relatives would then proceed to the groom's house.

* The ceremony would then take place at the groom's house.

* And sometimes for the wonderful occasion a special tent would be set up.

Weights shaped like ducks
were used by the ________.

* They would then have a "week long" wedding feast immediately following a brief marriage ceremony.

* During this celebration they would have lots of good-natured joking, singing and dancing.

* They would sing and dance to music made with flutes, castanets and tambourines.

* All the guests would take turns blessing the joyous couple.

* The Song of Solomon and the 45th Psalm and other poems about love would be recited to the joyous couple.

* Everyone in the community thought of weddings as being very important.

* The entire community was made stronger by the start of a new family.

* So for the first year of marriage the young groom did not have to serve in the army.

* "Friend of the bridegroom" or "steward of the feast" is what they called the groom's best man.

* Like at the wedding at Cana, one of the responsibilities of the best man was to make sure that all the guests have plenty of food to eat and wine to drink. (John 2:1-10)

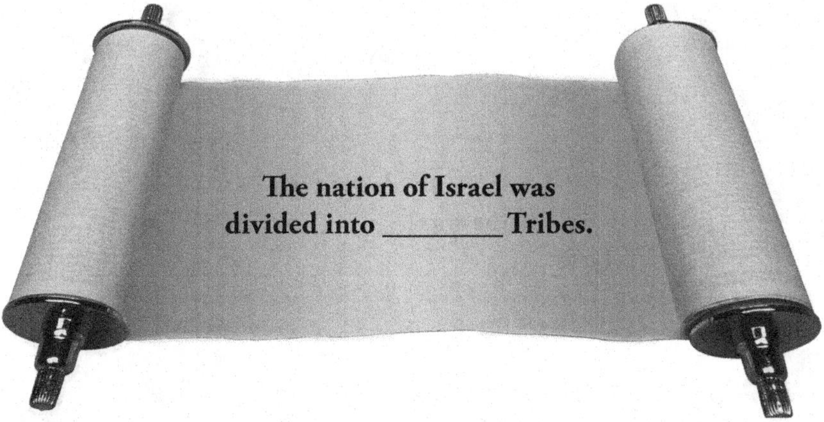

The nation of Israel was
divided into ________ Tribes.


* Scales and weights were used for transactions by sellers and buyers in the Old Testament.

* Simple "stone balls" were used by the Hebrews as weights.

* Weights shaped like "ducks" were used by the Babylonians.

* "Lion-shaped" weights were used by the Assyrians.

* By not using the correct weights, if they were too heavy or too light, is one way merchants would sometimes cheat their customers.

* God commands the Jews and us to use only "honest balances and honest weights" in all our transactions. (Leviticus 19:36)
* The nation of Israel was organized into 12 Tribes for several different reasons.
* For one, it was an effective and easier way to manage and govern such a large number of people.
* It also made things easier when it came time to divide up the Promised Land.
* Also because being known by their Tribe had always been a part of their culture and heritage.

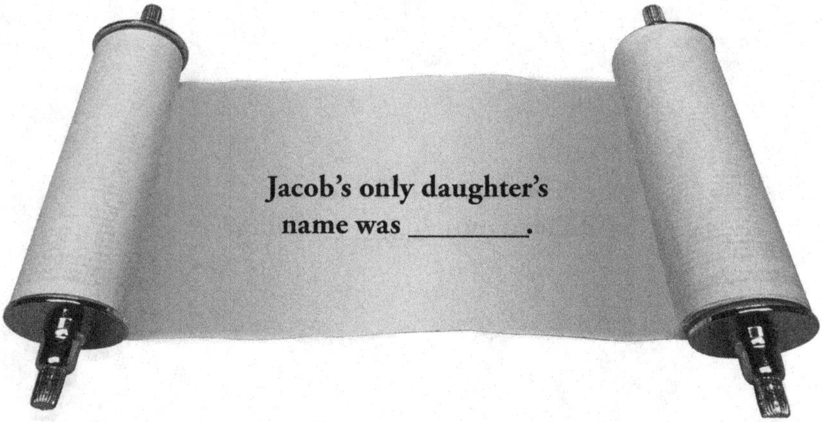
Jacob's only daughter's
name was ________.

* Since back then the only way to prove membership in God's chosen nation (which is Israel) was by genealogies or what we would call family history or family tree.
* So with everybody divided up into Tribes it made it so much easier to do.
* Because people were not known by their last name but by their family, Tribe and clan.
* This also made traveling in the wilderness much easier.
* People would keep up with their Tribes banner or flag and stay together.

* So they wouldn't get lost since there were approximately 2 million people counting men, women and children.

* The entire nation of Israel came from the 12 sons of Jacob.

* God may have changed Jacob's name to Israel for this reason as well.

* Jacob had only one daughter her name was Dinah.

* Dinah's mother's name was Leah. (Gen. 30:21)

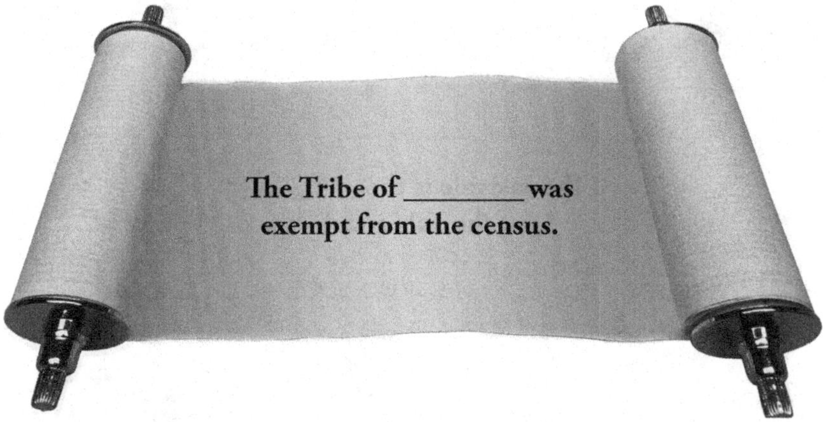

The Tribe of ________ was
exempt from the census.


* Here are the names of Jacob's 12 sons from the oldest to the youngest; these are the 12 Tribes of Israel.

* Reuben, Simeon, Levi, Judah, Dan, Naphtali, Gad, Asher, Issachar, Zebulun, Joseph and Benjamin. (Gen. 29:31 thru Gen. 35:18)

* These are the original 12 Tribes of Israel until they were in the 2nd year of leaving Egypt and were wondering in the wilderness with Moses. (Num. 1:1-34)

* Then the Lord told Moses that He wanted the people to build Him a Tabernacle.

* The Lord said He wanted one that they could take down and carry with them.

* The Lord told Moses to take a census of the whole community of Israel by their clans and families.

* He said to list all the men 20 years and older who are able to go to war.

* But God said to exempt the Tribe of Levi because they were going to take care of the Tabernacle.

* So Moses took the Tribe of Joseph and divided it up into 2 half Tribes.

* Moses took and made the Tribe of Ephraim and the Tribe of Manasseh from Joseph's 2 sons.

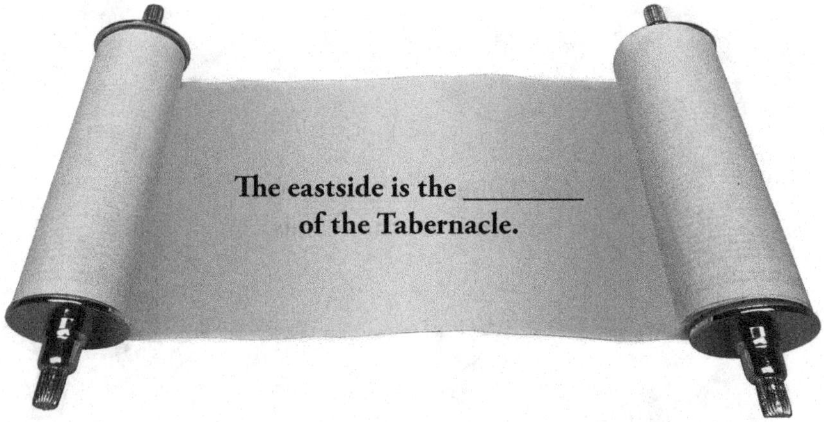
The eastside is the ________
of the Tabernacle.

* So the tribe of Ephraim and the Tribe of Manasseh replaced the Tribe of Joseph and the Tribe of Levi. (Num. 1:1-54 thru 2:19)

* The Lord told Moses and Aaron, "Each tribe will be assigned its own area in the camp..."

* "...and the various groups will camp beneath their family banners."

* "The Tabernacle will be located at the center of these tribal compounds." (Num. 2:2)

* The Tribes of Judah, Issachar and Zebulun camped toward the "sunrise" on the "eastside" of the Tabernacle.

* So the Tribes of Judah, Issachar and Zebulun all camped beneath their family banners.

* The "eastside" is at the "front" of the Tabernacle at the "entrance." (Num. 2:3-4)

* Between these 3 Tribes there were a total of 186,400 men that were old enough and able to go to war. (Num. 2:9)

* These 3 Tribes, Judah, Issachar and Zebulun, "led the way" they were "1st in line" whenever the Israelites traveled to a new campsite. (Num. 2:9)

* "David and Jesus" came from the Tribe of Judah.

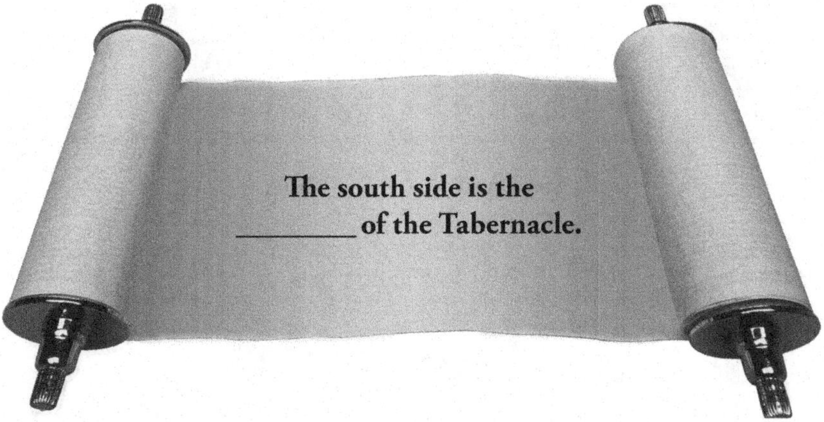
**The south side is the**
**________ of the Tabernacle.**

* Jacob's wife Leah was the mother of Judah, Issachar and Zebulun. (Gen. 29)

* The leader of the Tribe of Judah was Nahshon.

* Nahshon was also Aaron's brother-in-law. (Ex. 6:23)

* The leader of the Tribe of Issachar was Nethanel.

* The leader of the Tribe of Zebulun was Eliab.

* The Tribes of Reuben, Simeon and Gad camped on the "south side" which is the "left-side" of the Tabernacle.

* So the Tribes of Reuben, Simeon and Gad all camped beneath their family banners.

* Between these 3 Tribes there were a total of 151,450 men that were old enough and able to go to war. (Num. 2:16)

* These 3 Tribes, Reuben, Simeon and Gad were "2nd in line" when the Israelites traveled to a new campsite. (Num. 2:16)

* "Jephthah" may have come from the Tribe of Gad.

* Jacob's wife Leah was also the mother of Reuben and Simeon. (Gen. 29)

* Zilpha, Leah's servant gave birth to Gad.

* But Leah is the one that named Gad. (Gen. 29)

* The leader of the Tribe of Reuben was Elizur.

* The leader of the Tribe of Simeon was Shelumiel.

* The leader of the Tribe of Gad was Eliasaph.

* The Tribe of Levi also known as the Levites was a "priestly" Tribe.

* Levi had 3 sons, Gershon, Kohath and Merari.

* Moses took Levi's 3 sons and had them and their clans set up their camps "around" the Tabernacle.

* The Gershonite clans camped on the "west side" which is the "back side" of the Tabernacle.

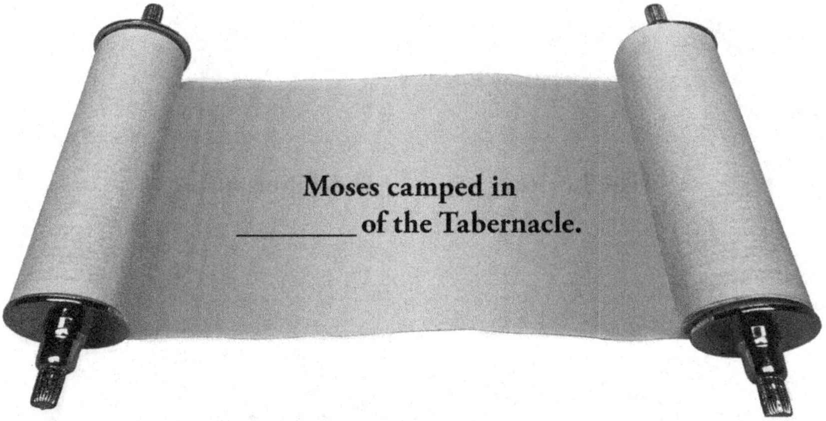
Moses camped in
________ of the Tabernacle.

* They set up their camp "in between" the Tabernacle and the Tribes of Ephraim, Manasseh and Benjamin.

* The Gershonite clans took care of all the material that covered the "outside frames" of the Tabernacle.

* They took care of the Tabernacle's layers of coverings, the entry curtains, the curtains that surrounded the Tabernacle and altar, the courtyard entrance curtain, the cords and all equipment related to them.

* The Kohathite clans camped on the "south side" which is the "left-side" of the Tabernacle.

* They set up their camp "in between" the Tabernacle and the Tribes of Reuben, Simeon and Gad.

* The Kohathite clans took care of all the things on the "inside" of the Tabernacle.

* One of their responsibilities was to take care of the Ark of the Covenant.

* They also took care of the table, the lamp stand, the altars, all the utensils used in the sanctuary, the inner curtain and all the equipment related to them.

* The Merarite clans camped on the "north side" which is the "right side" of the Tabernacle.

* They set up their camps "in between" the Tabernacle and the Tribes of Dan, Asher and Naphtali.

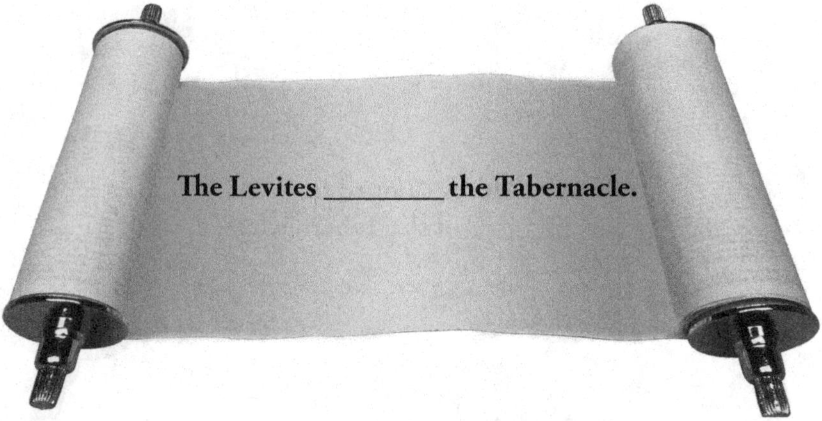
**The Levites ________ the Tabernacle.**

* The Merarite clans took care of the "outside framework" of the Tabernacle.

* They took care of the frames supporting the Tabernacle, the crossbars, pillars, bases, posts, pegs and cords and all the equipment related to them.

* Then Moses, Aaron and Aaron's sons camped on the "east side" which is the "front side" of the Tabernacle.

* They set up their camps "in between" the Tabernacle and the Tribes of Judah, Issachar and Zebulun.

* Moses and his group had the final responsibility for the sanctuary and going before the Lord in intercession for the people.

* Their responsibility was also to carry out the command of the Lord.

* The Lord said, "If anyone other than a priest or Levite came too near the sanctuary they were to be executed."

* The Tribe of Levi were to camp "around" the Tabernacle of the Covenant.

* They were to do this to offer the people of Israel "protection" from the Lord's fierce anger.

* So Levi's 3 sons, Gershon, Kohath and Merari, and all their clans camped beneath their family banners. (Num. 1:53)

__________ designed
the priestly garments.

* One of the responsibilities of the Levites was to "stand guard" around the Tabernacle. (Num. 1:53)

* There were a total of 22,000 males from one month old and up in the Tribe of Levi. (Num. 3:39)

* The Levites were "3rd in line" whenever the Israelites traveled to a new campsite. (Num. 2:17)

* "Aaron, Moses, Eli and John the Baptist" came from the Tribe of Levi.

* Jacob's wife Leah was the mother of Levi.

* The Levites were the only ones that could take down or set up the Tabernacle as they traveled.

* Because of dedicating their lives to the Lord one of their responsibilities of being "High Priest" was to represent the people before God.

* God wanted to express His righteousness and merciful love for His people.

* So He designed the "priestly garments" in a way that they would always see this.

* First the priest would put on a tunic and a mitre (turban) of fine linen.

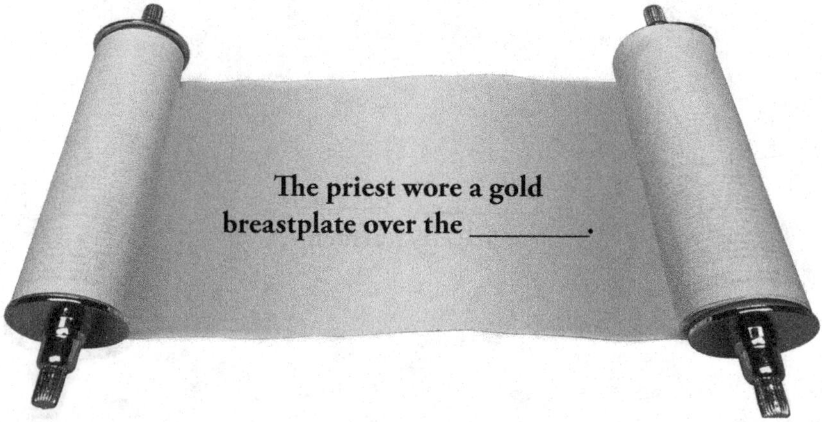
**The priest wore a gold breastplate over the ________.**

* The mitre (turban) had a gold plate on it which came down over the priest's forehead.

* The gold plate had an inscription on it which read "HOLINESS TO THE LORD."

* The Hebrew translation is "SET APART AS HOLY TO THE LORD."

* In order for the Lord to accept the sacrifices that the priest made on behalf of the people the priest had to always wear this in the Lord's presence.

* The "ephod," which is a vest or waist coat, and a "blue robe" were also always worn by the priests.

* On "each shoulder" of the "ephod" were the names of the "12 Tribes of Israel" inscribed in onyx stones.

* The priest would wear a "gold breastplate" over the ephod.

* The names of the 12 Tribes of Israel were inscribed in "12 different precious stones" on the "chest" of the "gold breastplate."

* To continually "remind the Lord of His people," the priest would wear this "over his heart." (Ex. 28:29)

* Also in a "pocket over his heart" is where the priest would keep the "Urim and Thummim."

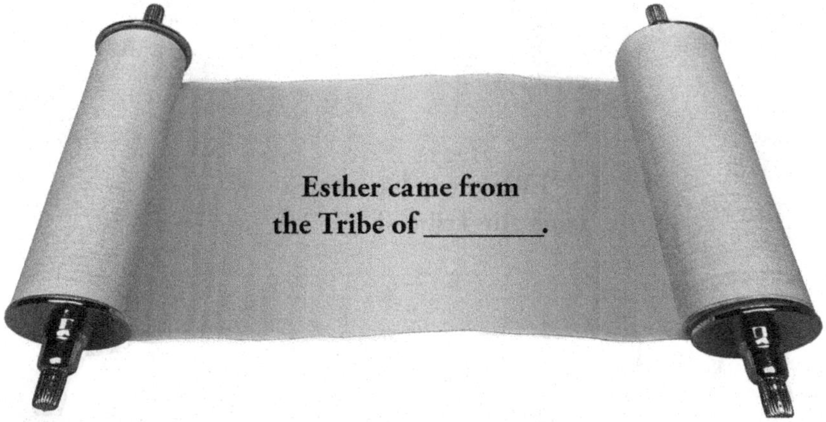
Esther came from
the Tribe of ________.

* To determine the Lord's Will for the people of Israel, the priest would use the Urim and Thummim. (Num. 27:21)

* The Urim and Thummim were probably some kind of stone or tokens, like dice or coins that had to land upright or upside down.

* They could give answers to true-false or yes-no questions.

* Only the High Priest could use them.

* There is no mention in the Bible of "Abraham, Moses, David or the prophets" ever using them.

* Neither the Urim or Thummim are mentioned in the New Testament.

* The Urim and Thummim were used a lot by the nation of Israel in its early years.

* They were not needed by the prophets, major spiritual leaders, or once the Holy Spirit was available to all believers.

* The Tribes of Ephraim, Manasseh and Benjamin camped on the "west side" which was the "back side or behind" the Tabernacle.

* So the Tribes of Ephraim, Manasseh and Benjamin all camped beneath their family banners. (Num. 2:18-19)

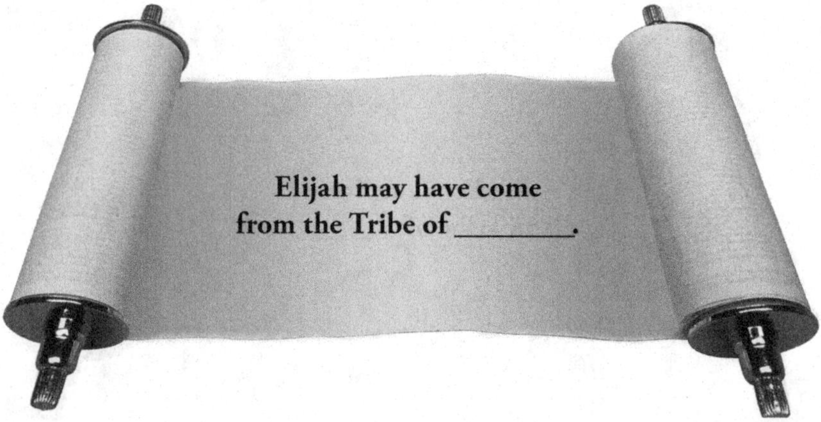
Elijah may have come
from the Tribe of ________.

* Between these 3 Tribes there were a total of 108,100 men that were old enough and able to go to go war. (Num. 2:24)

* These 3 Tribes Ephraim, Manasseh and Benjamin were "4th in line" in "behind the Levites," when the Israelites traveled to a new campsite. (Num. 2:24)

* "Saul, Esther, Gideon and Paul" came from the Tribe of Benjamin.

* The Tribes of Ephraim and Manasseh were originally the Tribe of Joseph.

* "Joshua and Samuel" came from the Tribe of Joseph.

* Jacob's wife Rachael was the mother of Joseph and Benjamin. (Gen. 29)

* Joseph's Egyptian wife Asenath was the mother of Ephraim and Manasseh. (Gen. 41:50)

* The leader of the Tribe of Ephraim was Elishama.

* The leader of the Tribe of Manasseh was Gamaliel.

* The leader of the Tribe of Benjamin was Abidan.

________ named both
Dan and Naphtali.

* The Tribes of Dan, Asher and Naphtali camped on the "north side" which was the "right side" of the Tabernacle. (Num. 2:25-26)

* The Tribes of Dan, Asher and Naphtali all camped beneath their family banners.

* Between these 3 Tribes there were a total of 157,000 men that were old enough and able to go to war. (Num. 2:31)

* These 3 Tribes, Dan, Asher and Naphtali were "5th in line" they were to "bring up the rear" whenever the Israelites traveled to a new campsite. (Num. 2:31)

* "Barak and Elijah" may have come from the Tribe of Naphtali.

* Bilhah, Rachel's servant, gave birth to Dan and Naphtali. (Gen. 30:6-8)

* But Rachel is the one who named both boys.

* Zilpha, Leah's servant, gave birth to Asher. (Gen. 30:12)

* But Leah is the one who named Asher.

* The leader of the Tribe of Dan was Ahiezer.

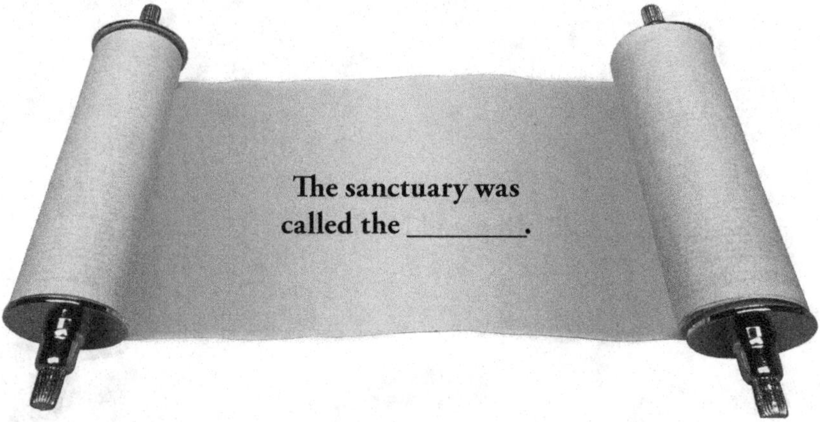
**The sanctuary was
called the ________.**

* The leader of the Tribe of Asher was Pagiel.

* The leader of the Tribe of Naphtali was Ahira.

* You know this had to have been a huge campsite!

* With the 603,550 fighting men, not to mention over 22,000 male Levites, all of the women and children, plus the Tabernacle, it probably would have taken about 12 miles to be able to set up enough tents for all these people.

* Taking a census was very important even though it was a very long and tedious job.

* Israel needed to know their military strength before they entered the Promised Land.

* The only way they could do this is to count how many men were old enough to fight.

* This "census" or "numbering of the people" is how the book of Numbers in the Bible got its name.

* The "sanctuary" of the Tabernacle was called the "Holy Place."

* The sanctuary or "Holy Place" was in one part of the Tabernacle.

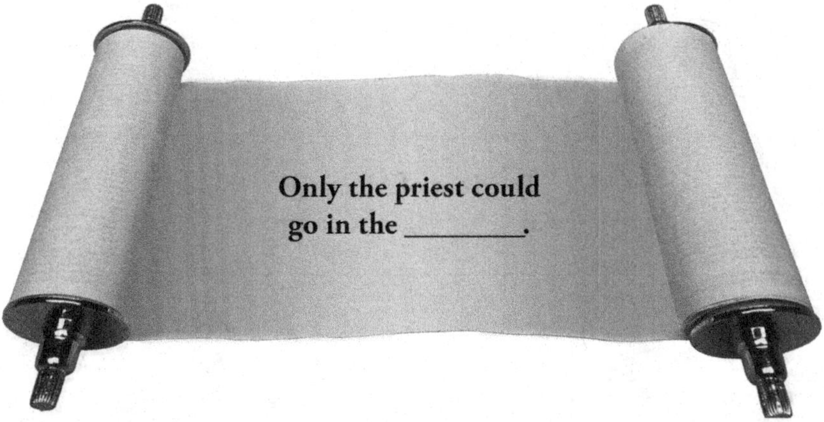
Only the priest could
go in the ________.

* The "Most Holy Place" or "Holy of Holies" was in another part of the Tabernacle.

* The "Ark of the Covenant" was located in the Holy of Holies.

* The Holy Place and the Holy of Holies were separated by a curtain.

* This "curtain" was called "the Veil."

* "The Veil" was a "barrier between" God and man.

* "The Veil" was 15 feet wide, it had winged cherubim facing each other embroidered into its heavy woven cloth.

* There was no opening in the middle of the curtain.

* Only the High Priest was allowed to enter the Holy of Holies.

* For the High Priest to be able to enter the Holy of Holies he would have to go around the curtain and enter from the side.

* Later, King Solomon's Temple was built in a similar fashion.

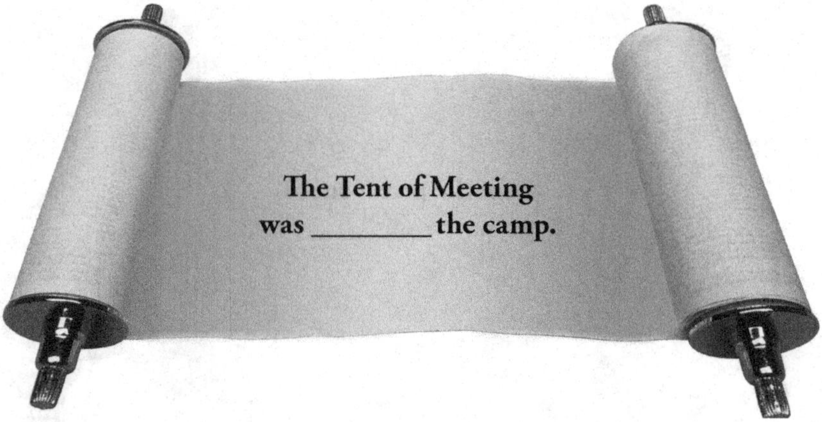
The Tent of Meeting
was ________ the camp.

* Aaron, the High Priest, would enter the Holy of Holies "once a year" through this "Veil."

* He would go into the Holy of Holies to intercede for the sins of the people of Israel.

* In the Holy of Holies is just one place where God would talk with Moses at. (Num. 1:1)

* "The Veil" of the Temple "was torn from top to bottom" by God, when "Jesus died on the Cross."

* The tearing of the Veil symbolizes that now through the death and resurrection of Jesus that it is not up to the High Priest anymore, but all believers can now come before the Throne of God.

* Now "Jesus is our High Priest," who is ALIVE and sits at the right hand of God in Heaven, interceding for us.

* In Exodus 33:7, it mentions a place before the Tabernacle was built where Moses met with God, called the "Tabernacle of the congregation" or "Tent of Meeting."

* It was Moses' custom to set up the tent known as the "Tent of Meeting" far outside the camp. (Ex. 33:7)

* Everyone that wanted to consult with the Lord would go there.

* When Moses would go to the Tent of Meeting the "pillar of clouds" would come down and "hover" at the entrance while the Lord spoke with Moses. (Ex. 33:9)

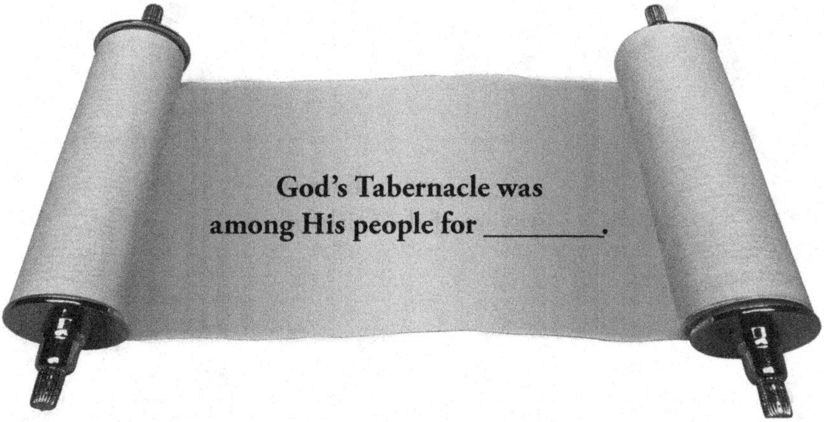
**God's Tabernacle was**
**among His people for ________.**

* "Inside" the Tent of Meeting the Lord would speak to Moses "face to face", as a man speaks to his friend. (Ex. 33:11)

* Many scholars believe that the Tent of Meeting and the Tabernacle served the same purpose.

* God had His people make the Tent of Meeting, the Tabernacle and then later the Temple.

* God did this because He wanted to dwell among His people. (Ex. 25:8)

* God wanted to talk with them and spend time with them.

* Through the Tabernacle, and later through Jesus, the Lord prepared a way for a sinful people to approach a Holy God.

* For "400 years" the Tabernacle is where God lived among His people.

* From the "Exodus" until King Solomon's Temple was built.

* The Tabernacle is discussed over a span of 50 chapters in the Bible.

* The Tabernacle was about the size of "half a football field."

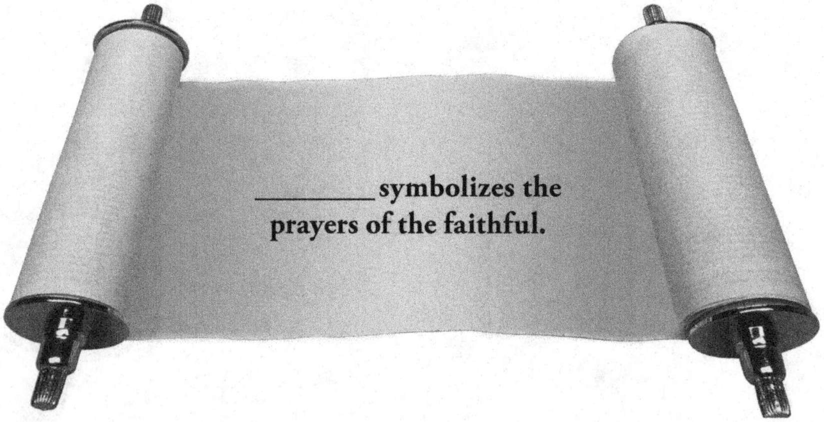
________symbolizes the
prayers of the faithful.

* The Tabernacle of the Old Testament was patterned after the one that is in Heaven.

* "They serve in a place of worship that is only a copy, a shadow of the real one in heaven. For when Moses was getting ready to build the Tabernacle, God gave him this warning: Be sure that you make everything according to the design I have shown you here on the mountain." (Hebrews 8:5)

* Our High Priest is Jesus Himself in this Tabernacle. (Hebrews 8:1-2)

* Many expensive materials were used in the building of the Tabernacle.

* Gold, silver, bronze, precious woods and rare cloth were all used.

* With today's prices the cost would well exceed $1 million.

* Everything was paid for by the "offerings" from the Israelites. (Ex. 36:5)

* The Israelites even gave more than what was needed.

* Moses had to command them to stop giving. (Ex. 36:6)

* One of God's commands was that they were to burn "special incense" constantly on the "altar of incense."

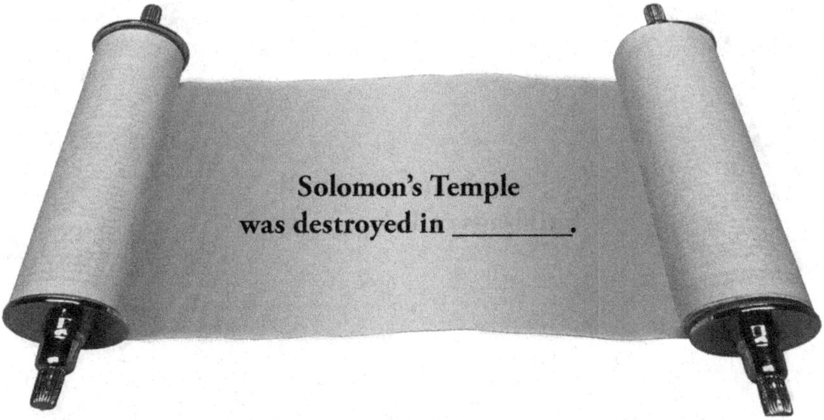
Solomon's Temple
was destroyed in ________.

* It was a special sweet mixture of incense that was to only be used for the Tabernacle. (Ex. 30:34-37)

* God gave specific instructions concerning this recipe.

* There was to be no other incense burned on the altar.

* Incense symbolizes "the prayers of the faithful." (Revelation 5:8 and 8:3-4)

* After settling in the Promised Land, King David wanted to build a permanent Temple to God.

* King David located a place on a hill in Jerusalem, so he purchased it for the site for the new Temple.

* But the Temple was actually built by David's son, King Solomon.

* This Temple was not only very beautiful but for the Jews it was the "one and only place of worship."

* This was, as stated in Jewish Law, "the only place where sacrifices could be offered to God."

* All year long the Temple was a very busy place.

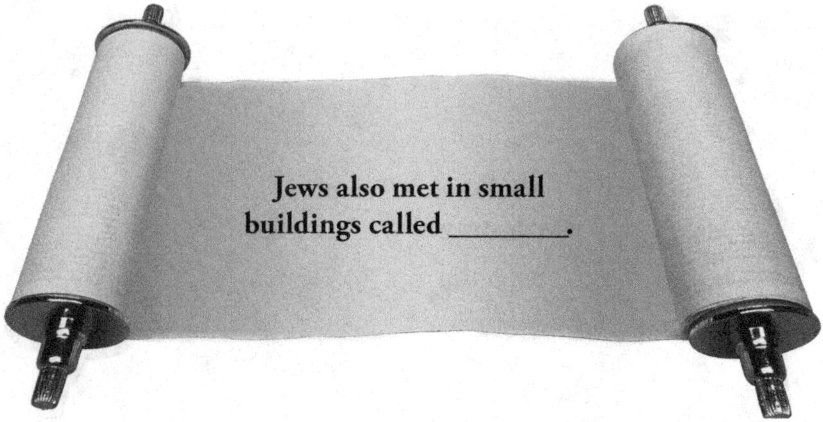
Jews also met in small
buildings called ________.

* Every day worshippers came for prayers and sacrifices.

* The annual pilgrimage festivals were the busiest times of the year.

* It was required for all Jews to come to Jerusalem and worship at the Temple at this time.

* When the Babylonians captured Jerusalem in "586 B.C." they destroyed Solomon's Temple.

* Even though it was rebuilt 71 years later in "515 B.C." it was still not as grand as the original.

* "495 years later" in 20 B.C. the Temple was rebuilt a second time by King Herod the Great.

* The Temple was built on a mound called the "Temple Mount."

* Even though the Jews began meeting in other places, Solomon's Temple continued to be the "official" place of worship.

* Jews began meeting in small buildings called "synagogues" for prayer and teachings.

* They would go to synagogues because these were located in their hometowns.

The angel had Joshua
put on ________ clothes.

* The Temple was eventually destroyed in "70 A.D." by the Romans.

* A section of "wall" on the Temple Mount is all that remains of the ancient Temple today.

* Today this "wall" in Jerusalem is called the "Wailing Wall," and Jews come from around the world to pray there.

* At religious events the wearing of clean clothes was showing a sign of respect.

* This respect was demanded by God of His people.

* After their Exodus from Egypt, while wandering in the desert God told Moses that He would let the people hear Him as He spoke to him. (Ex. 19:9)

* But first they needed to sanctify themselves (turn away from sin), and they had to wash their clothes. (Ex. 19:10)

* An angel of the Lord appeared before the High Priest Joshua whose clothes were very dirty.

* Before the angel delivered his prophecy, he commanded the Priest's assistants to "take off his filthy clothes," so Joshua could put on clean ones. (Zechariah 3:3-4)

* Purification (turning from sin) in the Bible was symbolized by the washing and changing of clothes. (Gen. 35:2)

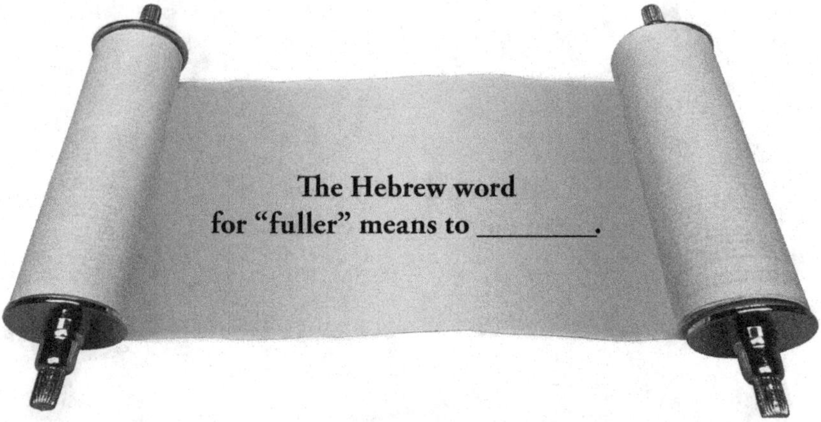
**The Hebrew word**
**for "fuller" means to ________.**

* The Israelites used a stream or a bronze cauldron to wash their clothes in.

* To loosen the dirt they would repeatedly step on them.

* Sometimes instead of stepping on them to get the dirt out they would beat the wet clothing with sticks or rocks.

* Most people washed their own clothes.

* If they could afford it they sometimes took them to a "fuller," which is a professional cleaner.

* The Hebrew word for fuller means "to trample," describing how the clothes were cleaned.

* A solution made from "olive oil, wood or plant ashes and powdered limestone" was used by the fuller, because there was no laundry soap.

* The fullers had to do the washing outside of the city gates because the solution smelled so bad.

* The clothes had to be rinsed many times to get the smell out.

* The clothes would then be left in the sun to dry, which often would bleach the cloth.

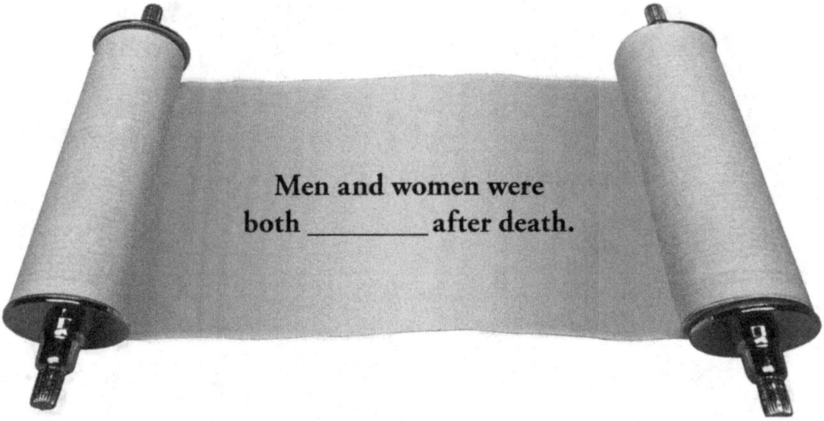
Men and women were
both ________ after death.

* Today, some people in the Middle East still wash their laundry the same way.

* When women went out in public, in ancient times, "veils" of light fabric were usually worn over their heads and faces.

* Only a husband was allowed to see his wife's face.

* Out of modesty, and to avoid being seen by men they didn't know, unmarried women also wore veils.

* This explains why "Rebekah" put on a veil when she met Isaac. (Gen. 24:65)

* Brides usually wore "veils" at their weddings that completely concealed their faces.

* Jacob was deceived at his wedding because of his bride's veil.

* Jacob thought he was marrying Rachel, but because the wedding was at night, and the bride wore a veil, he didn't realize until the next morning that he had actually married Rachel's oldest sister, Leah. (Gen. 29:22-26)

* Veils were not usually worn by men.

* But after Moses descended from Mount Sinai with the Ten Commandments his face was shining miraculously from being in the presence and glory of the Lord. (Ex. 34:28-33)

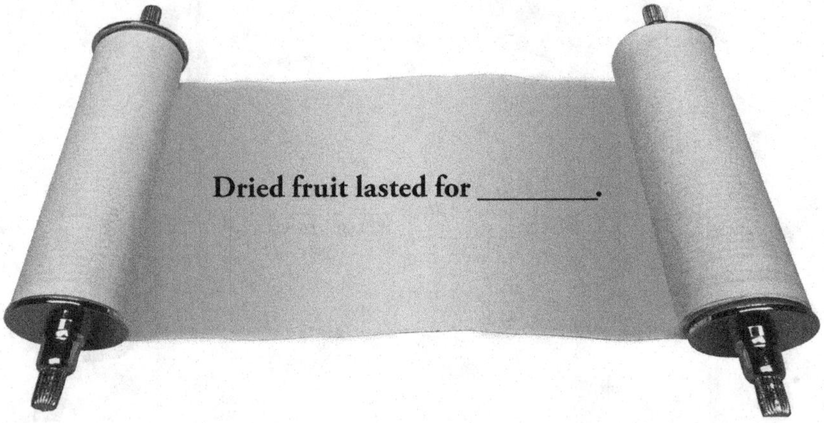


* Moses put on a veil to avoid scaring the Israelites when he returned.

* It was a tradition to cover the faces of the dead from view.

* Men and women were both veiled after death.

* In Genesis, God gives Adam and Eve "the seed bearing plants and all the fruit trees for their food." (Gen. 1:29)

* The Israelites ate mainly vegetables, grains and seasonal fruit which were plentiful in Biblical times.

* "Cucumbers, squash, onions, garlic and leeks" were the most popular vegetables.

* Because they could eat these vegetables raw or put them in stews with lentils or beans.

* Even though sometimes they would eat meals with no meat, only vegetables, it still provided them with strength and nourishment.

* Meals consisting of only "vegetables and water" were what the "Prophet Daniel, Shadrach, Meshach and Abednego" lived on for days, when they were taken captive by the Babylonians.

* And they became stronger than their Babylonian guards. (Daniel 1:3-16)

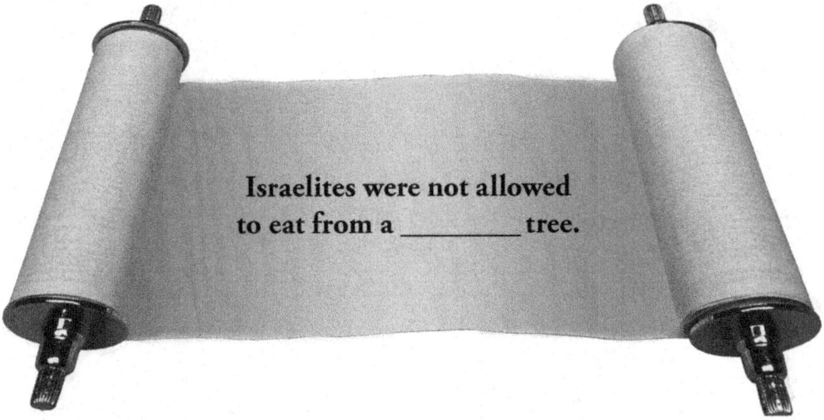

Israelites were not allowed
to eat from a ________ tree.


* The Babylonian guards ate meat and drank wine.

* The Israelites had an abundance of fruits such as "figs, olives, dates, grapes and pomegranates."

* "Apricots, peaches and cherries" were also in abundance in Biblical times.

* They would either eat the fruit fresh off the vine or they would dry some of it so they could use it in the future.

* Dried fruits came in handy because it would last for years and it could be taken with them on long journeys.

* They also turned some fruits into liquids.

* "Dates" were made into sweet syrup which is called honey sometimes in the Bible. "Olives" were made into oil and "grapes" into wine.

* It was forbidden for the Israelites to eat the fruit from a newly planted tree.

* For the "first 3 years" the fruit from a newly planted tree was "not harvested at all."

* Then in the "4th" year "all" the fruit was harvested and was "devoted to the Lord" as an outburst of praise.

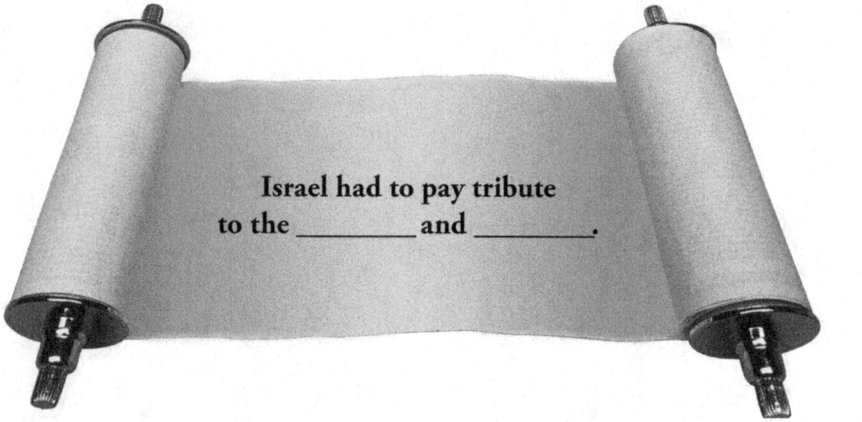

Israel had to pay tribute
to the ________ and ________.


* Finally in the "5th" year you may eat the fruit. In this way, its yield will be increased. I, the Lord, am your God. (Lev. 19:25)

* This made sure that fruit was only harvested from mature trees.

* For rulers in Biblical times, winning a war meant collecting "tributes" which was collecting payments from the losers.

* "Gold, silver or other products" could be used for these payments.

* It was expected for everyone in the community to pay his share.

* Weak nations, as the price for security gave tribute to their stronger neighbors.
* They did this in the hopes that they wouldn't get attacked by them.
* Forced labor could also be used as tribute.
* For example, the enslaved Jews built cities for Pharaoh in Egypt.
* "And they drave not out the Canaanites that dwelt in Gezer: but the Canaanites dwell among the Ephraimites unto this day, and serve under tribute." (Joshua 16:10)

The ________ collected
the tribute money.

* King David also collected "tributes" of gold and silver from the Moabites, Arameans and other tribes that he defeated in battle.
* "King David dedicated all these gifts to the Lord, along with the silver and gold he had set apart from the other nations he had subdued." (2 Samuel 8:11)
* King Solomon also collected tributes from people from the Euphrates River to the border of Egypt, and they served Solomon all the days of his life. (1 Kings 4:21)
* After Israel split, neither of the two kingdoms was strong enough to collect tribute from other lands.
* They had to pay tribute to the Babylonians and Assyrians.

* They did this in hopes of preventing them from invading them, but eventually they invaded them anyway.

* In the New Testament times the people of Judea paid tribute to the Romans.

* The tax collectors were the ones that collected the tribute money.

* There were not a lot of job openings for working on a ship in Biblical times.

* With the exception of King Solomon's fleet of ships, which traded successfully by sea.

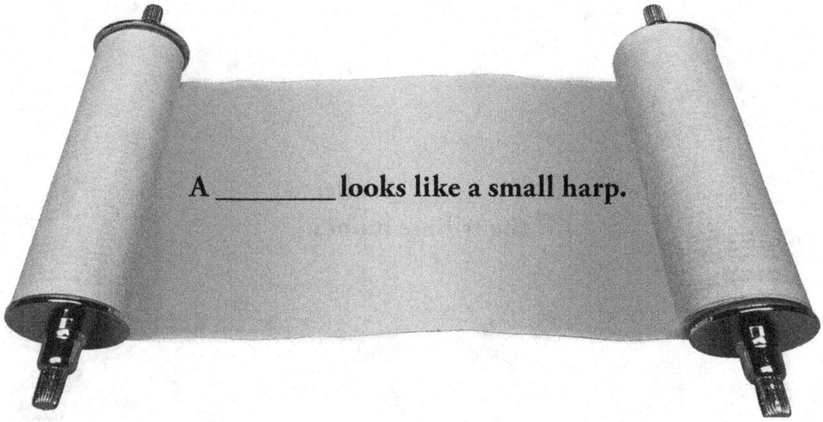
A ________ looks like a small harp.

* The Romans in the New Testament on the other hand were like masters of the seas.

* So Jews traveled and traded with the merchants who sailed on Roman ships.

* These ships were made from wood and powered either by teams of oarsmen working in unison or by sails.

* The Israelites used several different musical instruments as they danced and sang Psalms.

* One of these was a stringed instrument called a "nebel" in Hebrew.

* The "nebel" was a type of "lyre" which is an instrument that looks like a small harp.

* This type of lyre is similar to the musical instrument called a "kinnor," that David played when he was a teenager, to calm the moody Saul.

* The nebel is sometimes called a lyre in some Bibles.

* The nebel is called a "psaltery" in the King James Bible.

* The nebel had a small, hollow wooden sound box, with two arms that were arched upward that made it look like it was praising God.

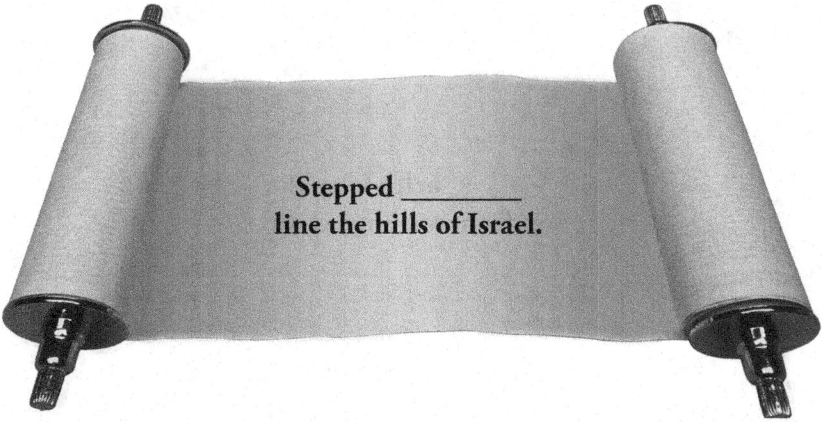
**Stepped ________**
**line the hills of Israel.**

* The arms were joined together near the top by a "yoke," which is a crossbar, and strings would run from this to the sound box.

* To play it you could hold the nebel in one hand, or in the bend of your arm, and then you would use the other hand to pluck the strings.

* The word nebel was not only used for a musical instrument, but in Hebrew it was also the name for a bottle made of skin.

* The bottle would take the shape of the musical instrument as it was being filled.

* Even though they are often called "harps," in the book of Psalms and other Old Testament books, the nebels and kinnors are mentioned together.

* King David danced to music played on the nebel as he was bringing the Ark of the Covenant to Jerusalem. (2 Samuel 6:5)

* The hills of Israel are lined with "stepped terraces."

* Stepped terraces slow down soil erosion and help retain water to help the crops grow.

* When the land of Canaan was divided among the 12 Tribes of Israel, Joshua told all the house of Joseph, and Ephraim and Manasseh…

* "Thou art a great people, and hast great power: thou shalt not have one lot only: But the mountain shall be thine; for it is a wood, and thou shalt cut it down…" (Joshua 17:17-18)

________ helps keep the
soil from washing away.

* One of the main occupations of the Israelites was farming.

* But with their land having so many hills, it posed a problem.

* They cleared the hillside from all the trees, plowed the ground up, and planted crops, but then the rain would come and wash it all away.

* So the Israelites decided if they were going to get crops to grow on these hills then they were going to have to use "terrace" farming.

* Terraces are low ridges of earth and rock built across the hillside.

* These ridges divided the slopes into a series of "benches."

* To get the extra water to run off to the level below they would dig a channel just above each ridge.

* By terracing the hillside this made rain water run down the slopes a lot slower.

* Which in turn would make more of the rain water soak into the ground.

* Which helped keep the soil from washing away and also helped the crops grow.

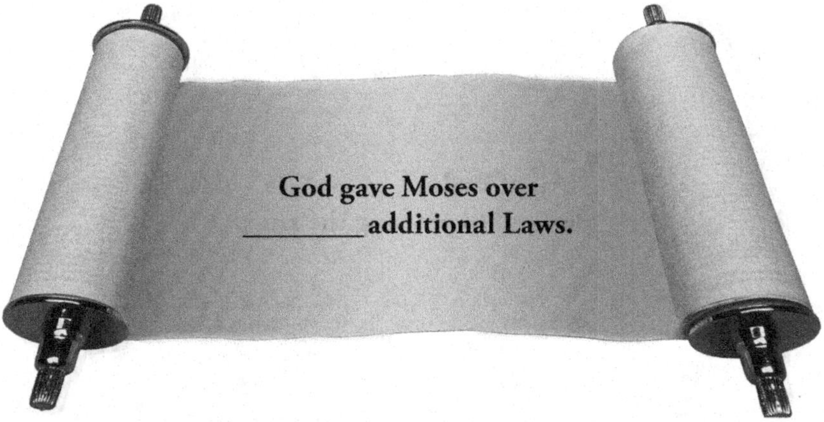
God gave Moses over
________ additional Laws.

* By terracing the land this also gave them more land that they could farm.

* So this helped the Israelites to be able to use all of their land.

* By terracing, the Israelites were able to produce generous harvests of "grain, olives, dates and figs" on land that was originally unproductive.

* These hillsides that the Tribes of Israel terraced back in the Old Testament are still terraced and farmed profitably today.

* When God talked face to face with Moses on Mount Sinai, He gave Moses His Laws in which He wants the Israelites and us to live by.

* God promised Moses that if His people, the Israelites and us would live by and follow these Laws, He would protect us all.

* God's Laws were not just the Ten Commandments that He carved on to the stone tablets.

* God gave us more than "600" additional Laws that Moses eventually wrote down later on.

* All these Laws were later put in the "1st five books" of the Bible.

* These books came to be known as "The Law" by the Israelites.

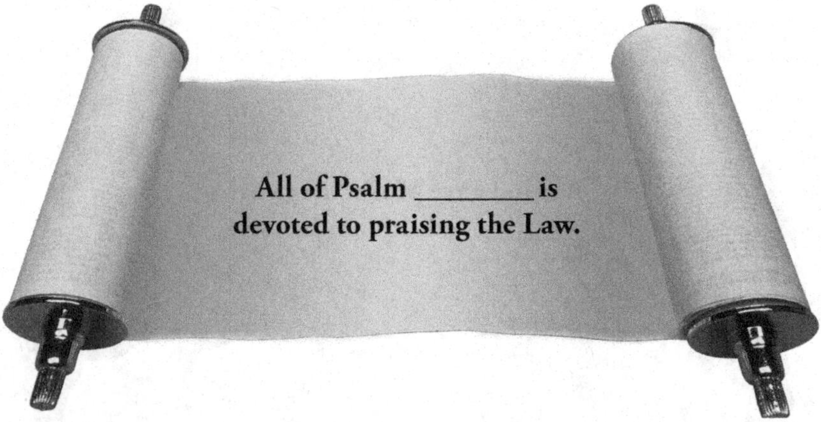
All of Psalm ________ is
devoted to praising the Law.

* Although laws had previously been handed down by the kings of Egypt and Babylon, they only covered civil matters.

* Their laws favored the upper classes and only covered property rights.

* "The Law" of the Israelites covered religious issues and civil matters.

* The "Jewish Law" also dealt with "matters of worship and protected strangers, widows, orphans and the poor," unlike other nations.

* "The Law" was not just some kind of rule to the Israelites, "it was a way of life."

* The Israelites would read from the Law and discuss it when they would gather together to worship the Lord.

* The Prophets would predict disaster when the people ignored or disobeyed the Law.

* The Prophets also predicted prosperity if the people would go back to obeying the Law.

* All of the 176 verses of Psalm 119 are devoted to praising "the Law" which is also the longest Psalm.

* The Egyptians went by a "solar calendar" in ancient times.

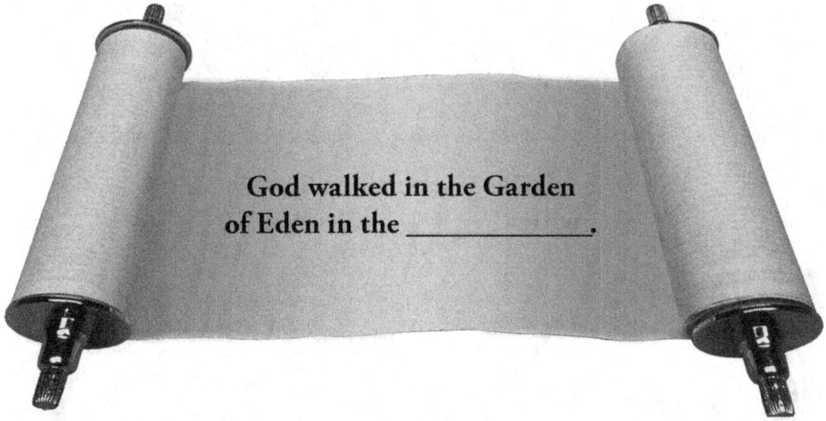
God walked in the Garden
of Eden in the ____________.

* A calendar that is based on the cycles of the moon is called a "lunar calendar" which is what most other people went by.

* There were only "354 days" in a 12 month lunar year.

* On a lunar calendar there were only "29 or 30 days" in each month.

* The Hebrew "week" was 7 days long.

* The "New Year" began in the "fall" and was celebrated with a festival.

* It took place when the farmers had finished with the harvest and were getting the fields ready for the spring crop.

* The new day "began" at "nightfall" on a lunar calendar.

* The "nighttime" began at "6 in the evening" and ended at "6 in the morning."

* According to the Hebrew calendar the "day" was divided into "3" 4-hour time periods, known as "watches."

* The day's "1st watch" was from "6am to 10am" in the morning.

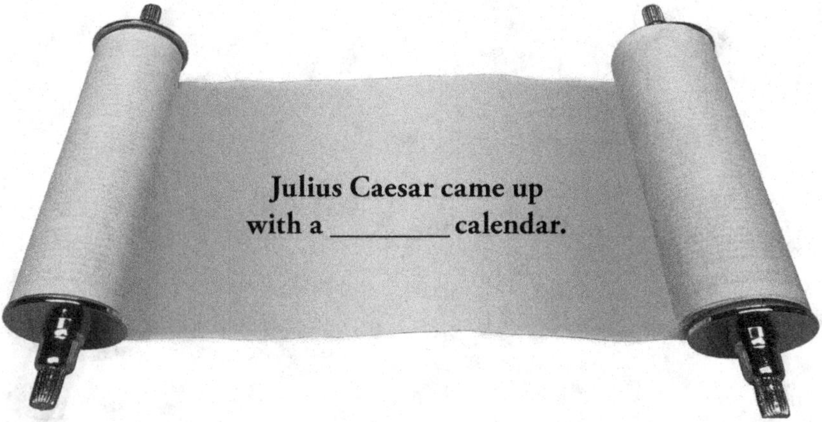
Julius Caesar came up
with a ________ calendar.

* The day's "2nd watch" was from "10am to 2pm" which was called the "heat of the day."

* The day's "3rd watch" was from "2pm to 6pm" which was called the "cool of the day."

* In the New Testament the Romans changed their own system to "4" 3-hour watches each night and day.

* God walked in the Garden of Eden in the "cool of the day." (Gen. 3:8)

* So to keep the seasons in order and at the same time each year, the Israelites had to add an extra month every so often, because the lunar year had less days.

* If they didn't then the harvest festival among other things would take place in the wrong season.

* It was the priest's responsibility to decide when to add the extra month.

* They would then let the people know when they did this by lighting bonfires.

* The Israelites considered the start of each month to be holy.

* In "47 B.C." Julius Caesar came up with a solar calendar, which is what we use today.

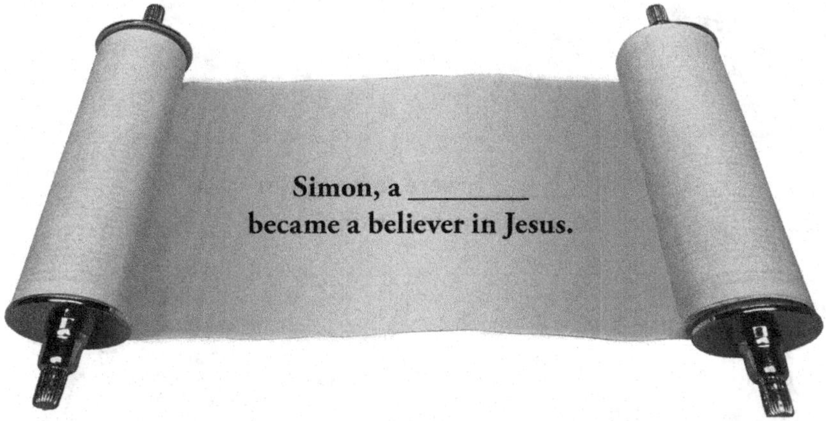
Simon, a ________
became a believer in Jesus.

* With our calendar we too have to adjust it every 4 years by adding a day, when we do this we call it a leap year.

* Magical rituals were used by many pagan religions.

* In the Bible God tells us that magicians are calling on evil spirits to perform their magic.

* All through the Bible, God's priests and prophets warned the people about not becoming a magician or being involved in any kind of magic in any way.

* Magicians who challenged God's miracles are mentioned throughout the Bible, and they were defeated every time.

* When Moses was trying to free the Israelites from Egypt he had several confrontations with Pharaoh's magicians.

* One occasion was when, through Moses, God turned all the water in Egypt into blood, killing all the fish and making the water undrinkable.

* "And the magicians of Egypt did so with their enchantments…" (Ex. 7:22)

* When God sent the plague of boils, Pharaoh's magicians saw that they were no match for God's superiority and power.

* God covered all the Egyptians, their animals and their magicians with boils.

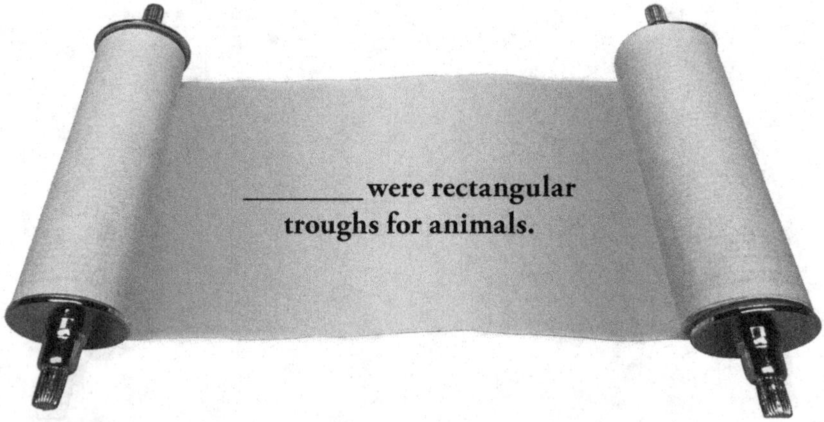
________ were rectangular
troughs for animals.

* Even though God was the ONLY one who could take the boils away, a lot of the people remained stubborn. (Ex. 9:8-12)

* In the New Testament, Philip the Evangelist met Simon the "sorcerer."

* Simon had bewitched the people of Samaria into thinking that he was "The Great One- the Power of God."

* But after the people of Samaria heard Philip preach about Jesus, they turned away from Simon and turned to Jesus.

* Then Simon himself became a believer in Jesus and was baptized. (Acts 8:9-13)

* "Mangers" were rectangular troughs, in which cattle, sheep, donkeys and horses all ate their food from.

* "Mangers" were usually carved out of stone, because wood was scarce, especially in Palestine.

* Ancient limestone mangers have been discovered by archeologists, measuring about 36 inches long, 24 inches deep, and 18 inches wide.

* To keep the animals from wandering off they would tie them to a tether.

* A tether is a rope or chain that was fastened through a hole that was cut into the side of the "manger."

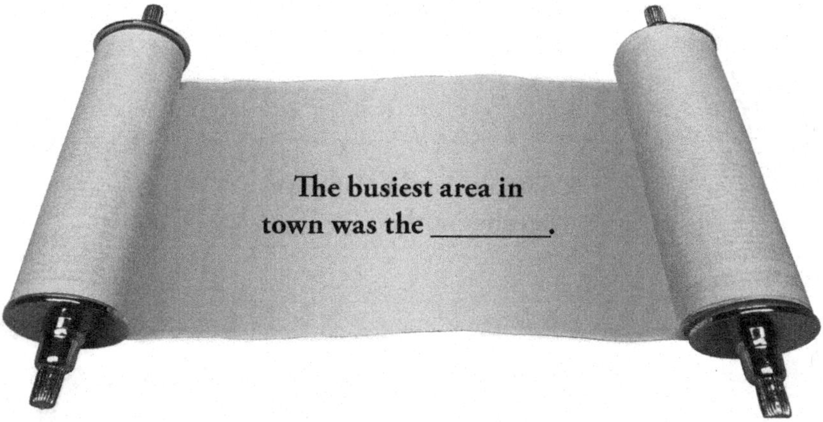
The busiest area in
town was the ________.

* In Palestine mangers were very common; some people even had mangers in their homes.

* Some people kept their animals in their homes because they couldn't afford a separate building for them.

* Some people used caves as stables for their animals; so they would carve a manger for them out of the rock in the wall of the cave.

* Jesus was born in one of these stables that was located inside of a cave in Bethlehem.

* And he was probably placed in one of these mangers that were carved out of the cave's stone wall. (Luke 2:7)

* "300 years later" a church was built over the cave where they believe Jesus was born.

* Today the church is called the "Church of the Nativity."

* A "star" marks the place where the "manger" is at.

* Written in Latin on the star are the words meaning, "Here Jesus Christ was born of the Virgin Mary."

* In Meggido, a city near northern Israel, mangers have also been discovered there by archeologists.

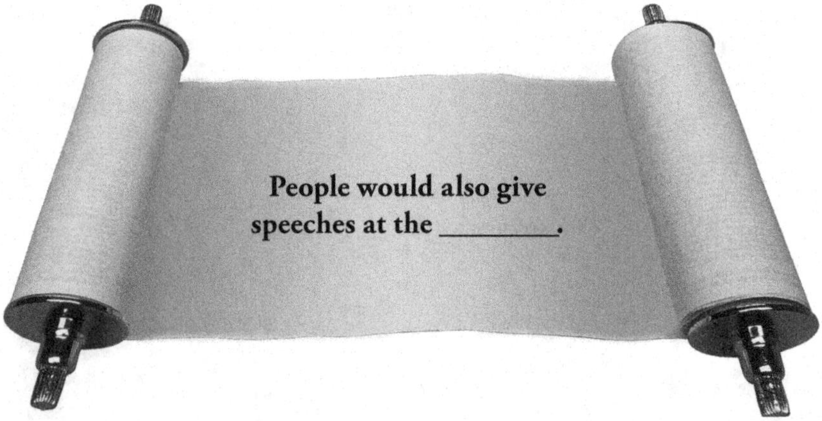
People would also give
speeches at the ________.

* It is believed that these mangers made out of limestone were made "800 years before" Jesus was born.

* These mangers are also believed to be part of the King of Israel's stables.

* Much like today, the "marketplace" in ancient times was the busiest and most exciting area of town.

* Markets could be found inside a city or just outside the city gates.

* Usually the marketplace inside the city was where all the tiny shops were gathered together on one particular street.

* If a shop owner lived on that particular street then he would just set up his shop in a room of his house that faced that street.

* Their store hours were from a little before sunrise to just before sunset.

* Sometimes at the city gate you could see local and foreign merchants with their goods laid out for everyone to see.

* If the city had several gates, then the merchants that had the same products would all gather at the same gate.

* For example, the fishermen in Jerusalem all sold their fish that they caught at the same main city gate.

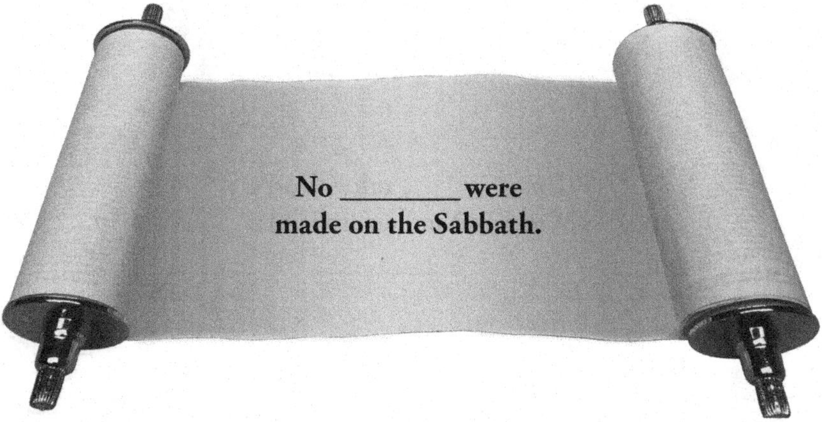
No ________ were
made on the Sabbath.

* So this city gate was called the "Fish Gate."

* Food, robes, pots, baskets, tools, jewelry and a lot more, could all be found at the marketplace.

* But the marketplace was not only a place to buy things, it was also a place where neighbors would spend time talking with one another.

* People would also give "speeches" at the marketplace.

* People would even hold "protests" at the marketplace.

* In Thessalonica, when Paul and Silas were preaching the Gospel, the Jewish leaders hired some thugs to start a riot in the marketplace.

* The Jewish leaders did this so they could arrest Paul and Silas. (Acts 17:5)

* In Philippi, because Paul and Silas cast the demon out of a girl that was a fortune-teller, her master got mad because she couldn't make him money anymore.

* So he had Paul and Silas beaten in the marketplace and thrown in prison. (Acts 16:19-22)

* People had to buy food daily because there was no refrigeration.

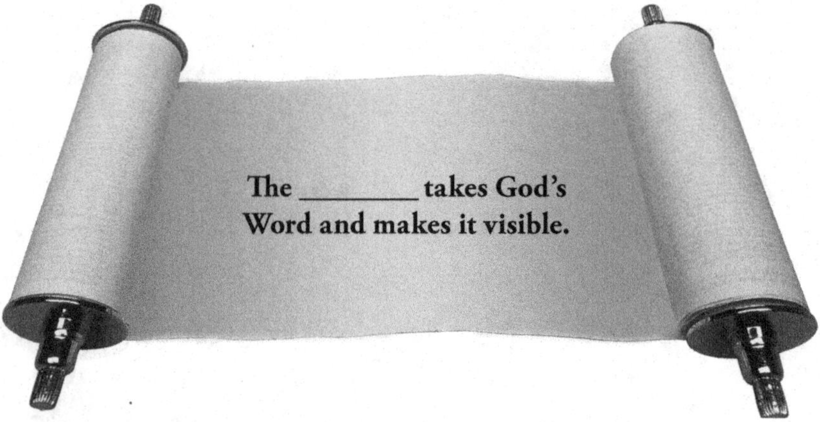
The ________ takes God's
Word and makes it visible.

* But on the Sabbath "no purchases" were made.

* God's Holy Spirit is at work all through the Bible, from the Creation in Genesis, to the return of our Lord and Savior Jesus Christ, to the Judgment Day in Revelation.

* Everything that is accomplished on earth is through God's "Holy Spirit."

* In Zechariah 4:6, the Lord tells us "…not by might, nor by power, but by My Spirit, saith the Lord of Hosts."

* The "Holy Spirit" is the vehicle that carries the voice of God.

* You cannot hear the Word of God without the breath of God, the "Holy Spirit," giving life to those Words.

* "In the beginning the earth was without form…," or not ready for habitation. (Gen. 1:2)

* The "Holy Spirit" was hovering over the face of the waters ready to bring into existence the very Words that would be spoken out of the mouth of God. (Gen. 1:2)

* One of the things that the "Holy Spirit" did in Creation was to take God's spoken word, which was invisible, and make it visible.

* He took it from the spiritual realm, and activated it into the natural realm, here on earth.

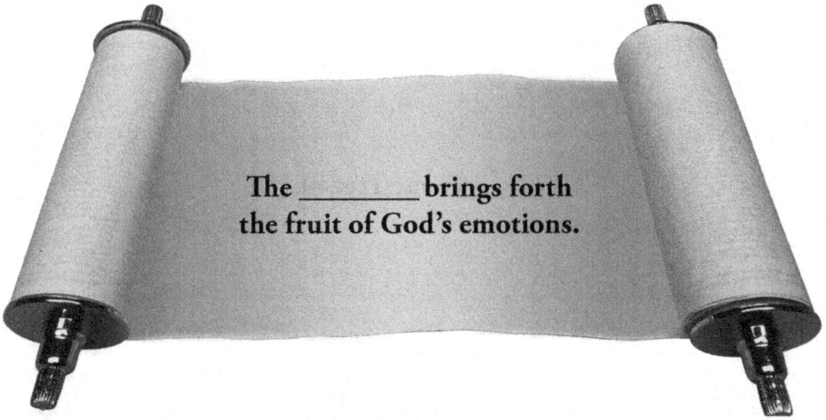
The ________ brings forth
the fruit of God's emotions.

* Genesis 1:26, is the first place where the Trinity is mentioned in the Bible (but not the word Trinity).

* When we speak of the Trinity, we are speaking of "God the (Father), God the (Son-Jesus), God the (Holy Spirit).

* In Genesis 1:26 God says, "Let "us" make man in "our" image."

* God put His character in us from the beginning, "love, kindness, patience, faithfulness, etc."

* But it is not fully activated or alive until we are born again through Jesus.

* Then the Holy Spirit brings forth the "fruit" of God's emotions that are inside of us, "love, kindness, patience, faithfulness, etc."

* Before Adam and Eve ate of the forbidden fruit of the "Tree of Knowledge," of good and evil, they only knew "good," they didn't know sin or evil.

* God's character was alive in them, in their spirit.

* Once they ate of the forbidden fruit they died spiritually and became sinners.

* When God told them not to eat of the "Tree of Knowledge," or they would die, He meant they would die spiritually and be separated from Him.

* He did not mean they would die physically at that time.

* God knew if they ate also from the "Tree of Life," that they would live forever in their sin state.

* "And the Lord God said, Behold, the man has become as one of "us," to know good and evil:"

* "…and now, lest he put forth his hand, and take also of the "Tree of Life," and eat and live forever." (Gen. 3:22)

* So the Lord drove them out of the Garden of Eden forever.

* But because God loves man so much, He had a plan to get man back to the way He originally created him, with no sin, and full of joy and life.

* That's why He sent His Only Son to die on the Cross and conquer death and the grave, to bring us back to Him.

* So now because of what Jesus did for us, when Jesus (our Tree of Life) returns, we can come back with Him with new bodies that will never die.

* And there will be no more sin, sickness, disease, sorrow or tears.

* We will be full of joy and life, the way God originally intended it to be in the beginning.

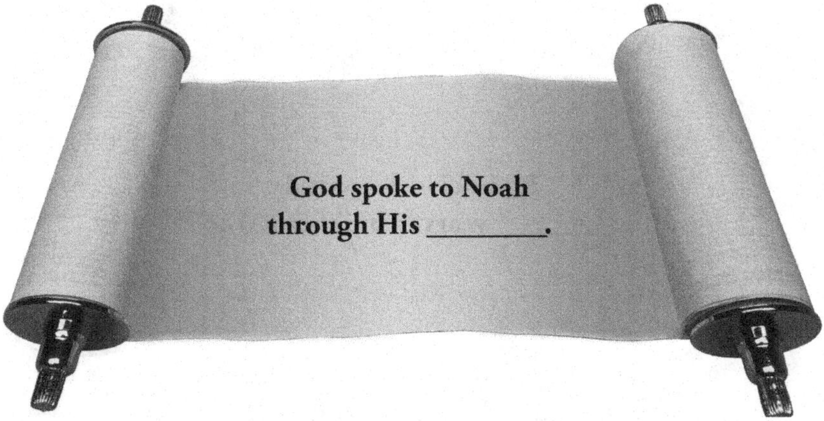
God spoke to Noah
through His ________.

* More than "700 years after the death of Adam," sin was everywhere in the earth. (Gen. 6)

* "Almost everyone" had turned away from God.

* There was "only 1 person" in the whole world that loved God, and that broke God's heart.

* "Noah" loved God, and he consistently followed God's Will and enjoyed a close relationship with Him.

* Noah found "favor" with the Lord.

* The Lord "thought" of him as a righteous man. (Hebrews 11:7)

* Noah was "500 years old" when God told him to build the Ark.

* Because He was going to flood the "entire earth" and destroy every living thing.

* God spoke to Noah through His Holy Spirit.

* Through the Holy Spirit, God told Noah the exact measurements of the Ark.

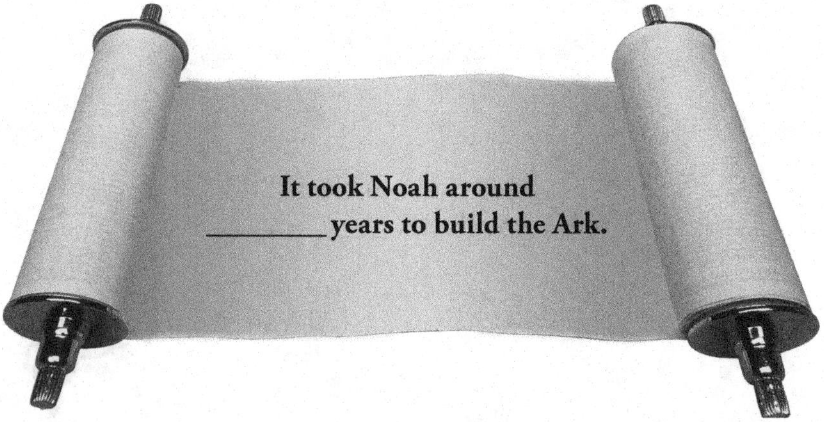
It took Noah around
________ years to build the Ark.

* It was to be 450 feet long, 75 feet wide and 45 feet high. (Gen. 6:15)

* God told him to make an opening all the way around the boat 18 inches below the roof, this was probably the window.

* God said put 3 decks inside the boat, a bottom, middle and upper, and put a door in the side.

* God even told Noah the "kind of wood" to use which was "gopher wood."

* He told him to seal it inside and out with "pitch" (tar). (Gen. 6:14)

* Noah was building a huge boat, it was the "length of one and a half footballs fields and as high as a four-story building."

* The "Ark" was exactly "6 times longer" than it was wide.

* Today, ships are still built by the same ratio.

* Noah was "600" years old when the Flood came.

* It took him approximately "100" years to complete the Ark. (Gen. 7:11)

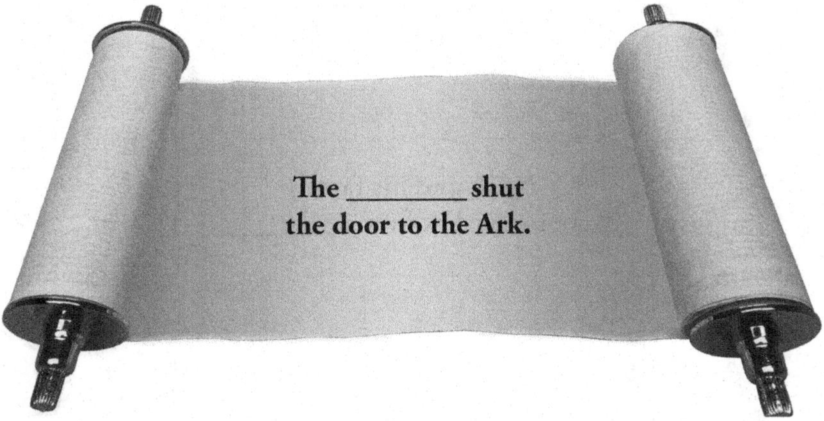
The ________ shut
the door to the Ark.

* Noah was the first major shipbuilder.

* Scholars believe that Noah was probably several miles from any body of water when he built the Ark.

* Noah's great, great grandfather was "Jared." (Gen. 5:18)

* Jared, "Enoch's father," lived to be "962" years old. (Gen. 5:20)

* "Jared" was the "2nd oldest" person whom ever lived.

* Noah's great grandfather was "Enoch." (Gen. 5:19)

* "Enoch" was "365" years old when "God took him," he never died. (Gen. 5:23-24)

* Noah's grandfather was "Methuselah," he was "the oldest" person whom ever lived.

* Noah lived to be "950" years old. (Gen. 9:29)

* "Noah" was the "3rd oldest" person whom ever lived.

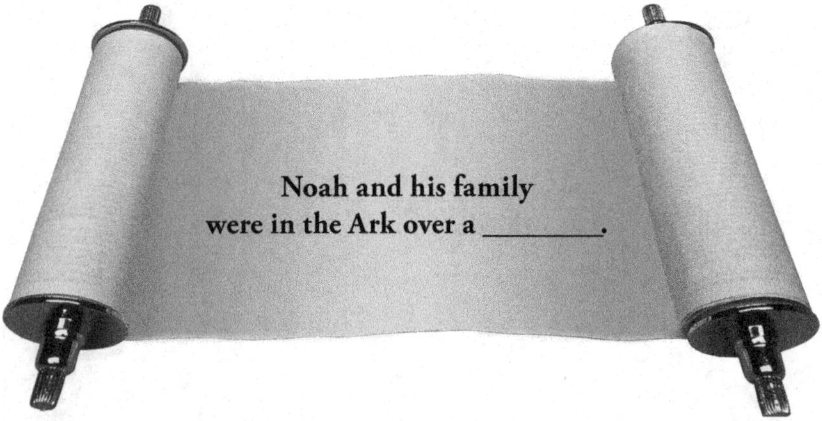

Noah and his family
were in the Ark over a ________.


* After Noah and his sons had completed the Ark, God told Noah that in a week the rain was coming.

* So Noah had a "week" to get everyone and everything on board. (Gen. 7:4)

* So Noah and his wife, with their "3 sons," Shem, Ham and Japheth and their wives, climbed into the huge boat along with all the animals.

* Then the "Lord shut them in." (Gen. 7:16)

* The rain came, not only did the rain fall in mighty torrents from the sky, but the underground waters burst forth as well. (Gen. 7:11)

* It rained for 40 days and 40 nights.

* The water rose higher and higher, until finally, the water covered even the highest mountains on earth.

* Water was standing more than "22 feet above" the highest peaks. (Gen. 7:18-20)

* After 150 days, exactly "5 months" from the time the Flood began, the boat came to rest on the mountain of "Ararat." (Gen. 8:3-4)

* On a "17,000 foot" mountain peak in "Ararat," in eastern Turkey, archeologists believe they may have found the resting place of Noah's Ark.

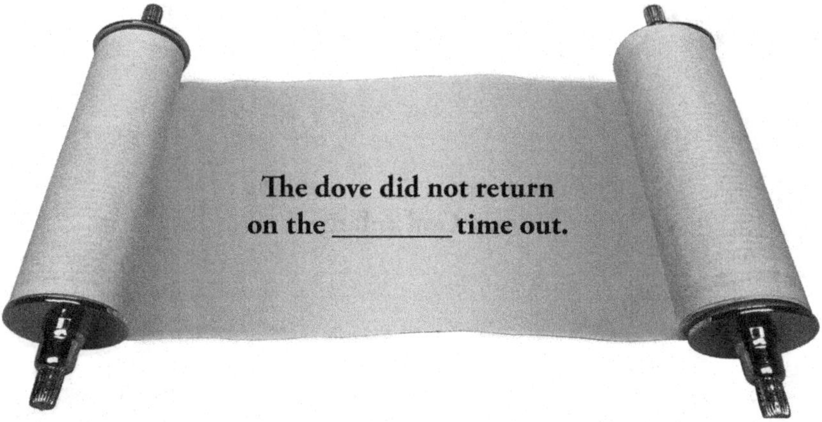

**The dove did not return on the ________ time out.**


* Noah, his family and all the animals were on the Ark for approximately a little "over a year." (Gen. 8:13-14)

* As soon as Noah came off the Ark he built an altar and made an offering to the Lord, to praise Him.

* God sent us a "rainbow" as a sign of His promise to "all of creation" that He would never destroy the "entire" earth with a Flood again. (Gen. 9:8-17)

* "And God blessed Noah and his sons, and said unto them, Be fruitful, and multiply, and "replenish" the earth." (Gen. 9:1)

* God spoke these "same" words to Adam and Eve, when He first created them in Genesis 1:28.

* The "2nd" time that Noah sent the dove out it returned with a fresh "olive" leaf in her mouth. (Gen. 8:11)

* "Olive" trees do not grow in high places, so Noah and his family were probably excited to see this, because this meant the waters were going down.

* Noah kept checking on the receding water levels by sending the dove out.

* And even though the dove didn't return on the "3rd" time out, Noah stayed on the boat for "2 more months."

* Noah did not leave the boat until "God told him it was time to leave." (Gen. 8:12-16)

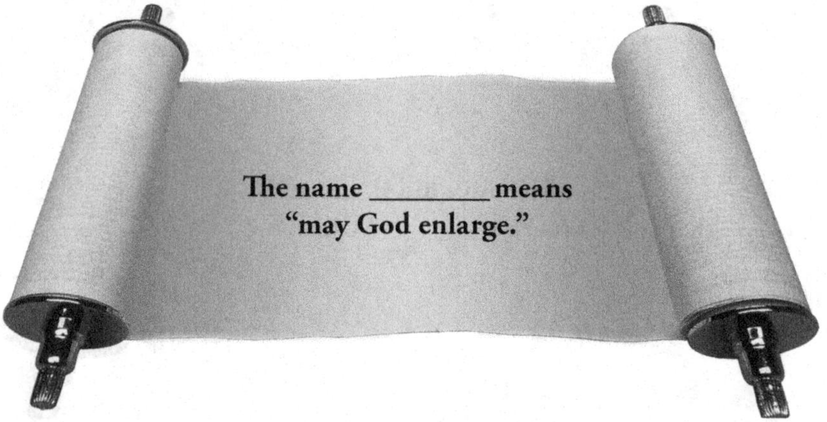
The name ________ means
"may God enlarge."

* The "Glory of the Lord was compared to the splendor of a "rainbow," by the Prophet Ezekiel. (Ezekiel 1:28)

* From Noah's 3 sons, Shem, Ham and Japheth, came all the people now scattered across the earth. (Gen. 9:18-19)

* Noah was a direct descendant of Adam.

* The name "Shem" means "renown."

* The name "Ham" means "hot."

* The name "Japheth" means "may God enlarge."

* "And "Ham," the father of Canaan, saw the nakedness of his father (Noah), and told his two brethren without." (Gen. 9:22)

* Out of respect, Ham should have covered his father; instead he went and told his two brothers.

* Noah "cursed" Ham, to be the lowest of slaves to his brothers, when he learned of this. (Gen. 9:25)

* "Shem and Japheth" took a robe and held it over their shoulders and walked backward into the tent and covered their father's naked body. (Gen. 9:23)

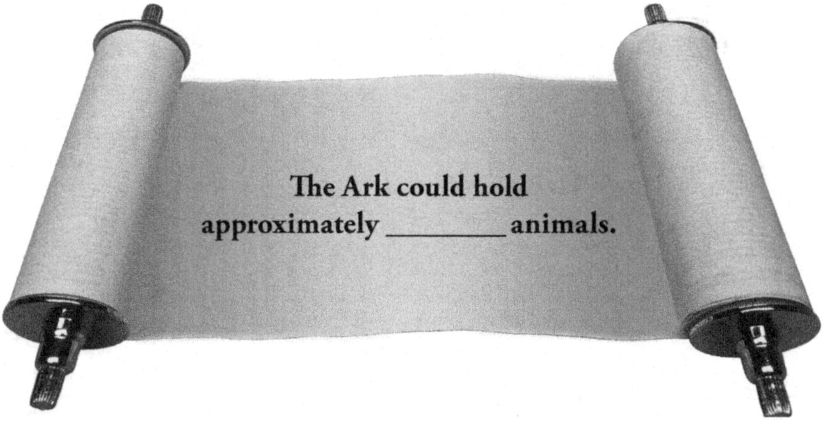
The Ark could hold
approximately ________ animals.

* So Noah "blessed" Shem and Japheth for doing the right thing. (Gen. 9:26-27)

* "Shem" had "5 sons:" Elam, Asshur, Arpachshad, Lud and Aram.

* "Ham" had "4 sons:" Cush, Egypt, Put and Canaan.

* "Japheth" had "7 sons:" Gomer, Magog, Madai, Javan, Tubal, Meshech and Tiras.

* "Shem's" descendants became "nomads" who traveled with their flocks from place to place.

* “Ham’s” descendants became “farmers” who lived in villages and towns.

* “Japheth’s” descendants became “seafarers” who lived on islands and coasts.

* “Ham’s descendants,” the Canaanites, were driven out of the Promised Land by “Shem’s descendants,” which caused “Noah’s curse to come to pass.”

* At the top of “Pilot Mountain,” in Pilot Mountain, North Carolina, there are layers of what looks like water rings around the top of the rock that could have only occurred from water being up that high, like from a “Flood.”

* The Ark could hold approximately “45,000 animals” according to scholars.

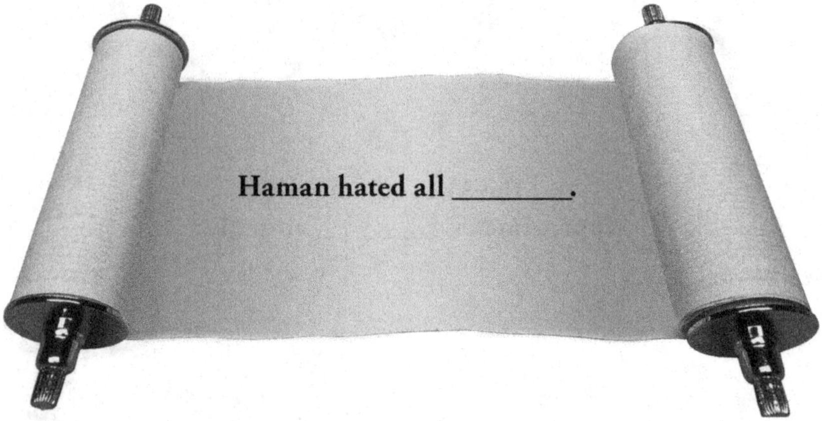


* After the “Flood,” God began shortening people’s life spans.

* From Noah at “950 years old,” until the time of Moses in Exodus, who lived to be “120 years old,” God had shortened our life spans by “830 years.”

* “Esther” was the beautiful young Jewish wife of King Ahasuerus of Persia.

* King Xerxes, as he is also known as, did not know that she was Jewish.

* But the King’s evil chief counselor “Haman” knew that she was.

* "Haman" hated all Jews, especially "Mordecai," Queen Esther's guardian and cousin, who "refused" to bow down to him.

* Haman tricked the King into signing a decree "to execute every Jew" within the vast Persian Empire.

* Haman did this because of his anger over Mordecai's disrespect to him.

* When Mordecai learned of this plan, he told "Queen Esther" that it was time to tell the King that she was Jewish in order to save her people.

* Esther hesitated at first.

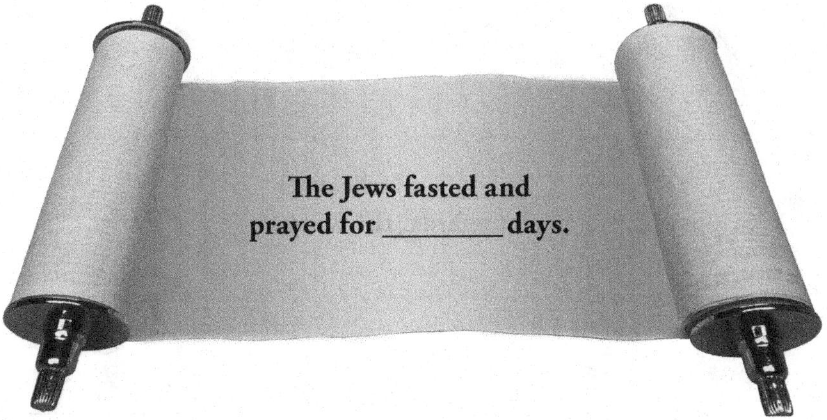
**The Jews fasted and**
**prayed for ________ days.**

* Because anyone who appears before the King in his inner court without being invited is doomed to die. (Esther 4:11)

* Esther knew it could cost her, her life, but it was what she had to do.

* But Esther knew she could only do this with God's help.

* And so she sought God for a plan of action. (Esther 4:16)

* So she called all the Jews to join her in "fasting and praying."

* She told them not to eat or drink anything day or night for "3 days." (Esther 4:15-16)

* By calling for the Jews to pray and fast with her, Esther was asking them to help her seek help from the Lord in this dangerous situation.

* So even though she was frightened, she approached her husband the King and he welcomed her into his court.

* He even offered to give her anything she wanted. (Esther 5:3)

* So Esther invited the King and Haman to "2 private feasts."

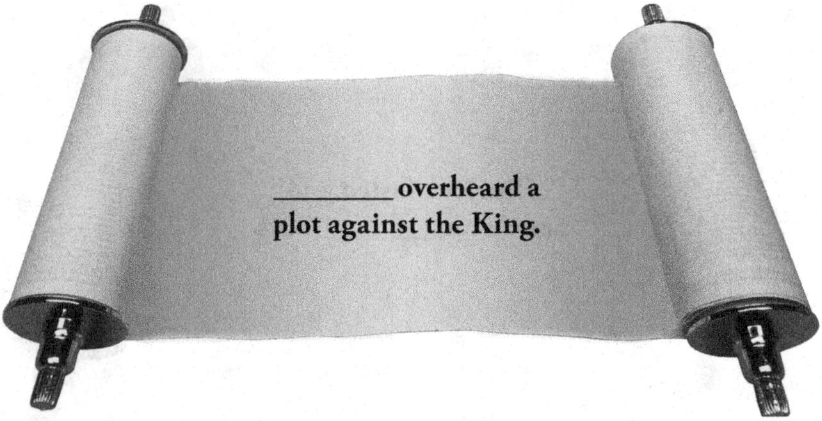
________ overheard a
plot against the King.

* And here is where she told the King about Haman's evil plot against her and the Jews and she begged him to save her people. (Esther 7)

* After hearing this, the King stormed out of the room, because he was very angry at Haman. (Esther 7:7)

* Haman fell on the couch where Esther was laying and pleaded with her for his life. (Esther 7:7-8)

* Just as Haman did this, the King returned and he saw Haman and thought he was assaulting his wife, so the King had him seized and hanged. (Esther 7:7-8)

* The King had Haman hanged on the very gallows that Haman had made to hang Mordecai on. (Esther 7:10)

* After this, the King gave Mordecai Haman's job as chief counselor.

* Through this position Mordecai now had the power and was able to protect the Jews throughout Persia. (Esther 8-10)

* The "Feast of Purim," which takes place in "March" every year, is where the Jews still celebrate Esther's bravery.

* God used Esther to save His people.

* God blessed Esther with beauty that He knew would appeal to the King.

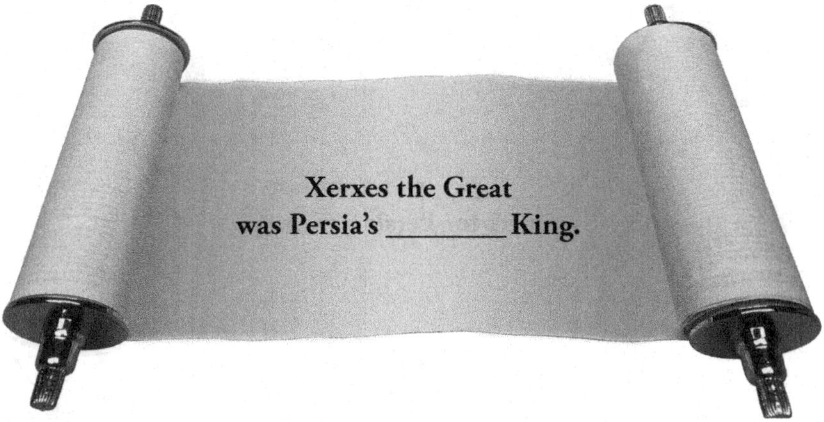
Xerxes the Great
was Persia's ________ King.

* All the Jews joined together and prayed and fasted.

* God made it possible for Esther to speak to the King.

* Mordecai trusted God to deliver him and his people.

* God made it possible for Mordecai to overhear a plot to assassinate the King.

* God made the King have trouble sleeping that night.

* So that he would be reminded and discover that he had never rewarded Mordecai for what he had done for him.

* Esther's story begins in "483 B.C."

* Her story takes place "103 years after" the captivity of the Jews by Nebuchadnezzar. (2 Kings 25)

* And "54 years after" God stirred the heart of King Cyrus of Persia to allow the Jews to return to Jerusalem and rebuild the Temple. (Ezra 1:2-3)

* And "25 years before" Ezra, a priest, scribe and descendant of Aaron led the "2nd group" to Jerusalem. (Ezra 7)

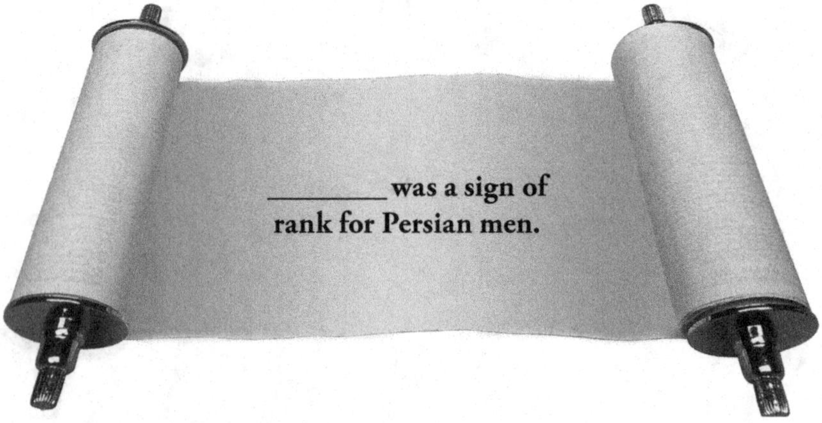
________ was a sign of
rank for Persian men.

* Esther lived in the kingdom of Persia.

* After Babylon fell in "539 B.C." the Kingdom of Persia became the dominant kingdom in the Middle East.

* Some of the Jews that were in exile chose not to return to Jerusalem; Esther's parents may have been among these.

* The "5th king of Persia" was Xerxes the Great, or King Ahasuerus, Esther's husband.

* He ruled from "486 B.C. to 465 B.C." approximately "21 years."

* King Ahasuerus also had a "winter palace" in Susa.

* The banquet that King Ahasuerus held that lasted for "6 months," was held in his winter palace in Susa.

* It was common for Persian Kings to hold great banquets before they went off to war.

* Persia was a "world power," so this made the King one of the wealthiest people in the world.

* The King used the 6 month banquet for planning his strategy of attack on Greece and to show that he had the wealth to back it up.

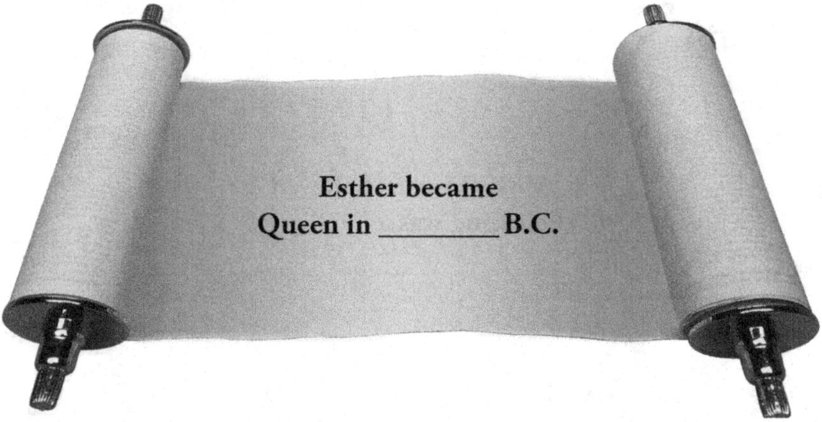
**Esther became**
**Queen in ________ B.C.**

* Persian Kings loved to show off their wealth any way they could, they would even wear expensive gemstones in their beards.

* Persian men used jewelry as a sign of rank.

* Even in battle, Persian soldiers would wear lots of gold jewelry.

* King Ahasuerus' first wife, "Queen Vashti" was dethroned in "483/482 B.C.

* She was dethroned because she disobeyed the King.

* The King had ordered her to come to him with the "royal crown on her head."

* Because he wanted all the men at the banquet to gaze at her beauty, but she refused to come. (Esther 1:11-20)

* So Esther was crowned "Queen" in "479 B.C.," she was Queen for approximately "14 years."

* In ancient records, during the reign of "Vashti's son, Artaxerxes," Vashti is mentioned as the "Queen Mother."

* "Artaxerxes" succeeded his father "Xerxes" on the throne.

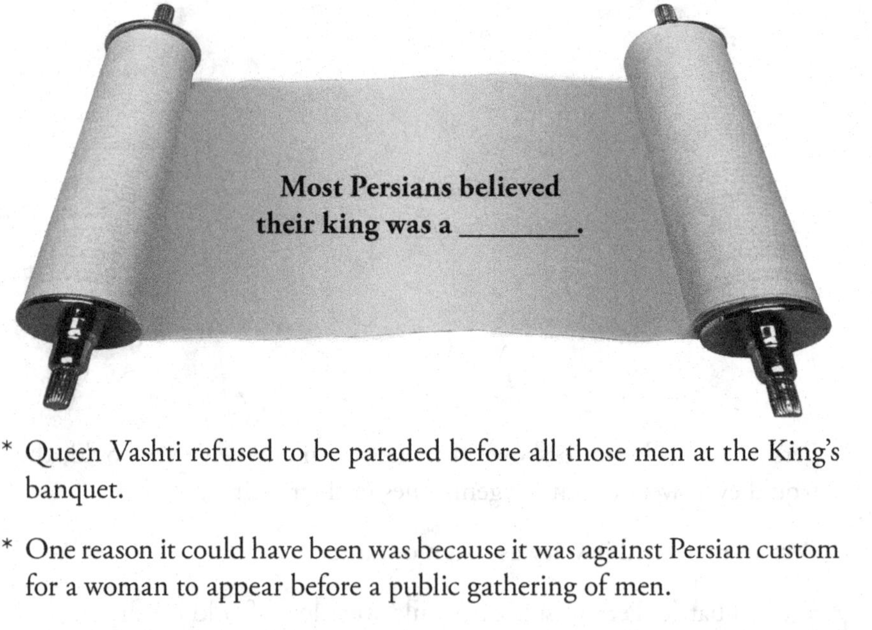
Most Persians believed
their king was a ________.

* Queen Vashti refused to be paraded before all those men at the King's banquet.

* One reason it could have been was because it was against Persian custom for a woman to appear before a public gathering of men.

* Some scholars believe that since she was pregnant with Artaxerxes, who was born in "483 B.C.," that she did not want to be seen in public like that.

* Middle Eastern Kings were not known to have a close relationship with their wives.

* "Xerxes" shows this in three ways.

* Xerxes had a harem. (Esther 2:3)

* He showed no respect for Vashti as a person. (Esther 1:10-12)

* And Queen Esther did not see him for long periods of time. (Esther 4:11)

* Persian Kings collected great amounts of jewelry and women.

* The King took "young virgins" from their home and put them in a building near the palace to live, called a "harem."

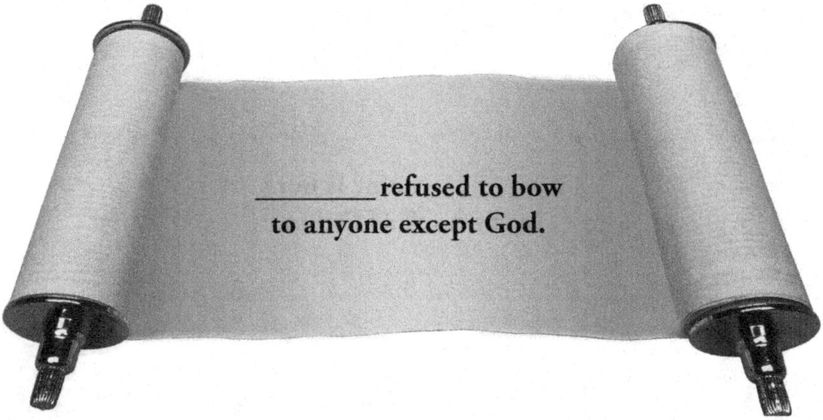
_______ refused to bow
to anyone except God.

* The only time they saw the King was if he needed them to serve him in some way or if he called on them for sexual pleasure.

* Most of the Persian people believed their King was a "god."

* So his laws or commands stood forever.

* Even if it was a bad law it could never be cancelled.

* But he could issue a new law to change the effects of the old one.

* Mordecai had a beautiful and lovely young cousin named Hadassah, who was also called Esther.

* After Esther's father and mother died, Mordecai adopted her into his family and raised her as his own daughter. (Esther 2:7)

* Mordecai refused to bow to anyone except "God."

* God had Esther in the right place at the right time.

* God placed her on the throne and got her in position because He knew what was getting ready to take place.

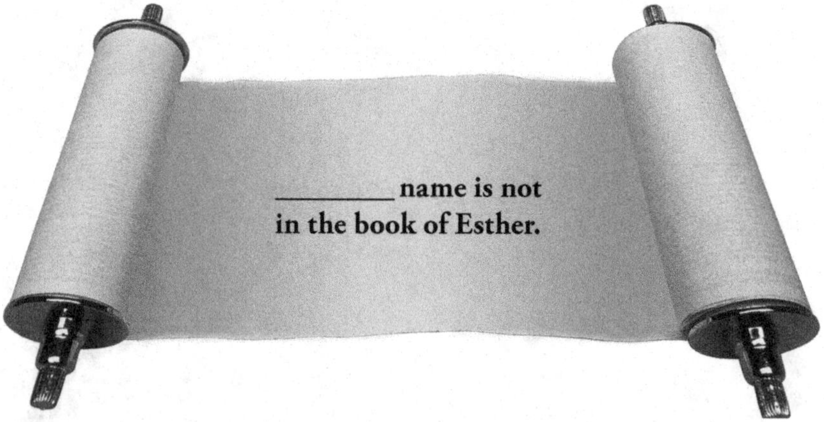

________ name is not
in the book of Esther.


* So that way God already had a person in place to offset the attack on His people.

* Haman's ancestors, the "Amalekites," and the Jews were ancient enemies.

* God had commanded the people of Israel saying, "...you are to destroy the "Amalekites" and erase their memory from under Heaven." (Deut. 25:17-19)

* King Saul of Israel, disobeyed God and "allowed King Agag of the Amalekites to live," and Haman is a descendant of this king. (1 Samuel 15:20)

* Haman's anger and hatred was not directed just at Mordecai.

* But his anger was directed at what Mordecai stood for.

* The Jews believe that God is the one and only true God and is the only One that is worthy of their praise, worship and reverence.

* To kneel before the evil Haman, to Mordecai, meant to acknowledge him as a "god," and Mordecai was not about to do that.

* In the book of Esther God is not mentioned by name.

* Even though God is not mentioned directly, you can still feel His presence and see His hand working all through the book.

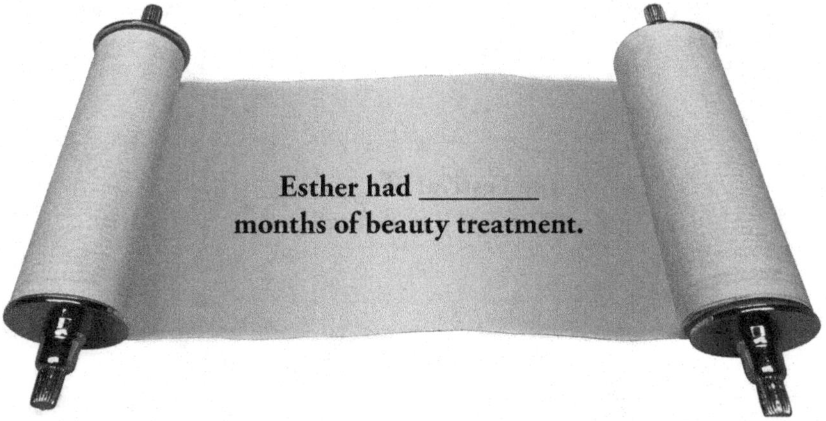
**Esther had ________**
**months of beauty treatment.**

* You can tell that the events that took place are not just coincidence.

* This shows us that God is in complete control over every area and everything in our lives. (Romans 8:28)

* When Mordecai stopped the assignation attempt on the King, no reward was given to him, but it was written in the history books.

* But Mordecai's reward came in God's timing.

* God promises to reward us for our good deeds, but we sometimes don't want to wait on His timing.

* So be patient, and wait on God, because He knows when it will do you the most good.

* The Persians would always place a "veil" over the face of someone who was condemned to death.

* Because Persian Kings would not look upon someone's face that was condemned to die.

* In "Susa" on "March 7th and 8th," King Ahasuerus gave a decree.

* He decreed that because of Haman's deceitfulness the Jews had a right to defend themselves against their enemies.

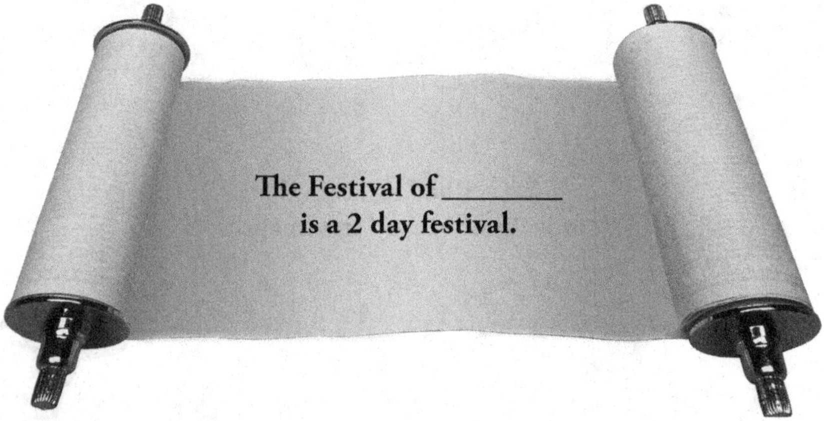
The Festival of ________
is a 2 day festival.

* So the Jews killed "800 people" in the city of Susa.

* In the rest of the cities on "March 7th" the Jews defended themselves against their enemies and killed "75,000 people" on that one day.

* Esther, just like the other young women in the harem, before she was taken to the King's bed, she was given the prescribed "12 months" of beauty treatment. (Esther 2:12)

* She had "6 months" with "oil of myrrh."

* Followed by "6 months" with "special perfumes and ointments." (Esther 2:12)

* When the time came for her to go in to the King she was given her choice of whatever clothing or jewelry she wanted to enhance her beauty. (Esther 2:13)

* Haman, son of Hammedatha, the Agagite, the enemy of the Jews, had plotted to crush and destroy them on the day and month determined by casting lots. (Esther 9:24)

* These "lots" were called "Purim."

* But when Esther came before the King he issued a decree causing Haman's plot to backfire. (Esther 9:25)

* Instead of Haman hanging Mordecai on the gallows,

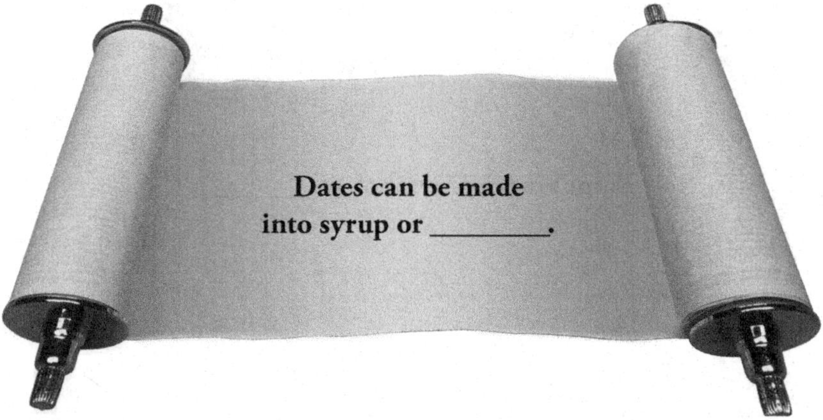
**Dates can be made**
**into syrup or ________.**

* "Haman and his sons" were hanged on the gallows. (Esther 9:25)

* That is why the celebration is called "Purim." (Esther 9:26)

* Because it is the ancient word for "casting lots."

* Heeding Mordecai's suggestion, an "annual 2 day festival" called "the Festival of Purim" is now celebrated on March 7th and 8th by all Jews.

* He suggested that they celebrate them with feasting and with joy and by "giving gifts to one another" and "to the poor." (Esther 9:22)

* In doing this they would be remembering and celebrating the time the Jews gained relief from their enemies. (Esther 9:22)

* "...when their sorrow was turned into gladness and their mourning into joy." (Esther 9:22)

* As it was in Biblical times, still today, the "Date Palm Tree," is important to the people in the "Holy Land" as a good source of food.

* The "palm tree" is very beautiful; it can grow up to "80 feet" tall.

* At the top of the palm tree it has a spreading plume of palms that can reach 10 to 20 feet long.

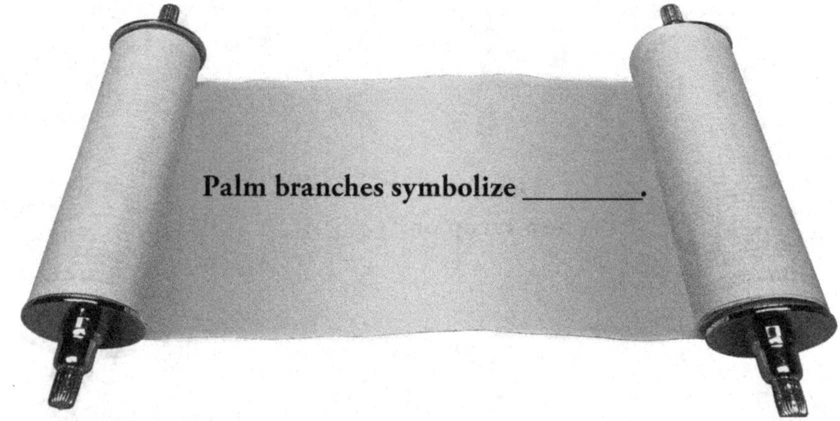
Palm branches symbolize ________.

* Some palms produce a fruit called "dates," which can be eaten fresh or dried.

* Some people that lived in the desert lived on nothing but dried dates and milk for months.

* Dates can also be made into "syrup or intoxicating liquor."

* "125 pounds" of dates a year could be produced by one pollinated "female palm tree."

* "Lumber" for houses and "fuel" for fires, came from the "trunk" of the palm tree.

* "Roofing" and fiber for "ropes, brooms and tent cloth," came from the "branches" of the palm tree.

* "Baskets, mats and even the sails for ships" were woven from the "leaves" of the palm tree.

* After the Jews left Egypt they lived in tents while in the wilderness.

* For "40 years" they wandered in the wilderness before God would allow them to enter the "Promised Land."

* Later, Jews celebrated the harvest each year by building huts and then covering them with "palm branches" and other plants to remember this time.

_________ seeds are among
the tiniest seeds of any plant.

* The symbol of "celebration" was "palm branches."

* After Judas Maccabeus drove the Syrians out of Jerusalem in "164 B.C." the Jews waved "palm branches" as he entered the city.

* "200 years later" on Palm Sunday, as "Jesus" rode into Jerusalem the Jews waved "palm branches" hailing Him as the "Messiah."

* Many Christians today still celebrate this custom.

* The "righteous" are described as being like the "palm tree" because it grows "straight and tall." (Psalm 92:12)

* "Mustard seeds" are among the tiniest seeds of any plant.

* In describing the Kingdom of Heaven, Jesus compares it to a "mustard seed" that is planted in the field.

* "Which indeed is the "least of all seeds:"

* "But when it "is grown," it is the greatest among herbs, and becometh "a tree,"

* "So that the birds of the air come and lodge in the branches thereof." (Matthew 13:31-32)

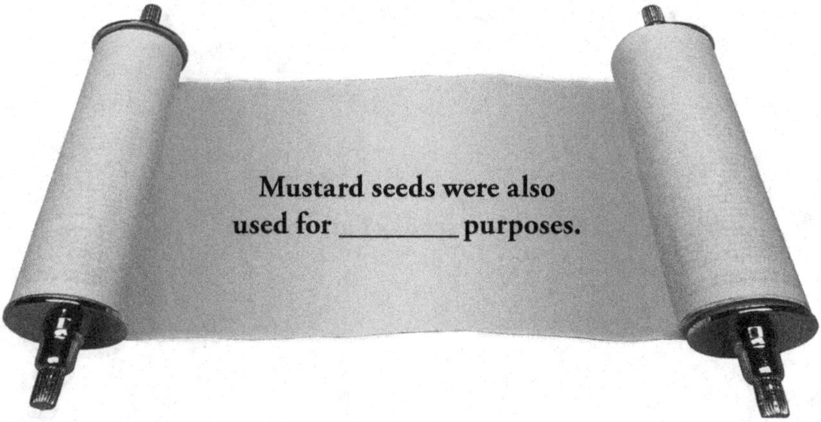
Mustard seeds were also
used for ________ purposes.

* The "black mustard plant" grew wild in the Holy Land; it may have been the mustard plant Jesus was referring to.

* It would grow even in "poor soil."

* These plants could reach a height of "4 or 5 feet" by the middle of the summer.

* But these seeds would produce even taller plants if someone planted them in their garden and took really good care of them.

* They would sometimes grow as high as a man on horseback.

* The stalks were so strong that small birds would sit on them to eat the plant's seeds.

* Many people in Biblical times used "mustard seeds" as a seasoning.

* The ripe seeds would be crushed to extract the tangy oil that was inside of them.

* Some people just ate the seeds themselves by sprinkling them over their food.

* Mustard seeds had "medicinal" purposes as well; they would crush the mustard seeds to make plaster.

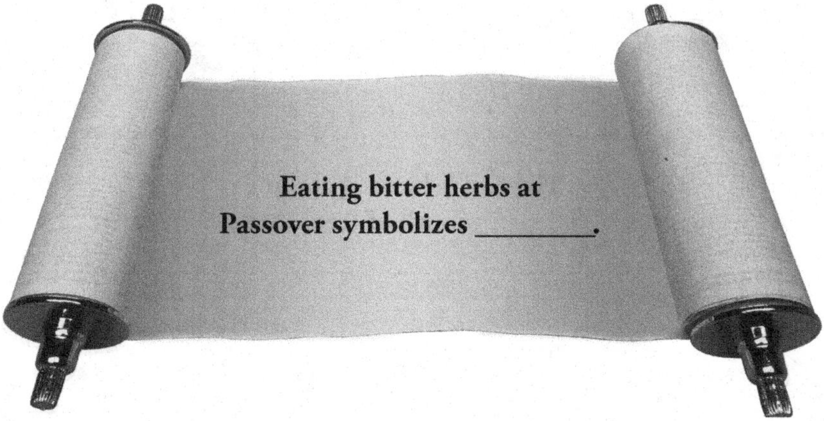
**Eating bitter herbs at**
**Passover symbolizes ________.**

* After crushing the seeds into powder they would then mix it with water and flour to create the plaster.

* Then they would put this mixture on to pieces of cloth and then lay it across someone's chest to relieve "lung congestion."

* One day, "the apostles said unto the Lord, Increase our faith." (Luke 17:5)

* "And the Lord said, "If ye had "faith as a grain of mustard seed," ye might say unto this sycamine tree, Be thou plucked up by the root, and be thou planted in the sea;..."

* "...and it should obey you." (Luke 17:6)

* At "Passover" the Jews eat several foods that have a symbolic meaning, such as "bitter herbs." (Ex. 12:8)

* At the "1st Passover" the Israelites were given specific instructions from God, by Moses and Aaron, as to what they should wear and eat, and why.

* The Jews celebrate the "Passover" festival in remembrance of their "Exodus" from Egypt.

* "And they shall eat the flesh (lamb) in that night…"

* "…roast with fire, and unleavened bread; and with bitter herbs they shall eat it." (Ex. 12:8)

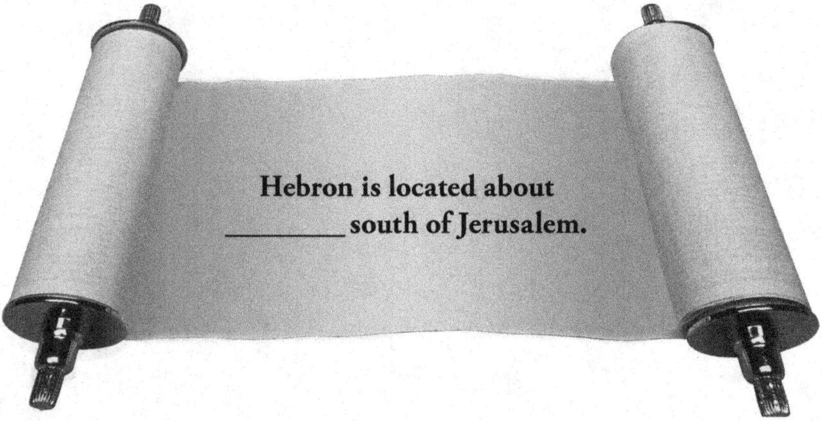
Hebron is located about
________ south of Jerusalem.

* When the Israelites were slaves in Egypt, Pharaoh was very cruel and hard on them.

* So the "bitter herbs" symbolize that "hardship" so they will remember what God did for them.

* Before they eat the bitter herbs they are to dip them in "saltwater" first.

* The "saltwater" symbolizes the "tears" they shed during their slavery.

* They were also supposed to eat it wearing their traveling clothes, with their shoes on their feet and their walking sticks in their hand.

* There is a shrine in the city of "Hebron," and in part of this shrine is the "burial place" of the Patriarchs.

* Also, in part of this shrine is a "wall" built by King Herod the Great.

* "Hebron" is an ancient city that is located in the heart of the "Judean hill country."

* Hebron sits more than "3,000 feet" above sea level on a mountain ridge.

* Hebron is located about "20 miles south" of Jerusalem and is well blessed with wells, springs and vegetation.

________ was crowned
King in Hebron.

* Because of its rich soil, the city has become the prime location for growing "grapes and olives."

* The city of Hebron dates back to the days of the Patriarch "Abraham."

* "Abraham" lived in Hebron for several years, and while he was there he purchased some land for a family burial plot.

* "Abraham, Sarah, Isaac, Rebekah, Jacob and Leah" are all buried in this family burial plot.

* When Moses, "700 years later," sent a scouting party made up of "12 men" on a "40 day journey" to the Promised Land, one of the cities they saw was Hebron.

* On the way to Hebron, near Ephrath, which is another name for Bethlehem, "Rachel" went into labor.

* "Rachel" died there after giving birth to her son "Benjamin." (Gen. 35:16-20)

* The city of Hebron was given to "Caleb" by Joshua after Joshua conquered Canaan.

* "Caleb" along with "Joshua" were both part of the "12 man scouting party" that Moses sent to check out the Promised Land.

* They are the "only 2" that came back with an encouraging report. (Num. 13 & 14)

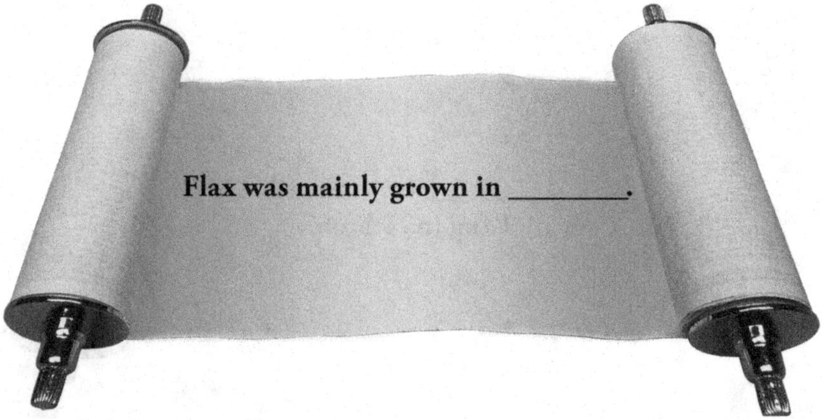
**Flax was mainly grown in ________.**

* "Young David" hid from King Saul near Hebron.

* In Hebron is where the "young David" was crowned "King of Israel," after Saul died.

* For "7 years" Hebron was King David's capital.

* Then King David conquered Jerusalem and made it the capital.

* When "Absalom" was trying to overthrow his father, King David, he tried to copy him by having himself crowned king at Hebron as well.

* The huge wall that King Herod the Great built around the "Hebron cave" was built shortly "before Jesus was born."

* The "holiest site" in Hebron is the "burial place" of Abraham and his family, called the "cave of Machpelah."

* It is sacred to "Jews, Christians and Muslims" alike.

* "Flax" could be found near Jericho and in Egypt, but it was mainly grown in "Galilee."

* The "sky-blue flowers" on the flax plant always bloomed in the spring.

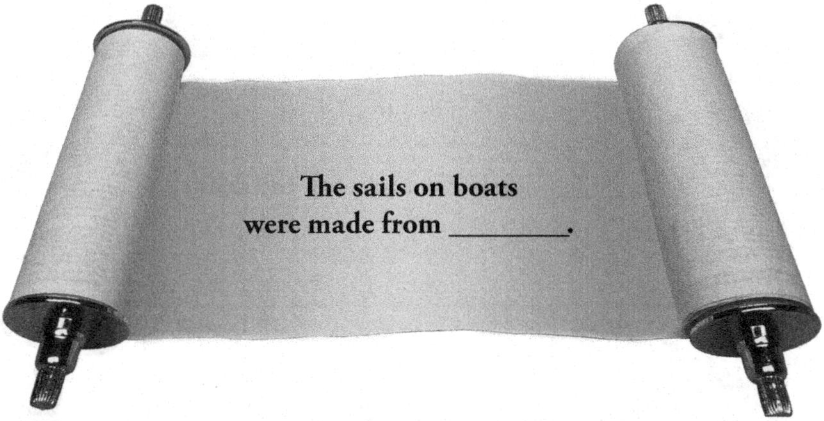
The sails on boats
were made from ________.

* Flax was the first crop harvested each year.

* The stems grew to about 2 feet tall and in clusters.

* To harvest them they would cut the stems close to the ground.

* Then they would soak them in water and lay them out to dry.

* "Joshua's spies" hid behind drying "flax stalks" when they crept into the city to spy on it.

* "Thread and woven linen" were made from "dried flax fibers" that had been separated from the stalks.

* They also made "undergarments, coats and priests cloaks" from this "whitish" cloth.

* The most popular and more abundant cloth was "wool."

* But the most comfortable cloth to wear in the warm climate was "linen."

* You can weave "linen" so fine that it is almost transparent.

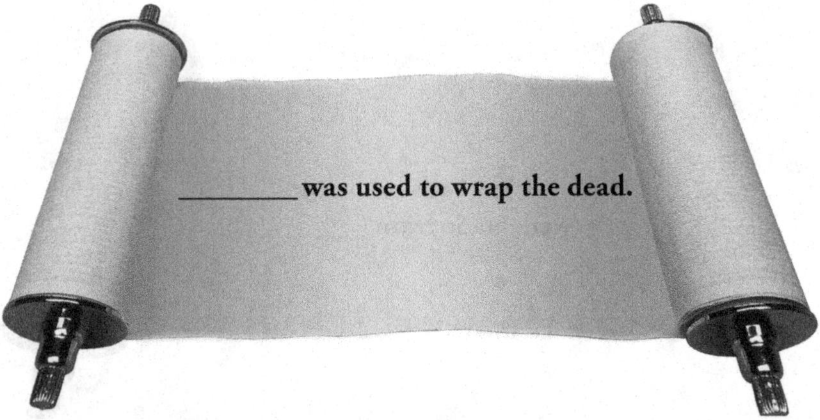
________ was used to wrap the dead.

* The "Prophet Isaiah" warned against wearing "linen garments" because it was so transparent. (Isaiah 3:23)

* The "sails" on boats were also made from "linen" because it was so durable.

* Flax fibers were also used as "wicks" for oil lamps because they were so flexible and porous.

* At night oil lamps were the main source of light.

* "Rope" was also made from "braided flax" which could then be used for "hunting, warfare and shipping."

* "Linen" is still today the fabric of choice for summer clothing.

* But what once was done by people long ago, is now done today by machines.

* The Israelites also "wrapped their dead" with "linen cloth."

* The "linen cloth," which is called the "Shroud of Turin," that was used to wrap "Jesus' body" in when He was placed in the tomb, was believed to have been discovered in France in the "14th century."

* Still today the flax plant is used to make "linen cloth, rope, wicks and linseed oil."

The American plane tree
is known as the ________ tree.


* A prickly fruit that is very common in the Holy Land comes from the tall "plane tree." (Gen. 30:37)

* The plane tree is referred to as a "chestnut tree" in the King James Version of the Bible.

* The Prophet Isaiah said God would show His might by making "giant trees grow in the desert."

* "I will plant in the wilderness the cedar, the shittah tree, and the myrtle, and the oil tree; I will set in the desert the fir tree, and the pine, and the box tree together:" (Isaiah 41:19)

* The amazing plane tree can grow more than "100 feet tall."

* "That they may see, and know, and consider, and understand together, that the hand of the Lord hath done this, and the Holy One of Israel hath created it." (Isaiah 41:20)

* In the Holy Land and in Syria, you will find the plane tree growing alongside streams and on the shores of lakes and rivers.

* The dark green large leaves of the plane tree are very shiny.

* The plane tree produces round, "inedible fruits" that are covered in spikes.

* These trees are very important because of their shade.

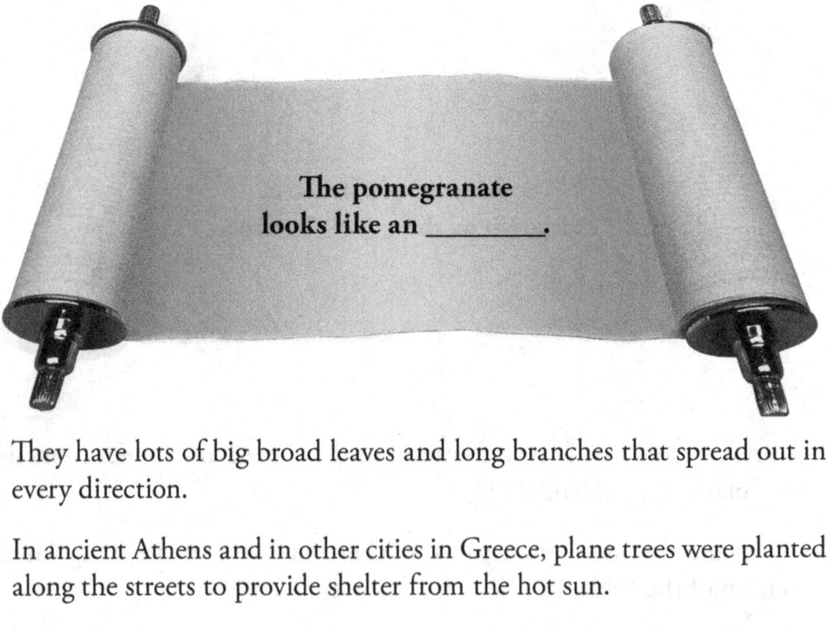
**The pomegranate**
**looks like an ________.**

* They have lots of big broad leaves and long branches that spread out in every direction.

* In ancient Athens and in other cities in Greece, plane trees were planted along the streets to provide shelter from the hot sun.

* In America, the plane tree is known as the "sycamore tree" and they also form a canopy over many streets in many cities today.

* "Armon" or "peeling off" is the Hebrew name for the plane tree.

* It is called this because of its unique bark.

* An inner surface is revealed when the outer layer of bark peels off.

* The inner surface is "mainly white," but it also has "spots of green, yellow and gray also."

* "Jacob" needed something with white stripes to influence the mating of his flock.

* So "Jacob" took "fresh shoots" from poplar, almond and plane trees and peeled off strips of the bark to make streaks in them. (Gen. 30:37)

* When Moses was telling the Israelites some of the things that were going to be in the Promised Land, "pomegranates" is one of the things he listed. (Deut. 8:8)

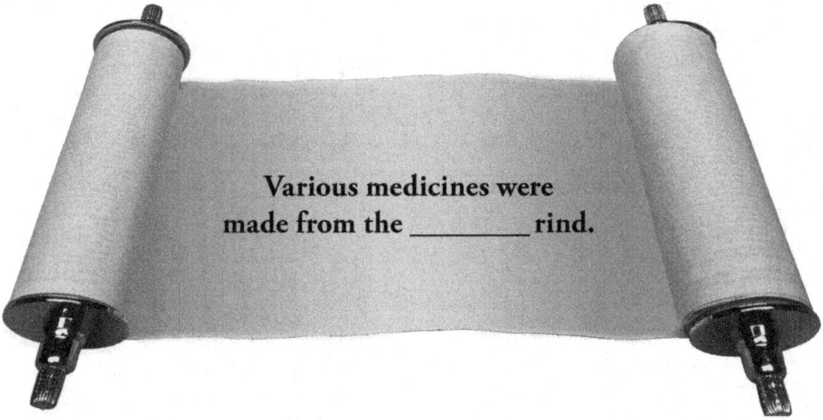
Various medicines were
made from the ________ rind.

* At first glance, the "pomegranate" looks like an apple.

* It is a shiny reddish-yellow fruit that produces a delicious juice that will quench your thirst on a hot summer day.

* The "pulp" has a pleasant but slightly sour taste.

* In Palestine and Egypt, "pomegranate" bushes have been planted next to houses and in gardens, since ancient times.

* In the spring orange-red flowers appear on the pomegranate bush which then produces refreshing fruit.

* In ancient times the pomegranate was used for many things, but it was mostly used for food.
* The main ingredient used in the making of the bright "red dye" that was used to tan leather came from the "hard rind" of the pomegranate.
* Various "medicines" were also made from the "pomegranate rind."
* Such as medicines for "diarrhea" and "different skin conditions."
* But an overdose could cause "vomiting and cramps."

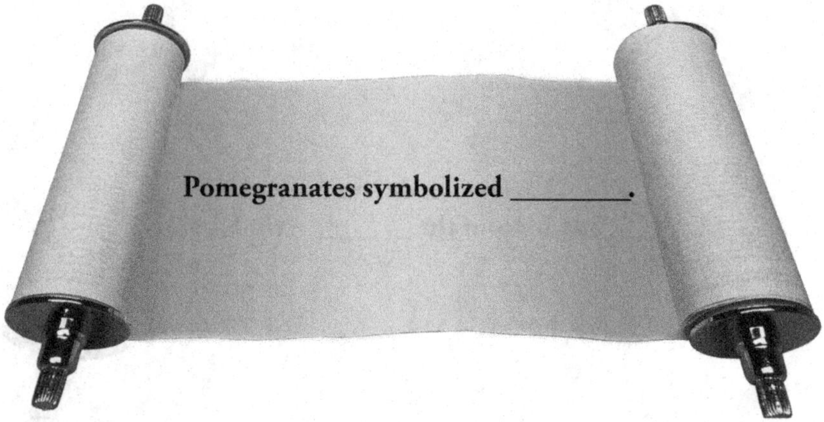
Pomegranates symbolized ________.

* To eliminate the parasite known as "tapeworm" people would ingest the "pomegranate's tiny seeds."
* Many artists were inspired by this colorful fruit and its tiny leaves.
* At the top of the "columns" of Solomon's Temple in Jerusalem were images of pomegranates.
* Designs of "blue, purple and crimson pomegranates" were sewn on the "robes" of the priests who served in the Temple at God's command. (Ex. 39:24-26)
* They alternated between "gold bells and pomegranates" all along the "hem."

* Aaron had to wear this robe whenever he entered the Holy Place to minister to the Lord.

* The bells on his robe would ring every time Aaron went in and out of the Lord's presence.

* The Lord said if he wears this robe he will not die. (Ex. 28:35)

* The pomegranate was a powerful symbol of "eternal life" in ancient times.

* It is dangerous to criticize or come against God's leaders or people in any way, even if you are one of His.

________ was embarrassed
by David dancing.

* God tells us in Psalm 105:15, "Saying, touch not Mine anointed, and do My prophets no harm."

* When we disobey this command the Lord says in Romans 12:19, "… Vengeance is mine; I will repay, saith the Lord."

* "Miriam" – She criticized Moses because he married an Ethiopian woman, and she was jealous of his leadership.

* Her Punishment - God struck her with leprosy. (Num. 12:1-16)

* "Korah, Dathan, and Abiram and their followers" – They and some of the Israelites came against Moses and his leadership. (Num. 16:1-30)

* Their Punishment – God had the earth open up and it swallowed up all the men, their families, their followers and all their belongings;

* Then the earth closed back up again. (Num. 16:31-33)

* "250 Male leaders who also followed Kohath" – They also rose up against Moses and his leadership.

* Their Punishment – Fire came forth from the Lord and consumed them all. (Num. 16:35)

* "All the congregation of Israel" – Everyone was murmuring against Moses and Aaron saying that they had killed the Lord's people.

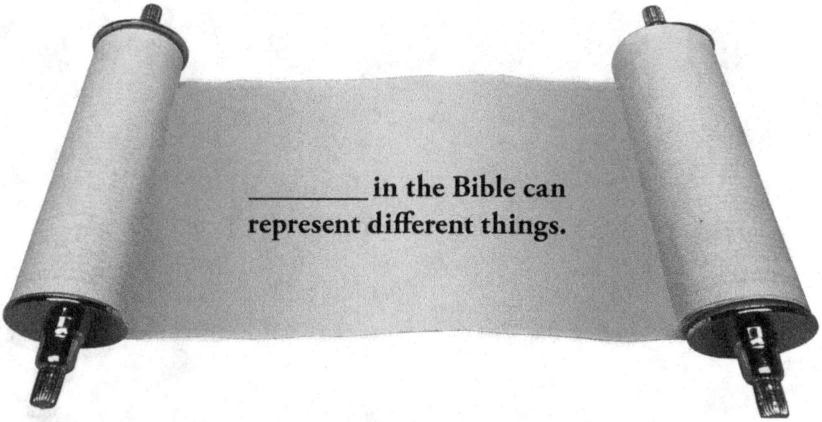
________ in the Bible can
represent different things.

* Their Punishment – God sent a plague upon them all and 14,000 people died. (Num. 16:41-50)

* "Michal" – She got upset with David because he embarrassed her by dancing before the Lord in public.

* Her Punishment – She was David's first wife, but God would not let her ever have any children. (2 Samuel 6:16-23)

* "Shimei" – He was a member of Saul's family he cursed and threw stones at David. (2 Samuel 16:5-14)

* His Punishment – After King David died, God had King Solomon execute him. (1 Kings 2:36-46)

* "Group of Youth" – They mocked Elisha and made fun of him because he was bald headed.

* Their Punishment – God had 2 female bears come out of the woods and they killed 42 of them. (2 Kings 2:23-24)

* Different "numbers" in the Bible represent different things.

* The number "2" represents "Agreement."

* The number "3" represents "Abundance, witness and the Trinity." (God the Father, God the Son (Jesus) and God the Holy Spirit.)

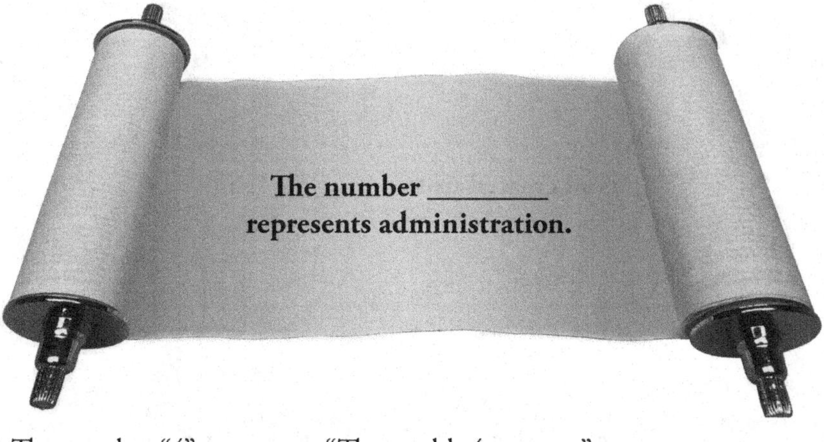
The number ________
represents administration.

* The number "4" represents "The world, 4 corners."

* The number "5" represents "Grace of God."

* The number "6" represents "Man, 6th day man was created."

* The number "7" represents "Divine perfection, completion."

* The number "8" represents "New Beginnings."

* The number "10" represents "Responsibility."
* The number "11" represents "Destruction."
* The number "12" represents "Administration."
* The number "120" represents "End of Judgment."
* The number "666" represents "The Anti-Christ."

* The sanctuary of a lot of churches are decorated by "banners and flags."
* Many churches also use "banners and flags" in Praise and Worship.
* They not only make the sanctuary look beautiful, but they also help people focus on the Lord.
* Banners and flags in a sanctuary are also used to remind the people to pray for certain things.
* Whatever the needs of the people are such as, faith, a deeper walk, healing, etc.

* They are also used to help people think about the things of God, "who He is, His character, His love, His mercy, etc."

* God created us to "worship" Him with every part of our being.

* So as we praise and worship Him, He not only "listens" to us, but He "watches" us as well.

* The history of banners and flags in the Bible can be dated back to the "12 Tribes of Israel."

* During the Exodus, banners and flags were used to line up each tribe in the march to a new campsite as well as in the camp itself.

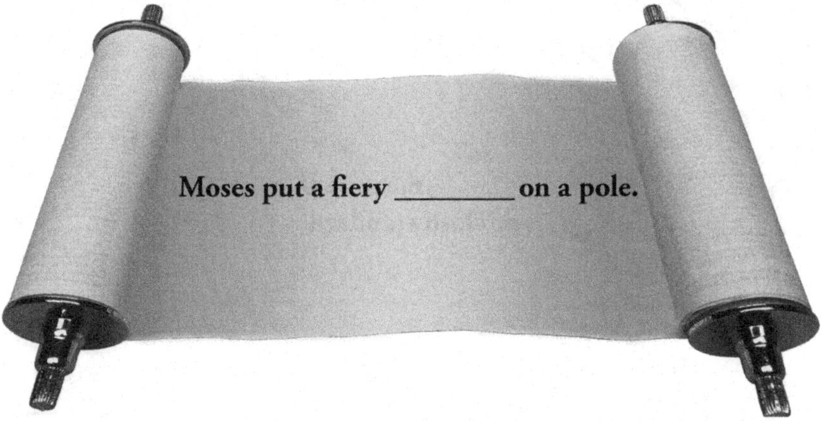
Moses put a fiery ________ on a pole.

* In the time of war, each tribe had a special place in the battle, and they used banners and flags to identify these places.

* Still today, small banners or flags are used by the military to identify a particular unit.

* While in the wilderness the Israelites complained against God and Moses.

* They complained about being in the wilderness with no bread or water, they even said they hated the manna that God had sent.

* So God sent poisonous snakes among the people and they bit the people and many died.

* Then they repented, so the Lord commanded Moses to make a "fiery serpent and set it upon a pole."

* And God said that when the people looked upon it they would be "healed." (Num. 21:5-9)

* This is showing that God used a "banner" to get a message to His people.

* In the Bible "flag" becomes the primary sign for lifting up a "standard" of God.

* A "standard" is what He stands for, who He is.

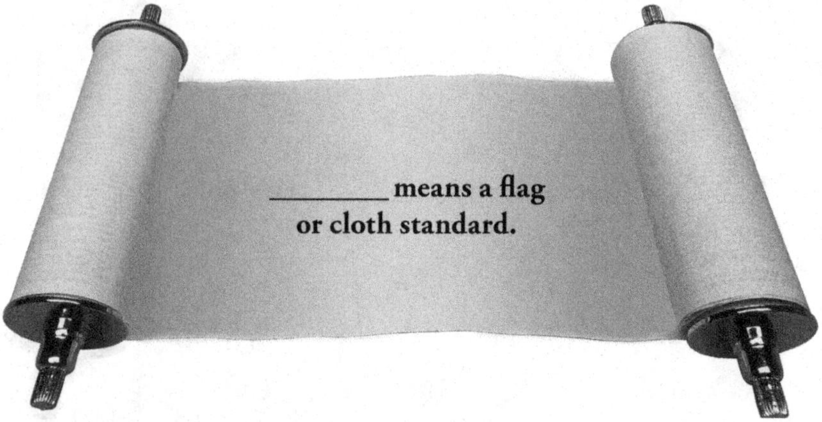
________ means a flag
or cloth standard.

* In the Bible the word "flag" is called a "standard or banner."

* Standard means a banner used with an emblem, marker, or rallying point. It could be a military or personal flag.

* An "emblem" is a picture or any object used to "symbolize" something.

* God commands Moses to tell the people of Israel to camp by their own "standard" (flag or banner) which represents their Tribe. (Num. 2:2)

* So there were "12 different" flags or banners for "12 Tribes."

* "Banner" means a flag or cloth standard.

* It is used symbolically to "describe" a part of God's character or one of God's names, such as "Jehovah Nissi, the Lord is my banner."

* "God's Salvation" is described and honored by "raising banners" in Psalm 20:5.

* "God's Truth" is described and honored by "raising banners" in Psalm 60:4.

* "God Himself" is described as a "banner of love" over us in Solomon 2:4.

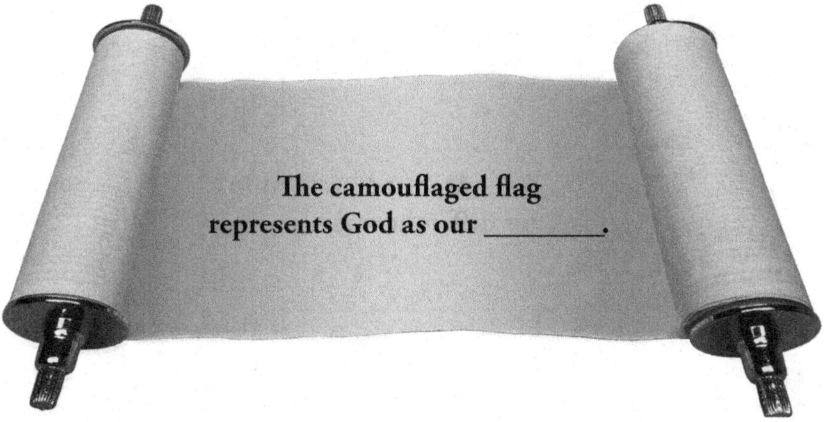
The camouflaged flag
represents God as our ________.

* God is "standard," and it is "His standard" that we are to live by.

* God said, "When the enemy shall come in like a flood, the Spirit of the Lord shall lift up a "standard" against him." (Isaiah 59:19)

* Which means Satan (the enemy) is defeated by "God's ways, God's truth, the Word (the Sword of the Spirit) and by our faith."

* God is calling us to lift up "His standard" and to declare it and proclaim it to the nations. (Jeremiah 50:2)

* "Flags and banners" represent "who God is, His power and authority, what He is doing on the earth on behalf of His people, and it lets the world know who He is to us."

* "Colors and numbers" are used by God throughout the Bible as symbols of Him, Jesus, the Holy Spirit and His Kingdom.
* "Flags and banners" are used by God the same way as symbols of Him, Jesus, the Holy Spirit and His Kingdom as well.
* As we "wave" a particular "flag," that "flag represents" who God is, what He is doing in His church, someone's life or on the earth.
* For example: If we "wave" the "camouflaged flag" it represents, "God as our warrior (who He is)."
* And it represents "God doing battle in our lives (what He is doing)."

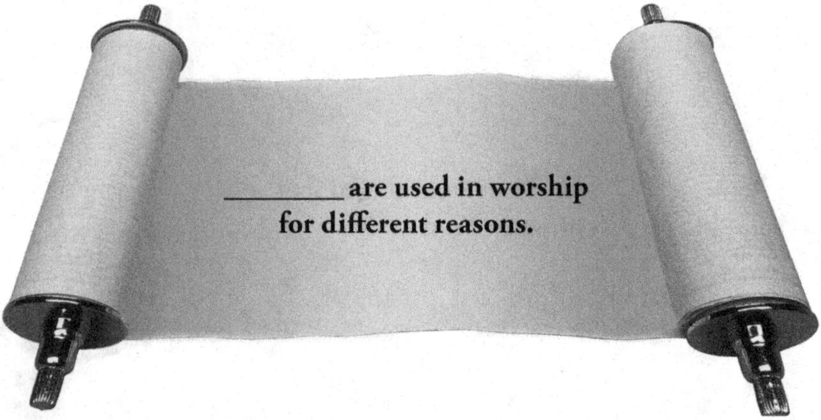
________ are used in worship
for different reasons.

* For example: You may "wave" the camouflaged flag "11 times" (11 symbolizing destruction) one way, then "11 times" another way; which could mean:
* "God is tearing down strongholds in our lives."
* Then you may "wave" the "white flag" (symbolizing purity) "8 times" one way, which could mean:
* Since God is tearing down the strongholds in our lives, God is giving us or that person a "new beginning."
* Because as we said earlier, "8" represents "new beginnings."

* There are several different reasons why "flags" are used in worship.

* They are used to "minister unto the Lord."

* They are used to "glorify Him."

* They are used to "show Him honor and give Him praise."

* They are used to "call out to God."

________ helps us know
God in a deeper way.

* They are used to "set the atmosphere for worship."

* So we can enter into the "presence" of the Lord.

* They are used to "tell of His Salvation to the lost."

* They are used to "declare victory over the enemy" through our worship of the Lord.

* They are used to "show what He is doing in a particular service."

* They are used to "welcome His presence."

* Using flags and banners in a service can heighten the level of the praise and worship where we can enter into the presence of the Lord where He wants us to be.

* They are used to "experience the power and authority of His Holy Spirit."

* Through worship we can come to know God in a deeper way.

* When we truly praise God and worship Him, His glory will fill our church and everything around us.

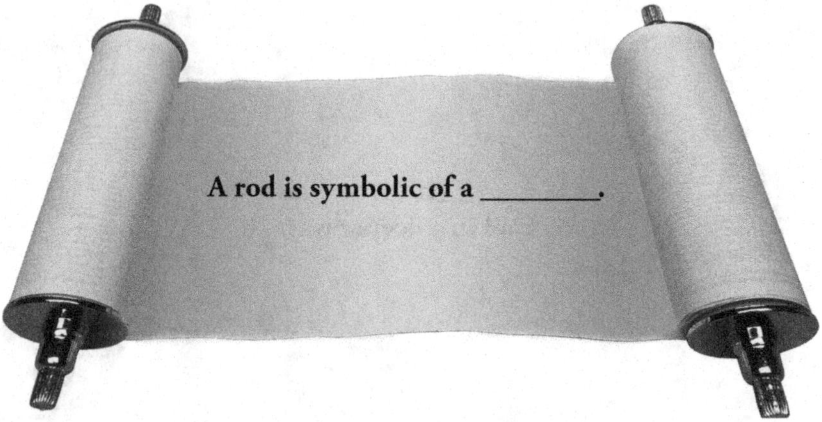


* They are used to "make a statement about God's character and His name."

* As we wave the flags we are showing God our love for Him.

* Waving the flags is like making a phone call to God and your prayers are represented by that particular "flag."

* We are seeking God in that particular part of His character that is represented by that particular flag.

* We are seeking Him to work that way in our lives or particular situation.

* If we wanted to honor God for being "Jehovah Roi (the Lord our Shepherd)," then we would raise the flag that symbolized that.

* That means that we are "seeking Him" as the "One who guides us, feeds us, protects and comforts us."

* We may be seeking Him for "restoration" or "to restore us."

* We may be seeking Him "to fight our battles" for us.

* Or we could be seeking Him "to guide us" in a particular situation.

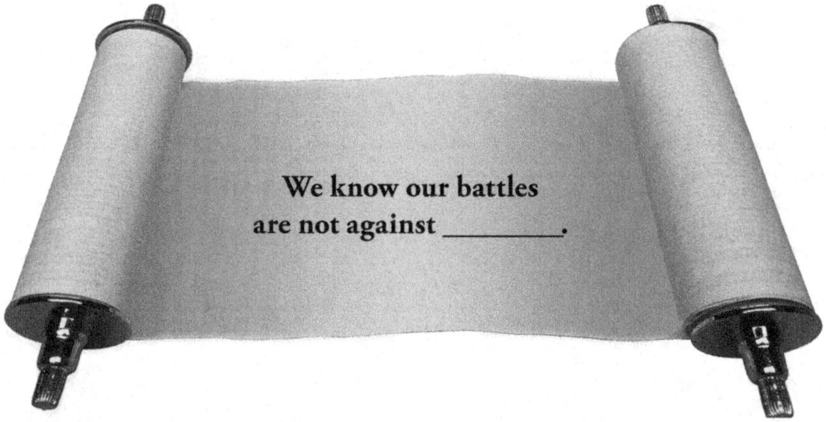
We know our battles
are not against ________.

* We lift those things up to Him as we are praising Him and we leave it at His feet and just wait on Him as He answers our prayer.

* Also during praise and worship "God will tell you" what He is doing or wants to do in that service or in you.

* And then "He will have you" wave the particular "flag" that represents that.

* Lifting flags in worship is like Moses lifting his rod as a sign of God's presence.

* A "rod" is a shepherd's staff, which is symbolic of a "flag."

* Flags are used as a sign to "rally the troops."

* "For we wrestle not against "flesh and blood."

* "But against "principalities, against powers, against the rulers of the darkness of this world, against spiritual wickedness in high places." (Ephesians 6:12)

* Raising a flag creates "unity in God's army."

* It encourages us to hold on to our faith and expect victory.

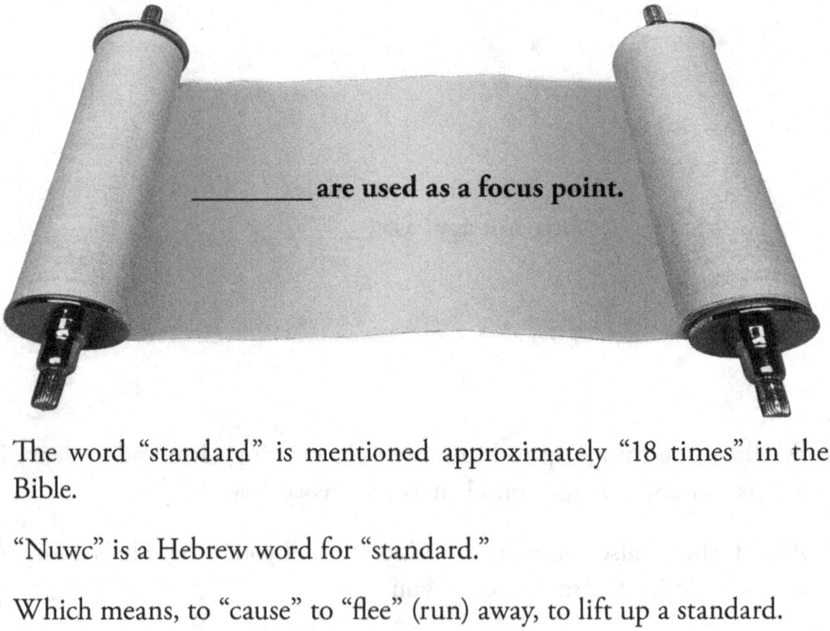
________ are used as a focus point.

* The word "standard" is mentioned approximately "18 times" in the Bible.

* "Nuwc" is a Hebrew word for "standard."

* Which means, to "cause" to "flee" (run) away, to lift up a standard.

* The waving of the flags "sends the enemy running," because it represents God.

* Ancient Egyptians used "flags" which were ribbons or fabrics tied to poles during battles to determine wind direction.

* That would help them determine how to aim and shoot their arrows.

* To show what is happening in the "spiritual" realm, a particular "flag" would be flown in the "physical" realm.

* This particular "flag" would show the direction in which the wind of the Holy Spirit is leading.

* When God had Moses put the serpent on the pole God was using it as a "focus point" for the Israelites "to receive their healing" through faith.

* "Flags" are also used as a "focus point" or visual aid for the people to see God in a particular way and to receive from Him.

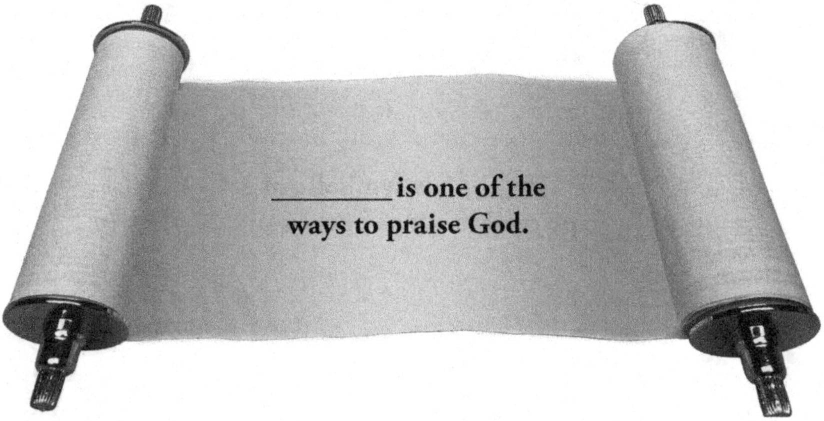
________ is one of the
ways to praise God.

* Flags are something you praise God with, just like you use a musical instrument to praise Him.

* Flags are also used to "celebrate an event."

* They can also be used to "declare a season," such as, a period of time set aside for fasting and prayer for a particular thing.

* Just like you combine the different number of waves of the flag to mean different things, you can also combine the different "colors on the flag to mean different things.

* To symbolize the "Royal Priesthood" you can use "gold and blue."

* To symbolize the "cleansing Blood of Jesus" you can use "red and white."
* To symbolize the "purifying Fire of the Holy Spirit" you can use "red, orange and yellow."
* When you put these 3 colors together in motion they "look like fire."
* "Dancing" as one of the ways to praise God, is Biblical as well.
* It says in Psalm 149:3 "Let them praise His name in the dance."

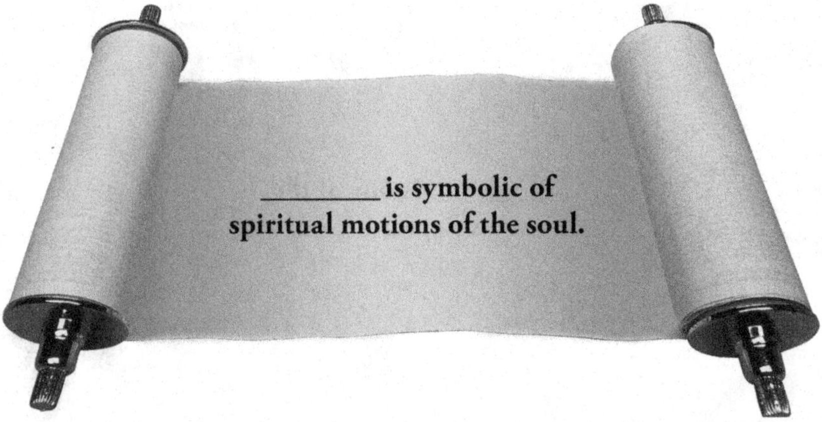
________ is symbolic of
spiritual motions of the soul.

* Also in Psalm 150:4 it says, "Praise Him with the timbrel and dance."
* Scripture describes praising God by "dancing" as a joyous celebration of praise.
* In the Hebrew tradition "dance" functioned as a "medium of prayer and praise."
* Dance was and is an "expression" of joy and deep love and respect for God.
* Dance was and is considered a go between or connection between God and humanity.

* The early Christian church used this kind of "holy" and joyous dancing before the Lord to praise Him.

* Dance was seen in the early church as a way to express to God their happiness and joy that He had given them.

* Dance continues within the church today, and should always be "holy" never profane.

* "Movement" when you praise and worship God brings "glory and honor" to Him.

* Dancing before the Lord helps you focus your whole being on God.

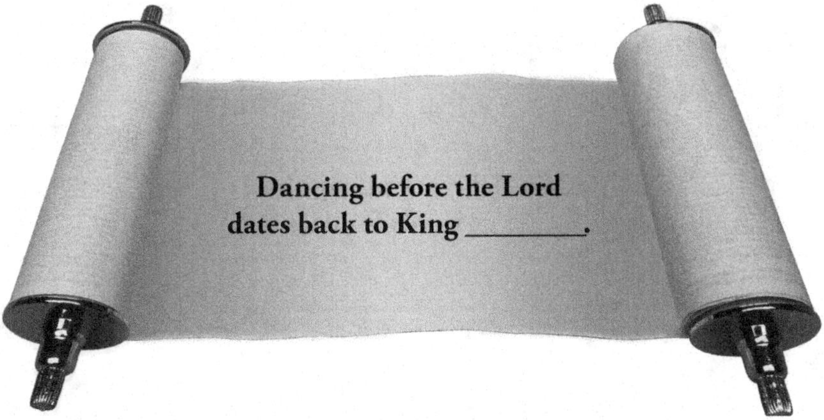
Dancing before the Lord
dates back to King ________.

* Dance is symbolic of "spiritual motions of the soul."

* The Lord enjoys and sees dancing before Him as "spiritual applause."

* Dancing before the Lord is a Jewish tradition and was adopted into the early church.

* Dancing before the Lord became an important part of "celebrations and worship."

* Today, dancing before the Lord is starting to become an important part of praise and worship in the church once again.

* The Biblical tradition of dancing before the Lord dates back all the way to King David.

* There are many forms and expressions of dance that are used in praise and worship.

* Such as dancing that is "choreographed" to dancing that is "spontaneous" by individuals of all ages.

* The ancient Israelites often used some form of dance as a part of their celebrations.

* They used dance in their praise and worship, their everyday lives, when they were victorious in battle and in their festivals.

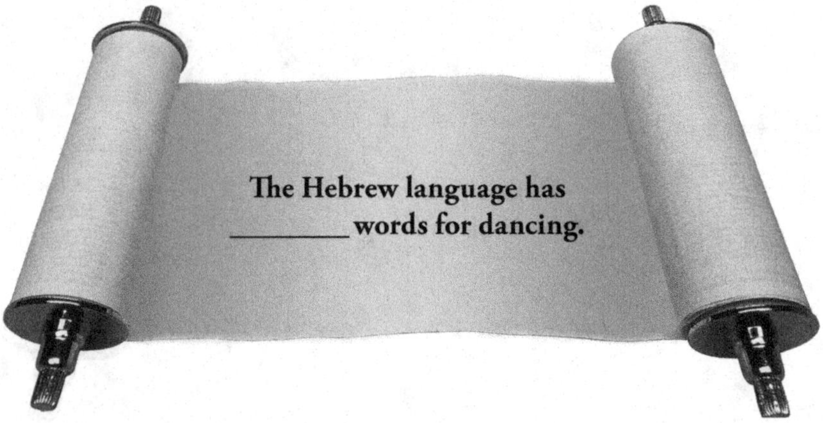
The Hebrew language has
________ words for dancing.

* The "holy dance" was a way to enter into God's presence.

* By dancing before the Lord it brought them into a closer relationship with God.

* In the Old Testament there are many references to dance as a form of praise to God.

* In the Old Testament the most frequent used root for the word dance is "hul."

* This refers to the "whirl" of the dance which means there is a lot of movement.

* The Hebrew language has "44 words" for the word dancing.

* There is only "1" word out of those 44 that may refer to "worldly dance."

* "Worldly dancing" and "holy dancing" are two totally different things.

* The "circular or ring dance" and the "processional dance" are just a couple of the dances used by the Israelites.

* "Specific events" were celebrated by using these types of dances.

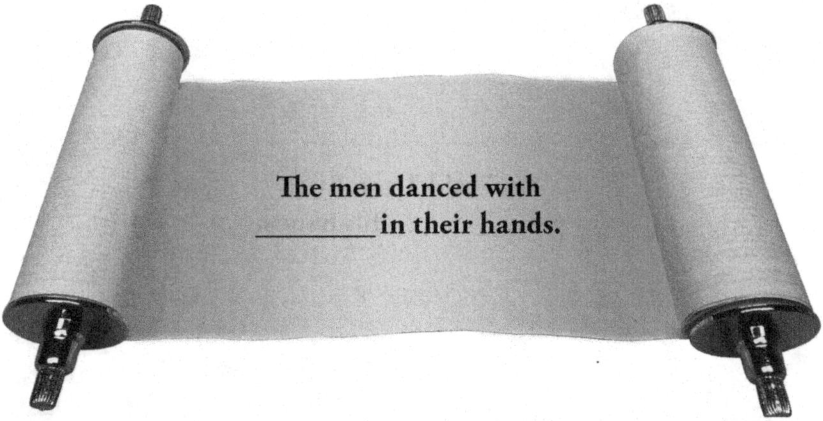
The men danced with
________ in their hands.

* Such as when the people of Israel danced before the "Ark of the Covenant."

* The "Ark of the Covenant" represented the "presence of God."

* King David did the "3rd type of dance" which included "leaping and whirling" which he used to express his joy about having the "Ark of the Covenant" back.

* When Pharaoh's army was defeated at the Red Sea, Miriam and all the women danced before the Lord. (Ex. 15:20)

* The Israelite women would dance and sing songs about King David's victories. (1 Samuel 29:5)

* Men who wanted to show reverence to God would dance at the "Feast of Tabernacles."

* The men danced with "torches" in their hands.

* The "Levites" would play music on all sorts of instruments as the men danced and sang songs of "joyful praise."

* The dancing and singing would last all night until a specific time in the morning.

* Dance was planted deep in the roots of the Christian church within the first 5 centuries.

Paul told Timothy to
pray ________ his hands.

* Because of the Hebrew tradition, dance became a very common and acceptable thing to do during worship and at festivals.

* There are not many "direct" references to dance in the New Testament as there are in the Old Testament.

* But dance was still a very important part of Jewish life.

* Jesus even used dance as showing expression of joy when He was describing that generation.

* Jesus said, "We have piped unto you, and ye have not danced." (Matthew 11:17)

* And also when Jesus was telling about the prodigal son returning home He mentioned dance.

* He told us how the father threw a party to celebrate his son's return, and there was music and dancing. (Luke 15:25)

* Paul talks about our bodies being the "Temple of the Holy Spirit" which should glorify God. (1 Corinthians 6:19-20)

* Paul tells us that even when we pray we should use our "whole body."

* He also teaches Timothy to do the same; he said to "pray lifting up holy hands."

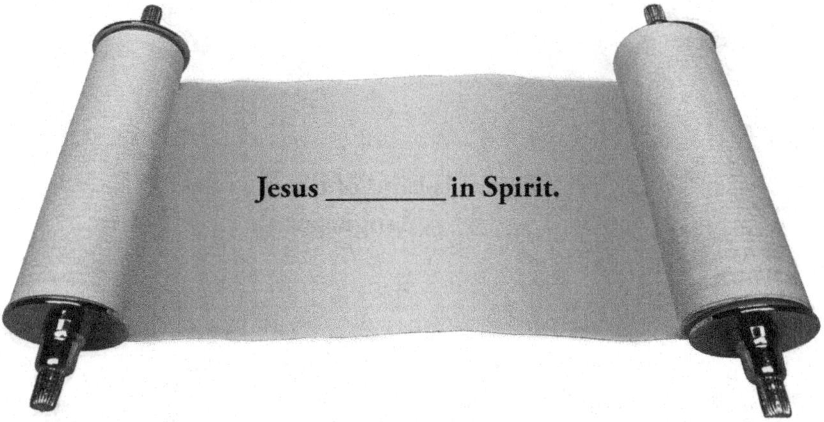


* In the Bible, for "most prayers" they would pray with their "hands and arms lifted up to God." (1 Timothy 2:8)

* If you were praying a "prayer of repentance" then you would "kneel or lay face down."

* If you were praying a prayer of "thanksgiving or intercession" then you would "stand with your arms raised."

* A lot of Jews spoke "Aramaic" and in that language the word for "rejoice" and "dance" are "the same."

* By combining "dance" with "rejoice," there are more references to "dance" than was first realized in the New Testament.

* Jesus says, "Rejoice" ye in that day, and "leap" for joy; for behold, your reward is great in heaven…" (Luke 6:23)

* It says in Luke 10:21 that "Jesus "rejoiced" in Spirit."

* Dance has always been a part of "praise and worship" for the Israelites, all through their history.

* When you speak of "dance" today people automatically think about how the world dances, because they don't know about the "holy dance" the dancing before the Lord.

* But in Colossians 1:16 it says, "…all things were created by Him, and for Him."

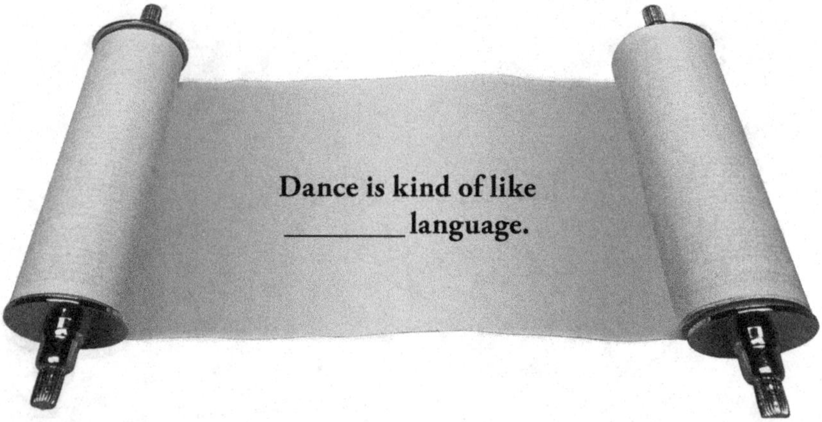
Dance is kind of like
________ language.

* Exodus 15:20, gives us the first mention that "dance" is a "type of worship."

* At the "School of the Prophets" they taught "praise dancing."

* Miriam was a "prophetess" and she "danced" before the Lord.

* The Bible does not mention any of Miriam's prophecies.

* "Dance" was treated as a "prophetic gifting" by the people of Israel.

* When you praise the Lord in "dance" you are "expressing your love to Him," not in words, but in "movement" kind of like sign language.

* A man after God's own heart, King David, is well known in the Bible for his "praise and worship."

* Today, Israel still uses "Davidic worship."

* In some of the Psalms written by "King David," he refers to "dance as a form of worship."

* Jewish style of worship was included in the New Testament church by both Jews and Gentiles.

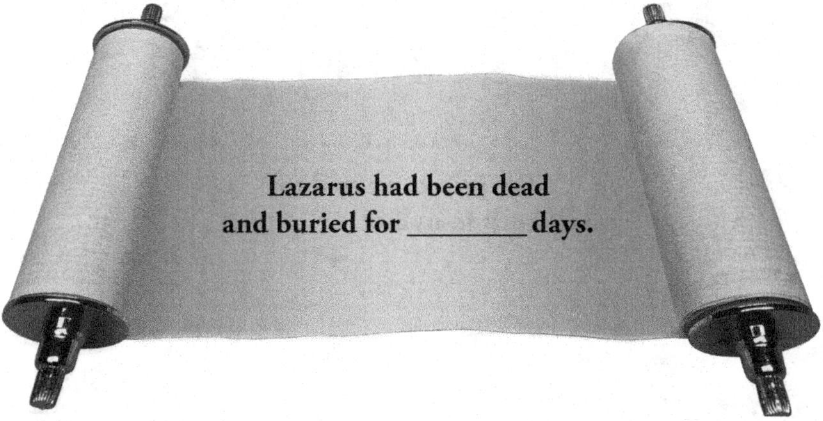
**Lazarus had been dead**
**and buried for ________ days.**

* In Acts 6, "Prochorus" was elected as one of the deacons of the Church.

* The name "Prochorus" means "leader of the circle dance."

* There is no age restriction on dancing before the Lord; Miriam was nearly "90 years old" when she danced before Him.

* "Lazarus" a man from Bethany, a village near Jerusalem, was a very close friend of Jesus.'

* He and his sisters, "Martha and Mary," were also disciples of Jesus.

* Not much is known about "Lazarus," except that his name came from the Hebrew name "Eleazer" which means "one whom God helps."

* Jesus did help Lazarus; He raised him from the dead.

* Lazarus' sisters sent for Jesus "when he became sick."

* At the time Jesus was east of the Jordon River in Perea.

* They begged Jesus to come because they knew that he could heal Lazarus.

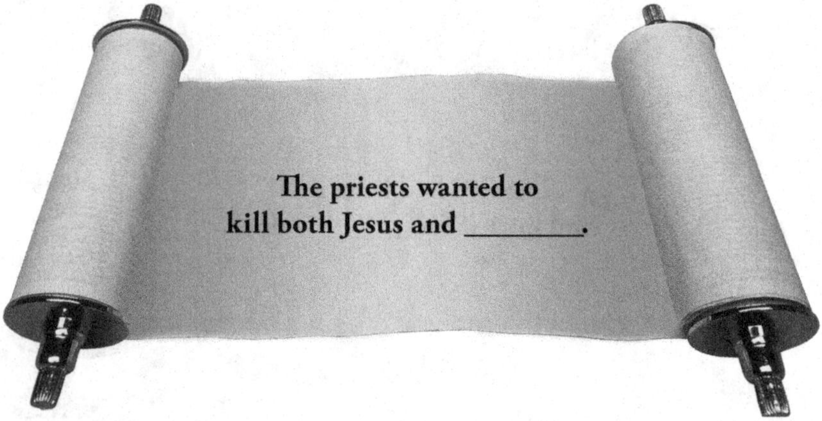

The priests wanted to
kill both Jesus and ________.


* Jesus waited "2 days" before going to Bethany where Lazarus was at.

* So the "miracle" would be even greater, Jesus waited to go.

* When Jesus arrived in Bethany He heard that Lazarus was dead.

* Jesus went to "Lazarus' tomb," he had already been "dead and buried" for "4 days."

* When Jesus arrived at the tomb, the Bible says that "Jesus wept." (John 11:35)

* "Jesus wept." This is the shortest verse in the Bible.

* "Jesus said, Take ye away the stone." (John 11:39)

* "Martha, the sister of him that was dead, saith unto Him, Lord, by this time he stinketh: for he hath been dead four days." (John 11:39)

* "Jesus saith unto her, Said I not unto thee, that, if thou wouldest believe, thou shouldest see the glory of God." (John 11:40)

* Then in a loud voice Jesus said, "Lazarus come forth!"

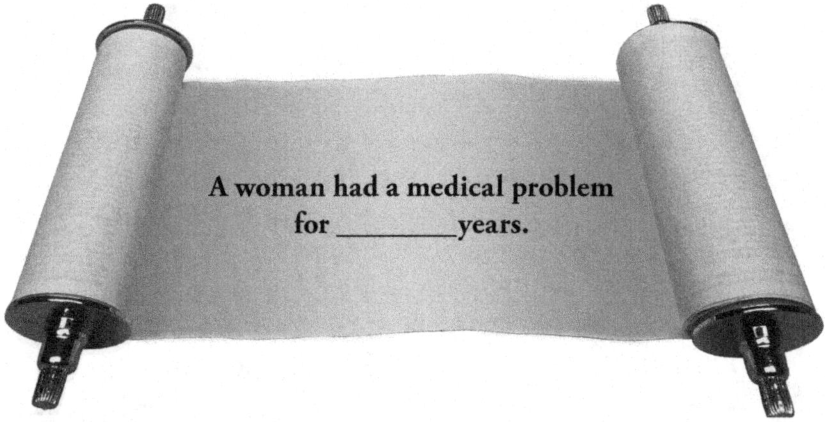
A woman had a medical problem
for ________years.

* "And he that was dead came out." (John 11:44)

* Many who witnessed this miracle then believed in Jesus. (John 11:45)

* Worried that Jesus would cause trouble with the Romans by causing an uprising, some priests in Jerusalem had a meeting to decide what to do.

* And their solution was to try to come up with a plan on how to "kill both Jesus and Lazarus." (John 11:53 and 12:10)

* "6 days" before the Passover ceremonies Jesus returned to Bethany.

* When He arrived He went to Lazarus' home where Lazarus' sisters had prepared a meal in Jesus' honor.

* So Jesus had dinner with Lazarus and his two sisters, Mary and Martha.

* The last thing that was said about "Lazarus" in the Bible was in John 12:10-11)

* "But the chief priests consulted that they might put Lazarus also to death;"

* "Because that by reason of him (Lazarus) many of the Jews went away, and believed on Jesus."

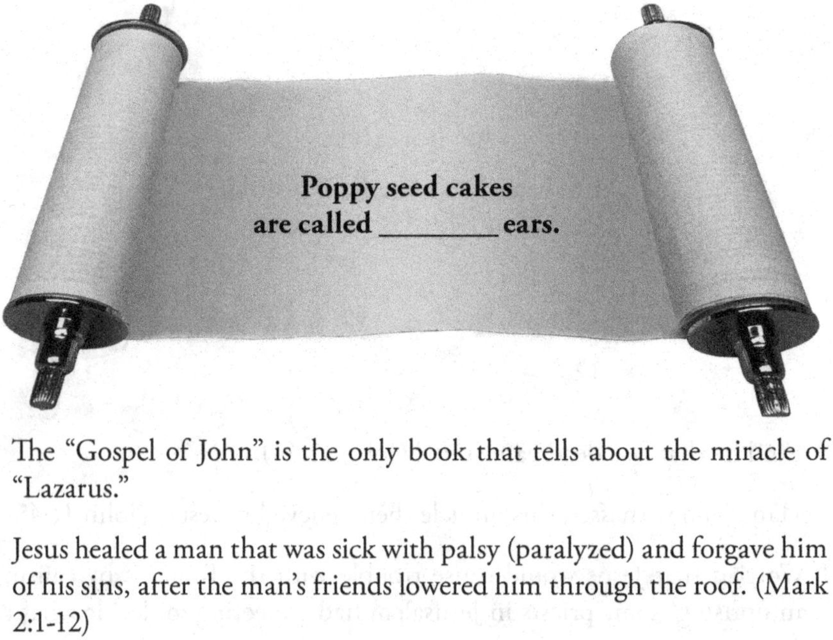
Poppy seed cakes
are called ________ ears.

* The "Gospel of John" is the only book that tells about the miracle of "Lazarus."

* Jesus healed a man that was sick with palsy (paralyzed) and forgave him of his sins, after the man's friends lowered him through the roof. (Mark 2:1-12)

* In the city of Nain, Jesus ran into a widow woman whose only son had died.

* Jesus had compassion on her and raised her son from the dead. (Luke 7:11-17)

* A woman who had an "issue of blood" for "12 years," spent all she had on doctors and was not getting better she was only getting worse.

* But when she touched Jesus' garment she was totally healed. (Mark 5:25-34)

* The wish of the "religious leaders" of having Jesus killed was fulfilled. (John 11:53)

* But their wish was undone when "JESUS ROSE FROM THE DEAD!"

* "Haman" which means "magnificent" or "illustrious," probably came to Persia as a "captive" of war.

* Haman became the "Chief Minister" to the King Ahasuerus of Persia; he was married and had "10 sons."

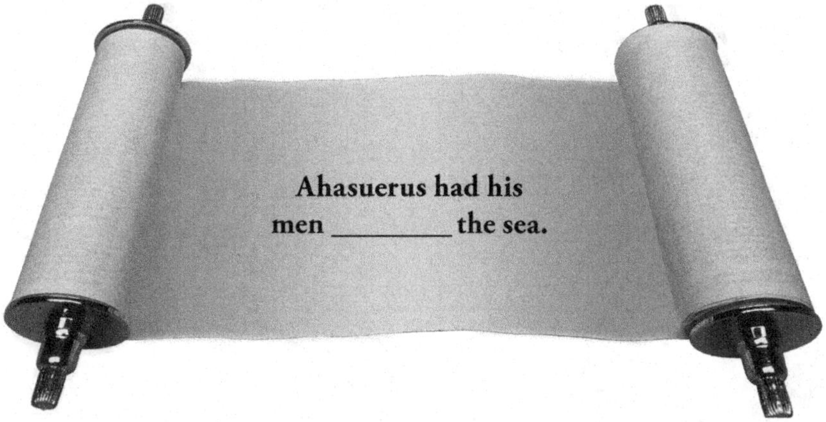
Ahasuerus had his
men ________ the sea.

* Whenever Haman passed by, all servants had to bow to him as ordered by the King.

* Jews baked "poppy seed cakes" called "Haman's ears" for the festival honoring Esther's bravery called "Purim."

* Cyrus the Great was King Ahasuerus' grandfather.

* Cyrus the Great "freed the Israelites" from captivity by defeating Babylon.

* When King Ahasuerus came to power in "486 B.C." the Persian Empire reached from "India to Ethiopia."

* This included "20" kingdoms, including "Judah."

* Any rebellions were crushed by Ahasuerus, who was a harsh ruler.

* He wanted to enlarge his territory by conquering "Greece."

* To do this, 2 boat bridges were built by his armies across the strait between "Northern Greece and Asia Minor" in "480 B.C."

* Ahasuerus got so mad because a storm destroyed the bridge that he ordered his men to "beat" the sea.

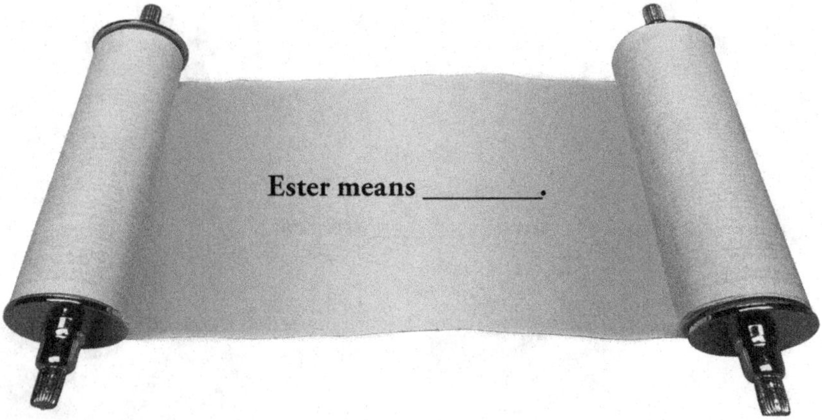


* Just like a disobedient soldier would be "whipped."

* After rebuilding the bridge his army went to "Athens" and "burned Athens to the ground."

* Ahasuerus was soon driven back to Asia by the "Greeks."

* In "464 B.C." Ahasuerus was "assassinated" by some of his subjects in his palace.

* This was not the same assassination plot that Mordecai warned him about.

* Today, in "Iran" you can still see the ruins of that elaborate palace, which was called "Persepolis."

* In a city east of the "Tigris River" called "Susa," is where "Esther" was born.

* "Esther's" family was very strong in their Jewish faith.

* They had come to that city almost a century earlier because of the "Babylonian exile."

* Even though the "Persians" had defeated the Babylonians and had made "Susa" their capital, they chose to stay.

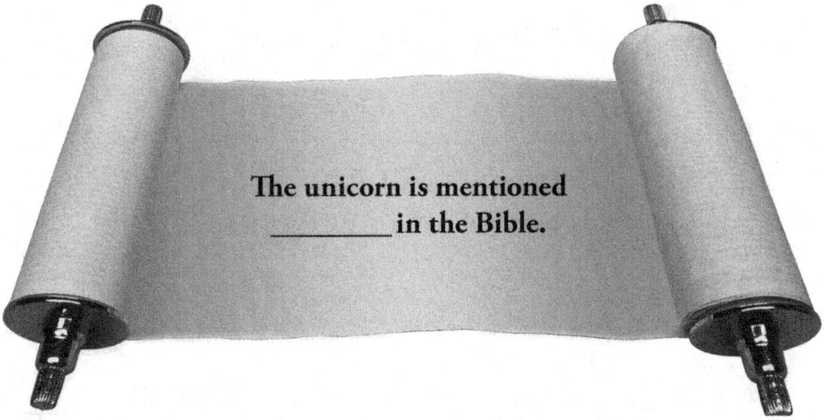
The unicorn is mentioned
________ in the Bible.

* "Esther" was her "Persian" name.

* Her parents had named her "Hadassah" which is "Hebrew" for "Myrtle."

* "Esther" means "star."

* The "unicorn" is a "mythical" animal.

* It has a horn in the middle of its forehead and a lion's tail, but it looks like a horse.

* The "unicorn" is mentioned in some "English" translations of the Bible, even though it never existed.

* It is mentioned at least "9 times" in the Bible.

* The "unicorn" is mentioned in the "King James" version in:

* Numbers 23:22, Numbers 24:8, Deuteronomy 33:17, Job 39:9, Job 39:10, Psalm 22:21, Psalm 29:6, Psalm 92:10 and in Isaiah 34:7.

* "Unicorn" legends go far back in time.

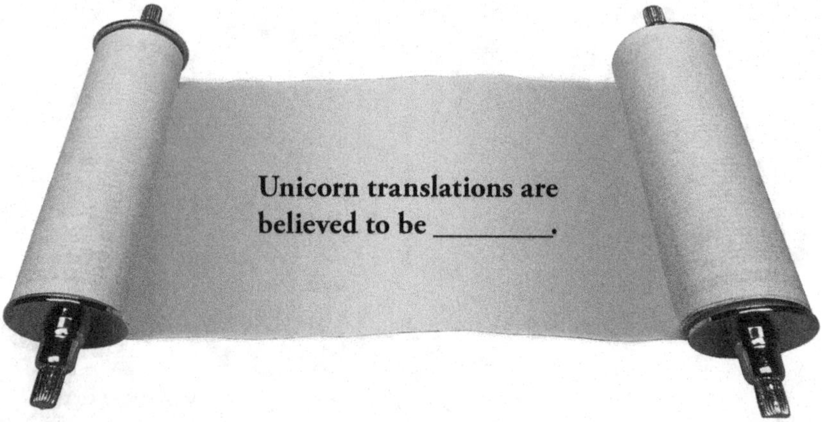
**Unicorn translations are**
**believed to be ________.**

* Early "Mesopotamian Art" contains "unicorns."

* The unicorn is said to have come from "India" according to "Greek" literature.

* The "horn" is supposed to be "white at the base" and has a "red tip" and is "black in the middle."

* "Epilepsy and stomach problems" were said to be "prevented" if you drank from the "horn."

* Several passages call it the "unicorn" in the King James Version of the Bible and some other earlier translations.

* These translations are believed to be "inaccurate" according to scholars now.

* The "wild ox" or "rhinoceros" are most likely the animal talked about in the Hebrew text.

* The "Middle Ages" belief was that "only" a "virgin" in its path could capture a "unicorn."

* Then the unicorn would jump into the girl's lap.

* Then she would nurse it.

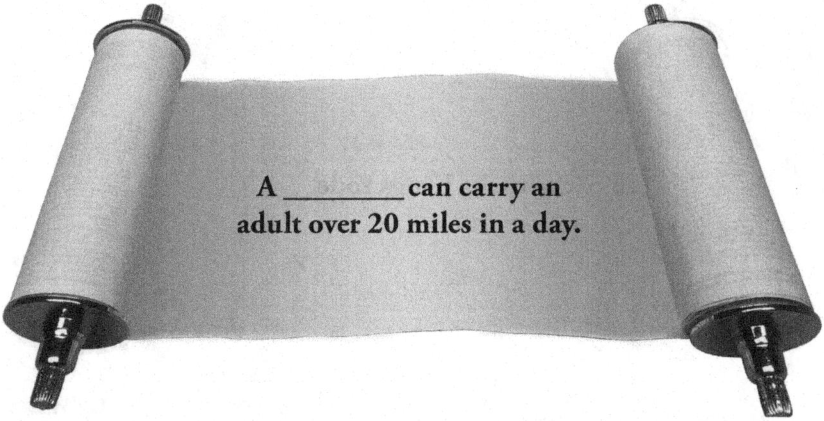

A ________ can carry an
adult over 20 miles in a day.


* The belief also was that you could not be poisoned if you drank from its "horn."

* People charged high prices, and sold "unicorn horns," that were nothing more than "rhinoceros horns."

* There are "3 main reasons" that prove that unicorns was an "inaccurate translation:"

* Unicorns never existed.

* For the Jews to believe in a "mythical animal" that had special powers was "forbidden" by God.

* For the virgin girl to nurse the unicorn was also "forbidden" by God.

* The camel is not as comfortable as the "donkey" to ride.

* In Biblical times "donkeys" were a popular form of transportation.

* Because a donkey is smaller than a horse it is much easier to get up on to ride.

* And a donkey can go "20 miles or more a day" carrying an adult.

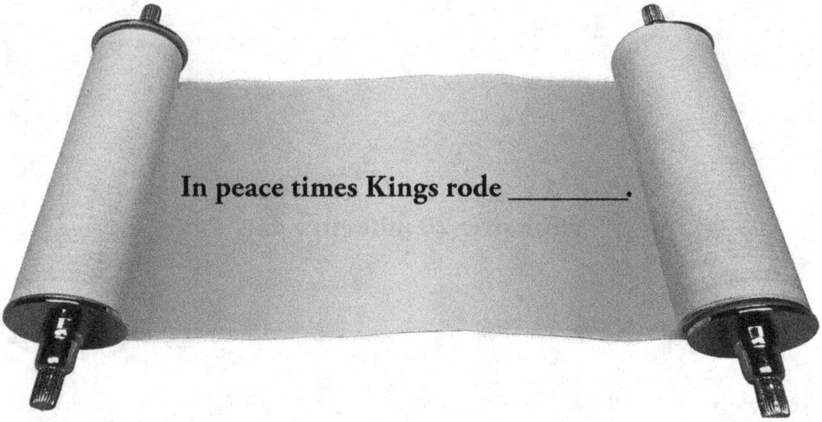
In peace times Kings rode ________.

* A donkey needs water "4 times sooner" than a camel.

* But the donkey takes the desert heat much better than a horse.

* When it drinks water the donkey has a "quick recovery" time, like the camel, from extreme thirst.

* "30%" of its body weight in water can be lost, and the donkey can still survive.

* Donkeys also pull plows and supply carts.

* They also loosen grain kernels from stalks that are used for making flour, by pulling boards covered with rocks across them.

* Swift horses were rode by "kings" in times of war.

* But in peace times "kings" rode donkeys.

* The "Prophet Zechariah" prophesied, "500 years before" it happened that Israel's King would be coming to Jerusalem riding on a donkey's colt, and He would be bringing lasting peace. (Zechariah 9:9-10)

* When "Jesus" rode into Jerusalem, "500 years later," riding on a "donkey's colt" He "fulfilled this prophecy."

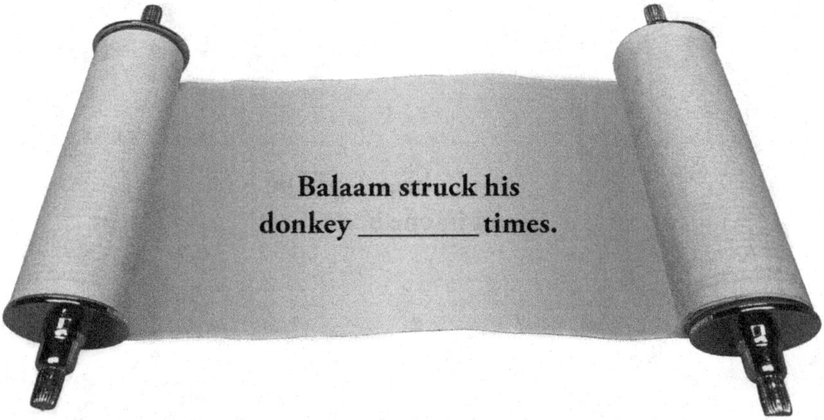
**Balaam struck his**
**donkey ________ times.**

* The "most famous donkey" not only in the Bible, but of all time, was the one that not only saw an "angel" but he also "spoke" to his owner.

* This donkey belonged to a man named "Balaam."

* The "Israelites" were invading the Moabites so the King of the Moabites wanted Balaam to curse the Israelites.

* But God sent an "Angel" to block Balaam's path, and to stop him from cursing the Israelites.

* The Angel stood in the middle of the road and when Balaam's "donkey saw him," he stopped.

* Balaam got very angry and he struck the donkey "3 times."

* But still the donkey would not move.

* Finally, the donkey had had enough and he "spoke up" and asked Balaam why he was hitting him.

* When God had the donkey speak, Balaam also saw the Angel and turned back.

* Still today in the Holy Land, the donkey is the favorite form of transportation because it is strong and reliable.

______ bees could be
found in one bee hive.


* Much like today, the people of ancient Palestine described "bees" as being very dangerous.

* In a song of victory in Psalms, "bees" are used to describe Israel's enemies.

* "They compassed me about like "bees;" they are quenched as the fire of thorns: for in the name of the Lord I will destroy them." (Psalm 118:2)

* The Israelites would gather "honey" from "wild bee hives."

* "Bee colonies" could be found in the desert as well as in wooded areas.

* During the battle with the Philistines, "Jonathan," Saul's son, ate "honey" from a honeycomb that he had found on the ground. (1 Samuel 14:2-30)

* The "Israelites" later began keeping "honeybees."

* The 1st people to domesticate "bees" in that area though were probably the Egyptians.

* The "Israelites" made hives from clay or reed woven together like a basket.

* The honeybee was used for "food and commerce."

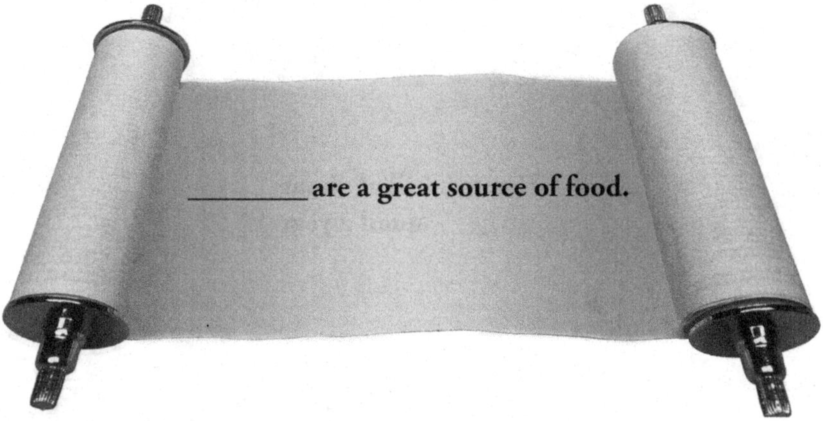
________ are a great source of food.

* "50,000 bees" could be found in one "hive.

* In one summer, that one hive could produce over "100 pounds" of honey.

* Honey was also used for "trading" for goods. (Ezekiel 27:17)

* They also ate the newly hatched bees that were in the honeycomb.

* Because "alcohol" could be made from "honey" it was not allowed to be part of a "burnt offering." (Lev. 2:11)

* For centuries there has been an abundance of "quail" in the "Holy Land."

* In the time of "Jesus" there was a writer who wrote a report about the migration of quail.

* In his report he told how one day during the migration of the "quail" that so many of them landed on a ship that it caused the ship to sink.

* "Quails" are a great source of "food."

* No wonder the Israelites, when they were complaining in the desert about being hungry, and they saw all those "quail" they got so excited.

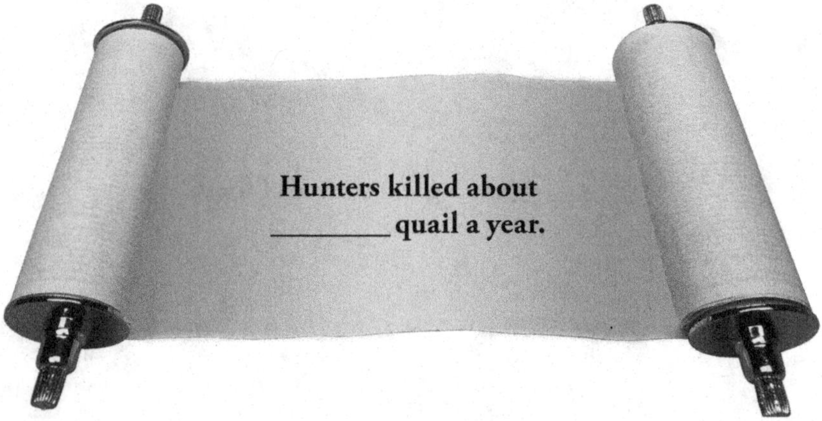
**Hunters killed about**
**________ quail a year.**

* Because God didn't just send a few, He sent them "thousands" of quails.

* Quails covered the landscape, they were everywhere.

* It took the Israelites "2 days" to gather up all that quail. (Num. 11:31-32)

* The quails that are in "America" are just a little bit different than the ones in Europe, Asia and Africa.

* Their "feathers" are "light brown" in color and have "streaks" of "black and white" in them, and they are about "7 inches" long.

* Quails are not known for their strong flying power.

* They need the help of a "tail wind" to fly long distances.

* When the wind stops, they have to land.

* And then it takes them about "2 days" to regain their strength.

* They have to be careful during this resting period, because they become easy prey for hunters or hungry wild animals.

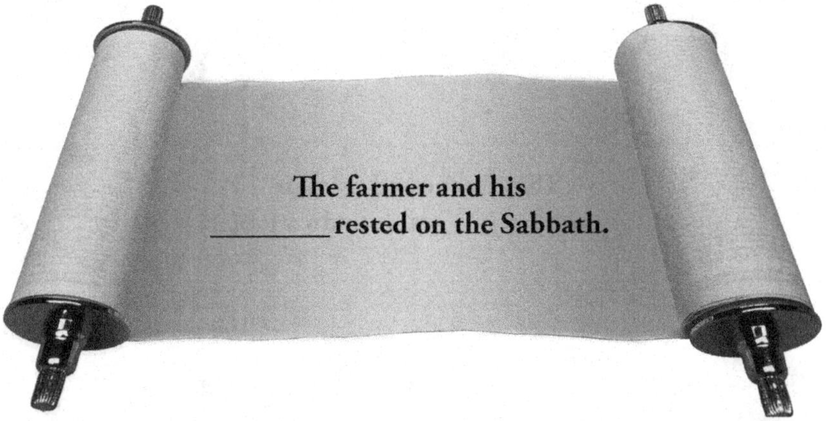
The farmer and his
________ rested on the Sabbath.

* Some of the hunters that would prey on the "quail" as they rested were the ancient Egyptians.

* Once they caught them they would be dried in the sun and then placed in clay pots to be kept for food throughout the year.

* Quails used to migrate in huge flocks up until about a century ago.

* But then, about "2 million" a year died by the hands of hunters.

* Because of this, today you will see much smaller flocks.

* Because the "oxen" were so strong and useful they were probably one of the most favorite animals of the ancient farmers.

* The "farmer" and "his oxen" always rested on the "Sabbath" in accordance with Jewish Law.

* Even in "Abraham's" day, people used "oxen" instead of horses or donkeys to pull a heavy wagon or plow.

* Oxen were slower than horses.

* Oxen could not work as many hours as horses; horses could work an hour or two longer each day.

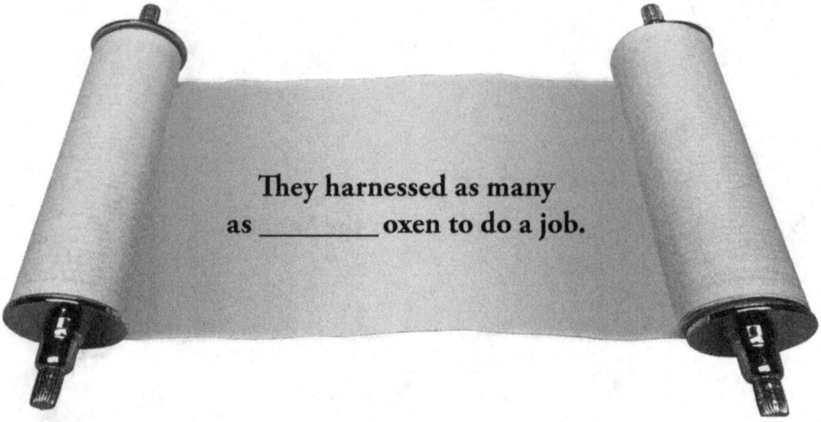

They harnessed as many
as ________ oxen to do a job.


* Oxen were more abundant in the Middle East than horses.

* Horses cost twice as much as oxen.

* So the oxen were a wiser choice because they were not only cheaper, but they were strong and steady on their feet as well.

* They were perfect for all that heavy farm work.

* When the job at hand was a little bit tougher they would yoke "2 oxen" together.

* To yoke "2 oxen" together they would put large collars around their necks.

* Then a wooden beam would be placed across their shoulders.

* Then the large collars would be attached to the beams.

* If the job got even tougher they would harness several teams of oxen together.

* Sometimes as many as "8 oxen" would be used at a time.

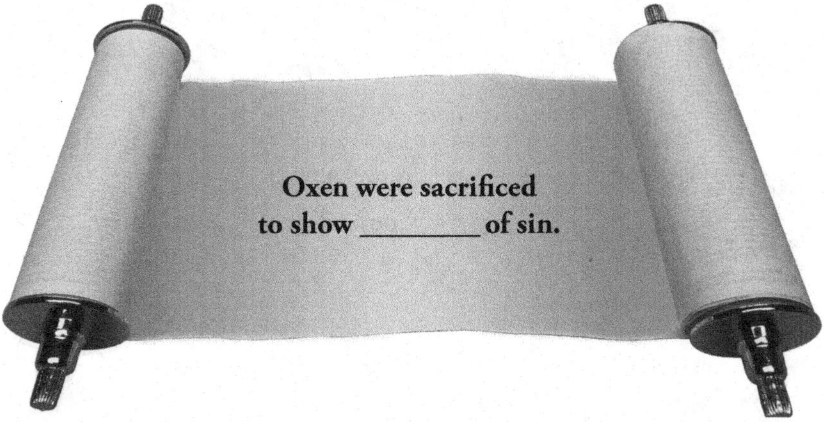
**Oxen were sacrificed**
**to show ________ of sin.**

* Oxen were also a source of food, unlike horses.

* By Jewish Law there were certain animals that the Israelites were not allowed to eat.

* They were not allowed to eat "horses, camels or pigs."

* But they could eat "cattle, oxen, sheep and fish."

* Oxen could also be used to make a sacrifice unto the Lord:

* To show "repentance of their sins."

* To "give thanks" for "God's blessings."

* To "give thanks" for the "birth of a child."

* To "give thanks" for being "healed from a sickness."

* There hasn't been many "lions" in the "Holy Land" since the "13th century."

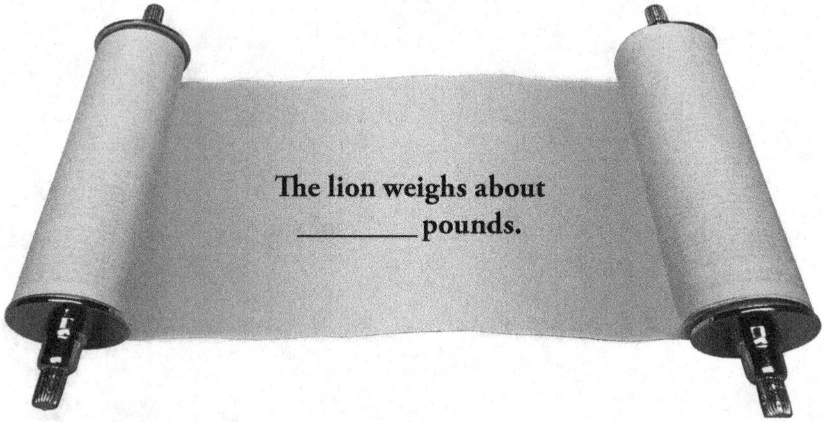
**The lion weighs about**
**________pounds.**

* But "lions" were a real threat to people and herds in Biblical times, in the Holy Land.

* In the Bible, God compares the "devil" to a lion.

* God says, "Be sober, be vigilant; because your adversary "the devil," "as a roaring lion," walketh about, seeking whom he may devour:" (1 Peter 5:8)

* The "lion" is mentioned in the Old Testament more than any other animal.

* Lions are well known for their "strength, fierceness and craftiness."

* Knowing this, the Israelites feared and respected them.

* "King Hezekiah" described the strength of the lion when he said, "as a lion, so will he break all my bones." (Isaiah 38:13)

* The lion is one of the strongest members of the cat family.

* The lion stands about "3 feet" high at the shoulders.

* It weighs about "450 pounds."

________ tore a lion
apart barehanded.

* Its body length is just "over 6 feet" including the tail.

* And its body is covered with short hair.

* Only the "male lion" has a majestic looking full mane, that's one reason people call it the "King of beasts."

* Lions are mighty hunters; they can kill domestic livestock and wild animals.

* Sometimes even people were attacked by them.

* "Samson" tore a "lion apart barehanded." (Judges 14:5-6)

* Sometimes "shepherds" had to risk their lives and fight off lions to protect their flocks.

* When David was a young boy and a "lion" attacked his flock, he hit the lion with a "stick" and snatched the lamb from its mouth. (1 Samuel 17:34-35)

* Proverbs 19:12 says that, "The king's wrath is as the roaring of a "lion."

* Lions have become a "symbol of royal authority."

David rescued ________
from lions and bears.

* As a "sign of power" lions were caught and were held in captivity by kings and nobles.

* "Daniel" was thrown into one of these lion pits by King Darius of Persia.

* But God is more powerful than a lion or a king, and God protected "Daniel" and brought him out safely.

* "Lambs" were symbols of "innocence and gentleness." (Jeremiah 11:19)

* Shepherds and farmers sometimes treated their "lambs" like members of the family.

* The Bible tells of a man who was poor, who took his "lamb" in to his home, "And it did eat of his own bread,"

* "And drank of his own cup, and lay in his bosom, and was unto him as a daughter." (2 Samuel 12:3)

* The young "David" rescued "lambs" from the mouths of both lions and bears. (1 Samuel 17:34-35)

* God was described as a "compassionate Shepherd" by the "Prophet Isaiah."

* "He shall feed His flock like a shepherd: He shall gather the "lambs" with His arm, and carry them in His bosom, and shall gently lead those that are with young." (Isaiah 40:11)

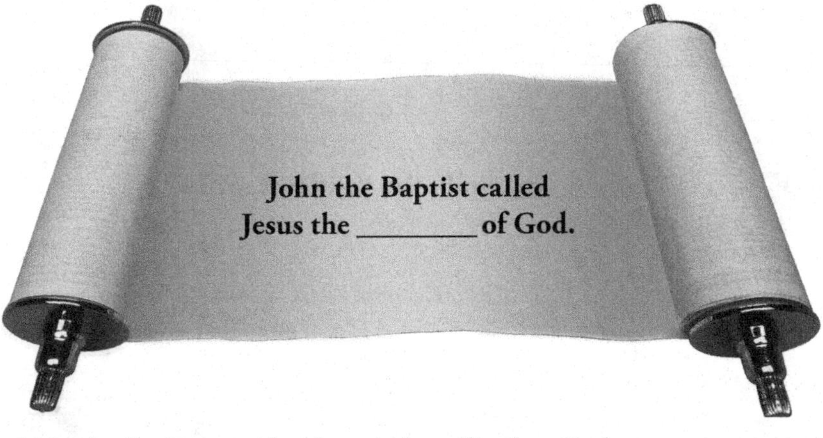
**John the Baptist called**
**Jesus the ________ of God.**

* Only the "purest sacrifices" could be offered to God.

* Once in the morning and evening an "unblemished lamb" was sacrificed.

* Every Jewish family that could afford to were suppose to sacrifice a "lamb" at the yearly Passover celebration.

* Then a piece of the "lamb" was to be given to everyone at the Passover meal to eat and enjoy.

* "Lambs" were sacrificed to make "atonement for sin" as well.

* "John the Baptist" proclaimed that "Jesus" was "The Lamb of God."

* And that like the "lamb" He would be "sacrificed" to "take away the sin of the world." (John 1:29)

* "Paul" wrote after Jesus was crucified, "For even Christ our Passover is sacrificed for us." (1 Corinthians 5:7)

* People believed that if while a "ewe" was breeding; if you put a "stripped object" in front of her then she would have "stripped lambs." (Gen. 30:37-39)

* The "grasshopper" was a good source of food to the Israelites. (Lev. 11:22)

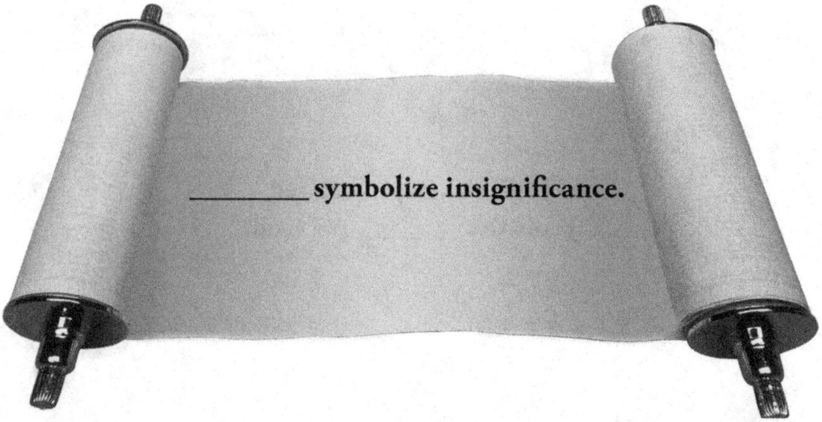
________ symbolize insignificance.

* The Hebrew have at least "12 ancient words" for the different species of "grasshopper and locust."

* Which makes it hard to figure out which one the Bible is talking about in a particular passage.

* The "grasshopper" is skinny, with long legs, and "2 pairs" of wings.

* In flight grasshoppers can reach speeds up to "15 miles per hour."

* Grasshoppers have even been seen "1,200 miles" out at sea.

* In ancient Palestine there were a variety of grasshoppers that were "1½ to 2 inches" long.

* "Grasshoppers" symbolize "insignificance" because they are so small.

* When the "scouts" that "Moses" sent out to check out the "Promised Land" gave their report, they said the men there looked like giants and that the Israelites looked like "grasshoppers" in comparison. (Num. 13:33)

* Grasshoppers look a lot like migrating "locusts."

* A swarm of flying "locusts" can destroy "all" the crops in its path.

Goats can go
________ without water.

* Grasshoppers on the other hand do not pose much of a threat to farmers.

* According to Jewish Law, the Israelites could eat "adult grasshoppers, beetles, and 2 kinds of locusts."

* They would eat them fresh or preserve them in "salt."

* Grasshoppers were a good source of "protein" for the Israelites.

* Today to honor the ancient tradition, in Yemen, a south-western country in "Arabia," the Jews still eat some types of "grasshoppers."

* "Goats" still today provide "meat and milk" for the people of the Holy Land.

* "Goats" can go up to "2 weeks" without water.

* "Goats" can drink approximately "7 gallons" of water at a time.

* Goats are very strong and can live about anywhere.

* Even in places where there is little plant life, such as the hot deserts of the "Holy Land."

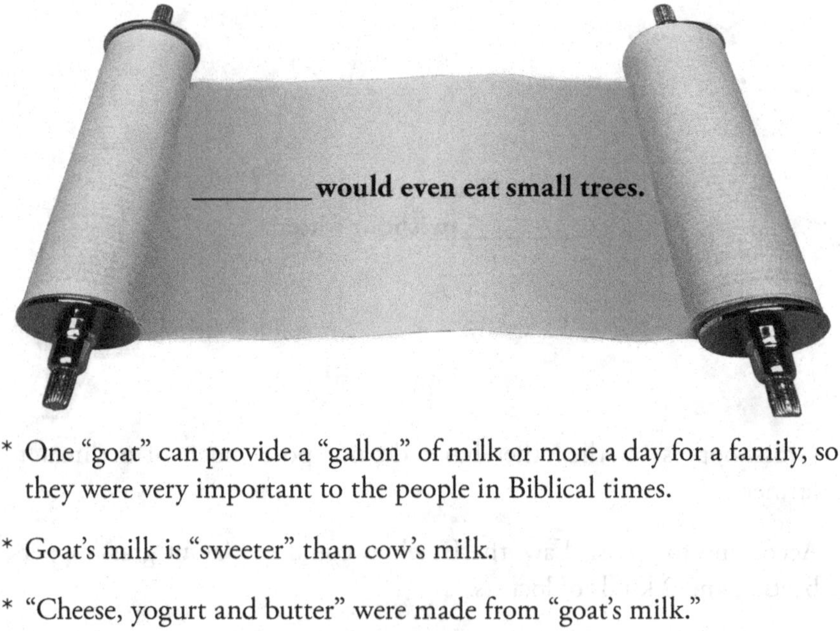
________ would even eat small trees.

* One "goat" can provide a "gallon" of milk or more a day for a family, so they were very important to the people in Biblical times.

* Goat's milk is "sweeter" than cow's milk.

* "Cheese, yogurt and butter" were made from "goat's milk."

* The Israelites would "cut" their "goat's hair" in the spring time.

* "Goat's hair" was used to make "tent covers, cloaks, carpets, sacks and even ropes," by weaving it into a "water-resistant" material.

* Goats were also an excellent source of "meat" for a family.

* They would then dry the "skins" in the sun and then sew them together to make strong "bags" that could hold water or wine.

* It was important to keep the "goats" constantly on the move or they would eat everything in the field.

* They would eat small trees, plants or whatever, all the way down to the roots.

* Sometimes, some goats would wander away from the rest of the herd and have to be rounded up.

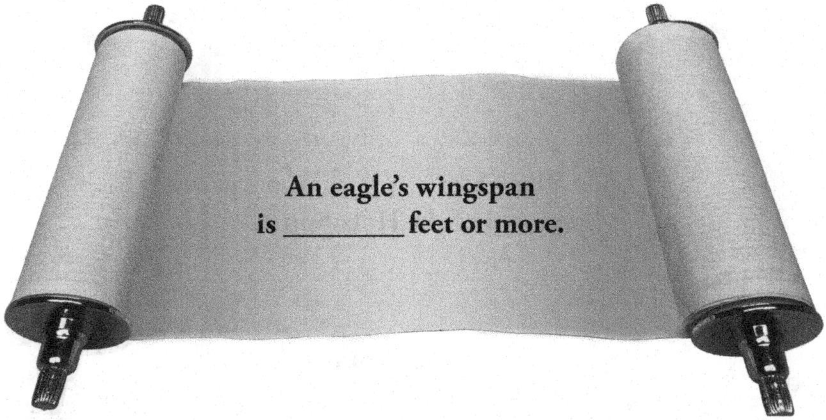
An eagle's wingspan
is ________ feet or more.

* Jews would sometimes "sacrifice goats" to show their "repentance for their sins."

* The Jews would sacrifice "one goat" once a year, in Jerusalem, for the "sins of the entire country."

* Once they sacrificed the "1st goat," they would then send a "2nd goat" out into the wilderness.

* This "scapegoat" as it was called, symbolized "sin leaving" Israel.

* "Eagles" are mentioned throughout the Bible.

* The "eagle" has a wingspan of "8 feet or more."

* Without having to flap its wings, the "eagle" is able to glide on the warm air that rises from the desert, almost like being carried by the wind.

* "Eagles" look for prey as they glide gracefully across the sky.

* When a "rabbit or some other small bird" is spotted, they swoop down and catch it.

* The "eagle" is the "largest flying bird" in the "Holy Land."

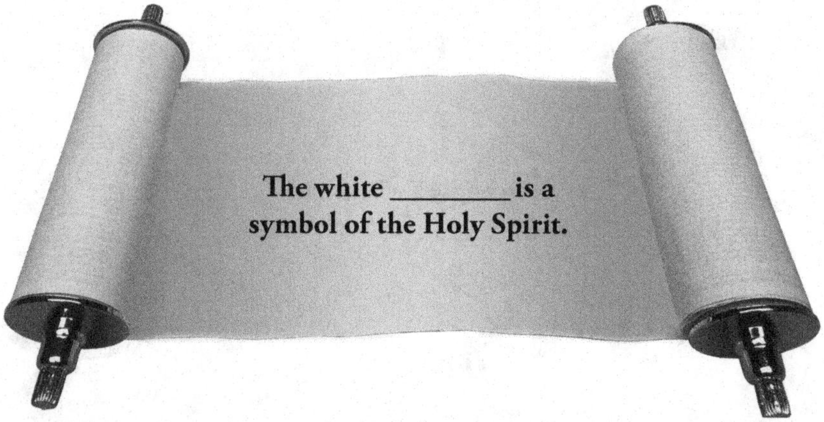

The white ________ is a
symbol of the Holy Spirit.


* An eagle's large nest is usually made out of sticks and branches.

* The eagle will usually build its large nest in a very high place, like a cliff or a very tall tree, to protect their young.

* Because of the eagle's "gracefulness, beauty, strength and rapid flight" it was associated with the "divine," by not only the Hebrews but also by other people in the Bible.

* "Moses" compared how God "cares for His people" to the way the "eagle cares for its young."

* "As an "eagle" strirreth up her nest, fluttereth over her young,"

* "Spreadeth abroad her wings, taketh them, beareth them on her wings: So the Lord alone did lead him, and there was no strange god with him." (Deut. 32:11-12)

* The "white dove" symbolizes the "Holy Spirit, peace, humility, purity and newness of life."

* "Doves" were also a good source of "food" for the Israelites as well.

* Doves also brought in good money for the merchants.

* They were easy to take care of, and since they were kept in coops it was easy to carry them to the marketplace.

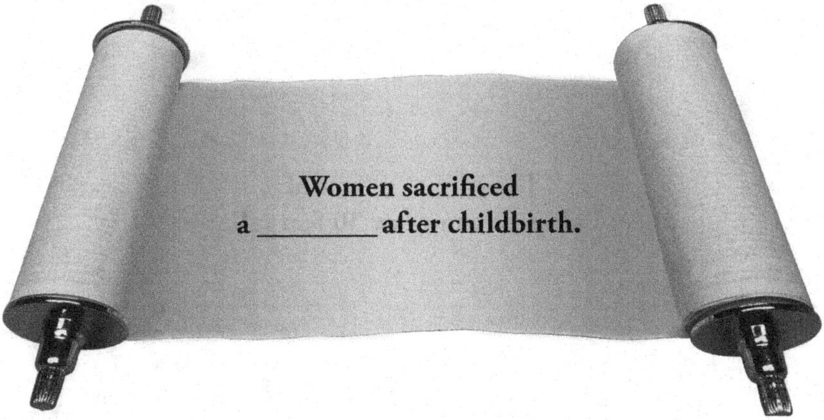
**Women sacrificed**
**a ________ after childbirth.**

* They would also release the "doves" so they could find their "own food."

* So there was no cost involved in feeding them.

* Doves were also used as "sacrifices."

* "Doves" were inexpensive, so if they couldn't afford a larger animal for an offering they could purchase a dove in the courtyard of the Temple.

* Doves were also used in "rites of purification."

* After "giving childbirth" a woman would "sacrifice a dove."

* After the birth of Jesus, "Mary" sacrificed a "pair of doves." (Luke 2:24)

* The "Flood" in Noah's day is probably where the "dove" as a symbol of "peace and new life" originated.

* When "Noah" sent out a "dove" to check for "newness of life," it returned with an olive leaf.

* This showed the "new beginning of life" on earth, and "peace."

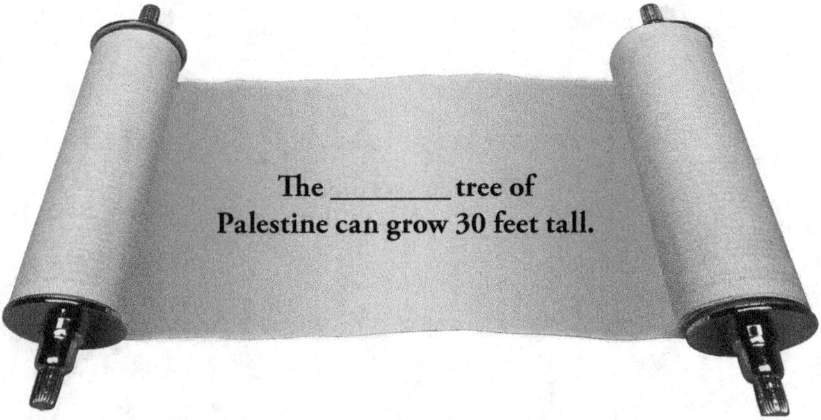
The ________ tree of
Palestine can grow 30 feet tall.

* The most popular story about a "dove" can be found in the Gospels, in the New Testament.

* Where it says that after "Jesus was baptized," that "...the Holy Ghost descended in a bodily shape like a "dove" upon Him..." (Luke 3:22)

* The "dove" is also a symbol of "love and forgiveness."

* You can find the "Judas tree" in southern "Europe, Asia and the Middle East."

* The "Judas tree" is part of the "redbud tree" family which has always grown in the Holy Land.

* As legend has it, the original "flowers" used to be "white."

* Then after "Judas," betrayed Jesus, he hung himself from a "redbud tree."

* Then the "flowers" turned "red" from his "blood."

* The "flowers turning red" symbolized "Judas' betrayal and death."

* In another legend, it says, that the "flowers turned red" because they were "burning with shame," because he used that tree.

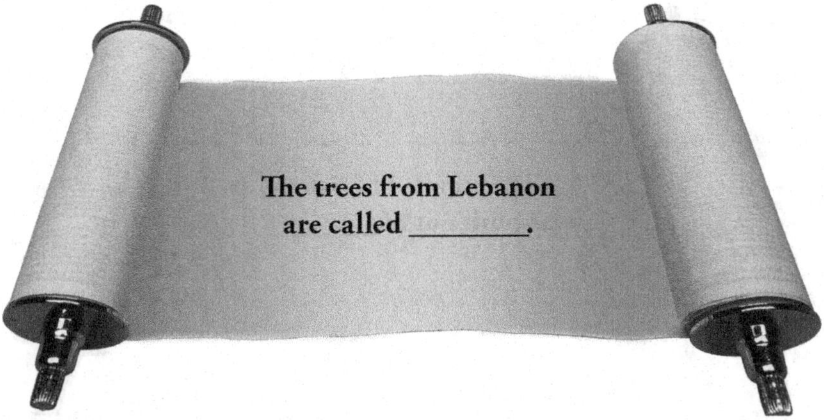
The trees from Lebanon
are called ________.

* People all over the world see the "redbud blossoms" as symbolizing that "spring" has arrived.

* Its "red or purplish-pink blossoms" are a welcome sight after a long winter.

* The "eastern North American redbud tree" can be found in the "United States" and can grow as tall as "40 feet" high.

* The "Judas tree of Palestine" rarely grows taller than "30 feet."

* The "California redbud tree" grows to almost "15 feet" tall.

* The "California' redbud's leaves" are the same as "Palestine's Judas tree."

* The "leaves" on a "redbud tree" are either "heart-shaped" or "kidney-shaped."

* The leaves on a redbud tree change colors in the fall from a bright green to a bright yellow.

* In and around "Lebanon" the forests were full of "cedar trees" in Solomon's day.

* These forests were called "Cedars of Lebanon." (Judges 9:15)

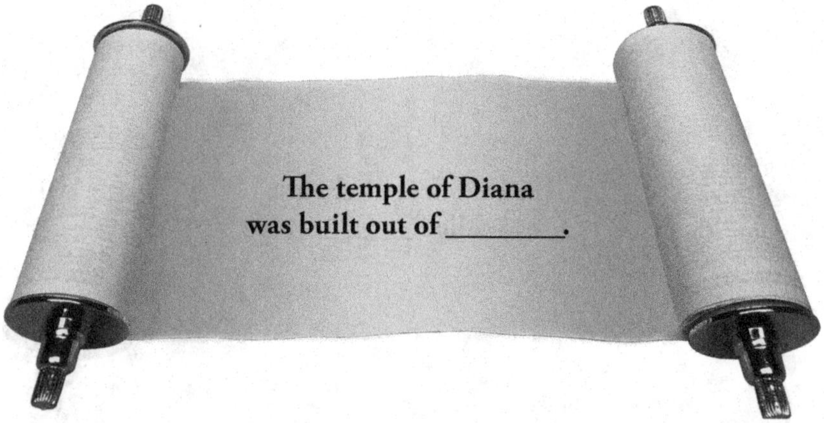

The temple of Diana
was built out of ________.


* Today in the Holy Land there are not many "cedar trees" left.

* Ancient builders liked the "cedar trees" the best.

* Because the "red wood" from a "cedar tree" is very durable and has "no knots" in it.

* These trees also gave off a "scent" that smells good and it "repels insects."

* The "Egyptians" used cedar to build their "ships."

* The "temple of Diana," which is one of the "7 wonders" of the world, was also built out of "cedar" by the "Ephesians."

* Roads were built by King Nebuchadnezzar just so he could transport "cedar" to Babylon.

* King Solomon wanted the "Temple" to "reflect God's majesty."

* So he only used the best building materials, such as "gold, silver and cedar" from Lebanon.

* It took "30,000 workers" to cut the "cedar trees down" off the mountains of Lebanon.

* At altitudes of "4,500 to 6,000 feet" these trees grew up to "100 feet" tall and "50 feet" around.

* Then to get them to the coast of Joppa, they had to be hauled down the mountain to the "Mediterranean Sea" where they then floated "200 miles."

* Then they had to carry them "25 miles" to "Jerusalem."

* Cedar was used for many things.

* Cedar was used for "fuel, embalming fluid, perfume and a protective coating for parchment."

* All these things were made from the "resin" of the "cedar tree."

* Cedar is now "scarce" in the Middle East today because it was used so much in ancient times.

* The "cedar" symbolizes "strength and beauty."

* The Bible speaks of the "Cedars of Lebanon" many times.

* In Psalm 104:16 it says, "The trees of the Lord are full of sap; the "cedars of Lebanon," which He hath planted;"

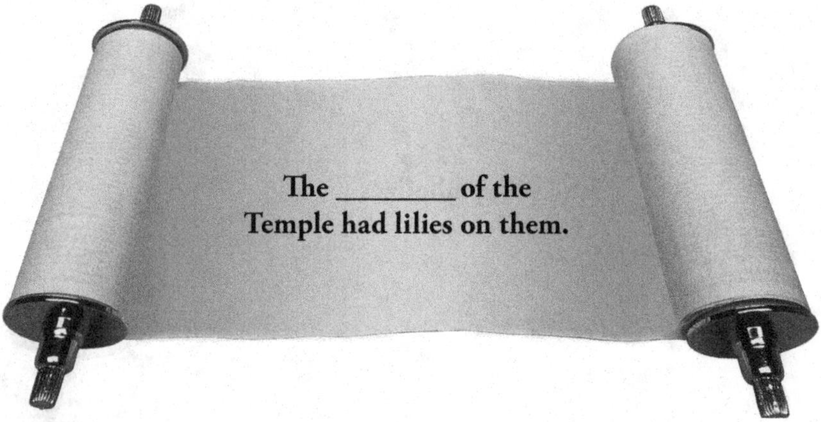
The ________ of the
Temple had lilies on them.

* The "lily" symbolizes "purity."

* The Bible refers to many flowers that grow from "bulbs" as "lilies."

* The following are some of the "flowers" that were all called lilies, "tulips, irises, crocuses, sweet-smelling blue hyacinths, poppy like anemones and lotuses, known as water lilies."

* The ancient "Egyptians" had "lotus lily" designs in their temples.

* "King Solomon" had these designs also in "God's Temple" that he built in Jerusalem.

* The Bible says that the "pillars" of the "temple" were decorated with "lilies."

* The "lily of the valley" mentioned in Solomon 2:1, was probably the "hyacinth" not the modern day "lily of the valley."

* The "lily" used to describe the "lover's lips," in Solomon 5:13 was probably the "scarlet martagon lily."

* The "martagon lily" is "native" to the Holy Land.

* The "lily" mentioned in Solomon 6:3, where it says "pastures his flock among the lilies" was probably the "trumpet shaped white lily."

The Sea tank could
hold ________ gallons of water.


* The "trumpet-shaped white lily" was named the "Madonna Lily" after Jesus' mother, "Mary."

* This "lily" was "rare" in Israel, but could sometimes be found in "Galilee."

* As a symbol of "Mary's purity" this lily can be seen in "paintings of the Annunciation."

* Jesus used the lilies to show how "God cares for and provided for all His creation." (Matthew 6:28-34)

* The "Sea" was a very large 'tank" that was used to hold a lot of water.

* It was designed for the "priests."

* It was placed in the "courtyard of the Temple" near the "altar" where burnt offerings were performed.

* The "Sea" (tank) was for the priests to "wash themselves before" offering sacrifices or entering the Temple.

* The "walls of the Sea" were about "3 inches" thick.

* Its "rim" flared out like a "cup" and resembled a "lily blossom." (1 Kings 7:26)

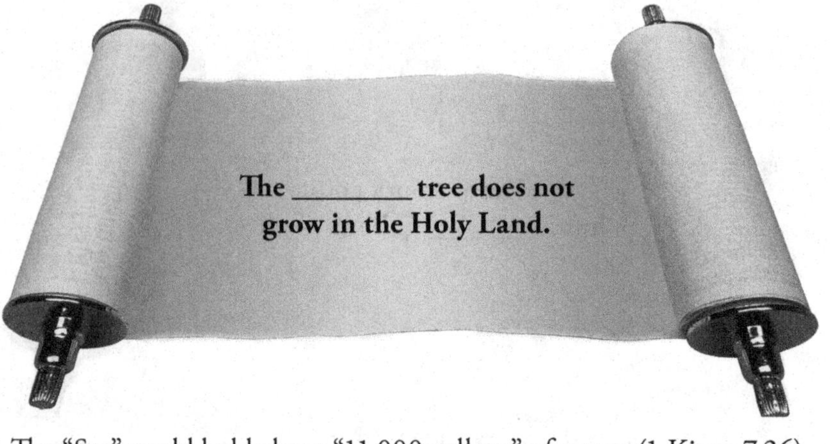

The ________ tree does not
grow in the Holy Land.


* The "Sea" could hold about "11,000 gallons" of water. (1 Kings 7:26)

* The "Sea" was made of "cast bronze; it was "7½ feet deep" and "15 feet across." (1 Kings 7:23)

* "12 bronze oxen" supported the "basin's weight;" there were "3" on "each side," facing north, south, east and west. (1 Kings 7:25)

* The "bronze Seas" was also called the "Molten Sea" and was built by Hiram.

* King Solomon asked "Hiram of Tyre" to come and make furnishings for the Temple.

* As a "skilled craftsman" Hiram was able to work very well with "bronze."

* Hiram was "half Israelite," since his "mother" was a widow from the "Tribe of Naphtali."

* And his "father" had been a "foundry worker" from Tyre. (1 Kings 7:14)

* For a long time people have associated the "dogwood" with the "Crucifixion."

* A lot of the people call the "dogwood" the prettiest flowered tree in the world.

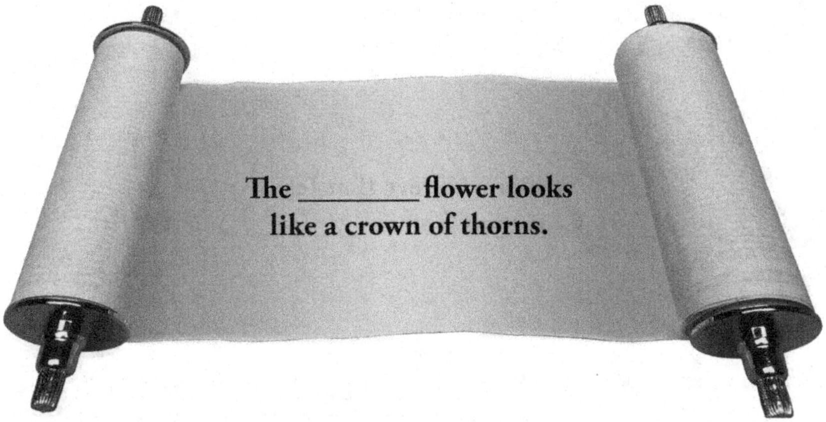
The ________ flower looks
like a crown of thorns.

* The "dogwood tree" blooms in late spring, usually "after Easter."

* It has "green leaves" and "white and pink flowers."

* The "dogwood" does not grow in the "Holy Land" and is not mentioned in the Bible.

* But because of a "folk legend" the dogwood is associated with "Jesus' Crucifixion."

* Legend has it that the dogwood used to be a tall tree.

* But because it was tall and strong it was cut down and used as "Jesus' Cross."

* But the tree was ashamed for being used for that purpose.

* So when Jesus was nailed to the Cross He could sense how the dogwood felt.

* And He felt sorry for the tree and promised it that it would never be used for a cross again.

* The legend says that since then, the dogwood trees have never grown tall or sturdy again.

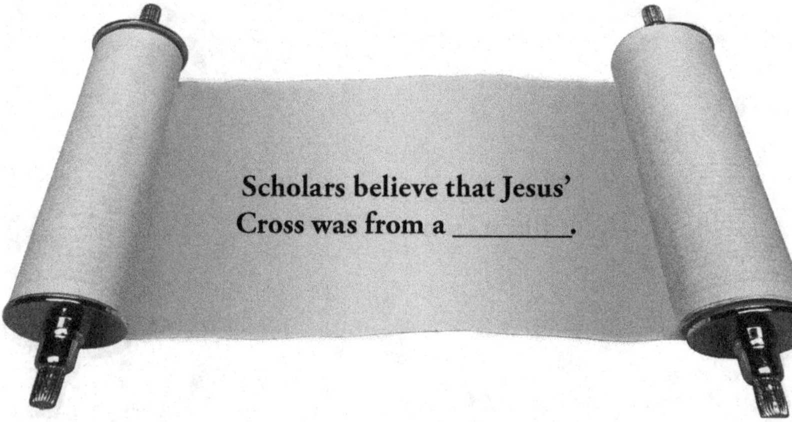
Scholars believe that Jesus'
Cross was from a ________.

* They became too slender and twisted to be made into crosses anymore.

* But legend has it that you can still see traces of that sad day in the "dogwood's blossoms."

* Because the "pink or white leaves" grow in the "shape of a cross" around the flower.

* Legend also says that the "brown stain" that is on "each leaf" is the "rust from the nails" that was driven into Jesus' wrists and feet.

* And some think the "flower" looks like a "crown of thorns."

* The legend says that, the dogwood symbolizes Jesus' suffering and newness of life through Him.

* Scholars today think that "Jesus' Cross" may have been made out of "pine."

* The "pine tree" grew very strong and straight and was abundant in "Palestine" during the New Testament times.

* Most "willow trees" grow near rivers and streams and are mentioned in the Bible several times.

* The "willow tree" grows quickly, and can grow up to "40 feet" tall.

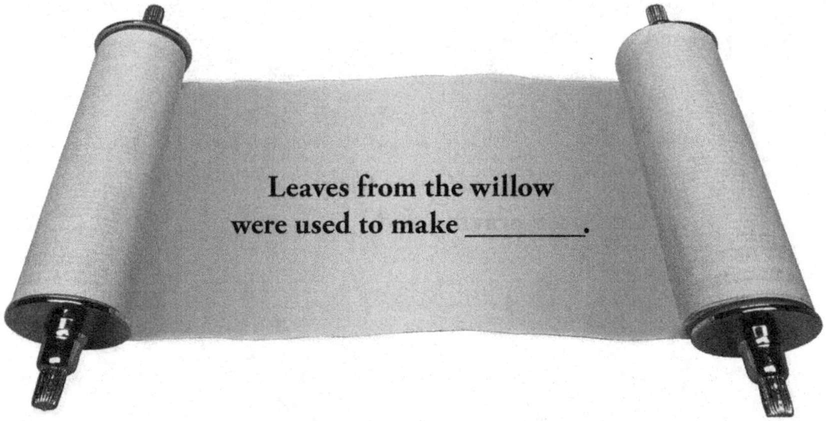

Leaves from the willow
were used to make ________.


* The "Prophet Isaiah" compares how "God's people will thrive" to that of a "willow tree," when He pours out His blessings upon them.

* "...I will pour My Spirit upon thy seed,"

* "And My blessing upon thy offspring:"

* "And they shall spring up as among the grass, as "willows" by the water courses." (Isaiah 44:3-4)

* The ancient Israelites had some type of use for about every part of the "willow tree."

* They used the "wood" from the tree to make small objects, like "handles for tools."

* They used the "branches" to weave "baskets."

* They used an ingredient from the "bark" to "tan leather."

* They used the "fiber" in the "seeds" to make "wicks" for their "oil lamps."

* They used the "leaves" to make "dye" to color "women's veils."

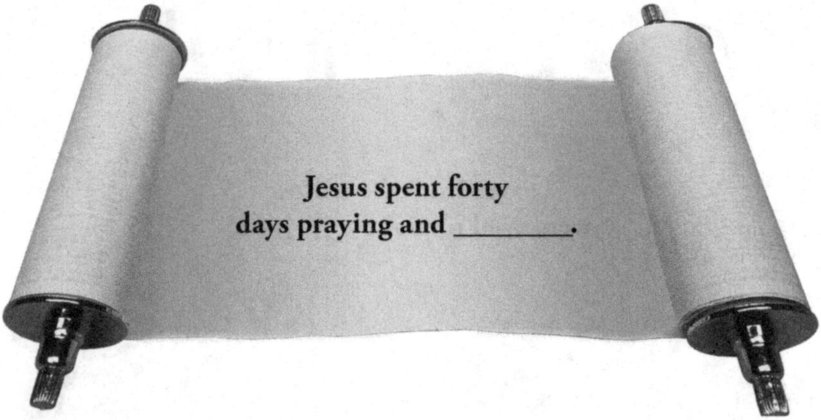
Jesus spent forty
days praying and ________.

* They used "willow and other tree branches" to build "huts" to celebrate the "Harvest Festival of Succoth."

* The "most unusual thing" involving the "willow tree" in the Bible is mentioned in Psalm 137:1-4.

* Where the Jews are held captive in Babylon and they are too sad to sing.

* So they "hung their harps" on the "willow tree."

* "How shall we sing the Lord's song in a strange land?" (Psalm 137:4)

* Still today, the Jews associate the "weeping willow tree" with this time in their history.

* The "willow tree" symbolizes "sadness" as well because of its drooping branches and leaves.

* "Salicylic acid" is a main ingredient in "aspirin" it comes from a type of "willow tree."

* After "Jesus" was baptized, and then was affirmed by the Holy Spirit, He began preparing Himself for His mission.

* He did this by being led by the Holy Spirit into the wilderness of Judea, which is a few miles northwest of Jericho.

Satan tried to get Jesus
to turn ________ into bread.


* It was a hot, dry, barren place.

* There, "Jesus spent 40 days praying and fasting."

* "After" Jesus prayed and fasted for "40 days and 40 nights," Satan showed up and approached Him with the "1st temptation."

* Satan was "twisting the meaning of God's Word" in order to try to trick Jesus into disobeying God.

* Just like Satan did with Adam and Eve.

* Satan told Jesus that if He was the "true Son of God" then He wouldn't have to go hungry.

* Satan tried to get Jesus to doubt God and disobey Him by turning the "stones into bread" to satisfy His hunger.

* But "Jesus refused," He held on to His faith in God.

* Jesus told Satan, "It is written, Man shall not live by bread alone, but by every Word that proceedeth out of the mouth of God." (Matthew 4:4)

* The "scripture" Jesus "quoted" is found in "Deuteronomy 8:3."

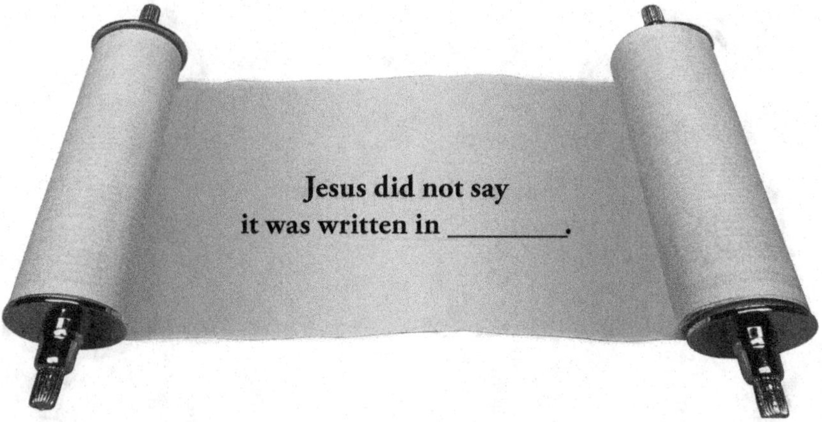

Jesus did not say
it was written in ________.


* That verse says, "And He humbled thee, and suffered thee to hunger,"

* "And fed thee with manna which thou knewest not, neither did thy fathers know;"

* "That He might make thee know that man doth not live by bread only,"

* "But by every Word that proceedeth out of the mouth of the Lord doth man live."

* Jesus didn't quote it exactly word for word, but He was still saying what was "written" in that verse.

* Jesus also didn't say it was written "in Deuteronomy 8:3."

* Because the Bible had not been broken down into chapters and verses at that time.

* That wasn't done until over "1,000's of years later."

* Jesus showed us that "it's okay" if we "don't know where" it is written in the Bible.

* As long as we know that "it is written" in there.

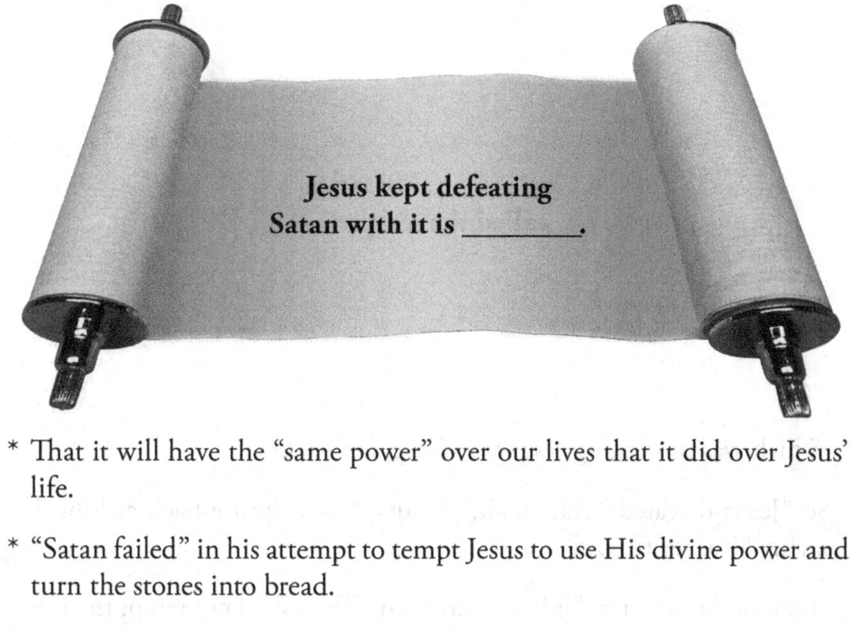
Jesus kept defeating
Satan with it is ________.

* That it will have the "same power" over our lives that it did over Jesus' life.

* "Satan failed" in his attempt to tempt Jesus to use His divine power and turn the stones into bread.

* But Satan didn't give up, he figured if that didn't work, then he would try something else.

* So Satan tried a "2nd time," this time Satan "took" Jesus to the holy city of Jerusalem.

* And then Satan "placed" Jesus on the highest part of the Temple.

* Then the devil said to Jesus, "If Thou be the Son of God, cast Thyself down:" (Matthew 4:6)

* Then Satan "twisted the meaning" of the scriptures again, as he quoted it to Jesus, trying to get Him to disobey God.

* Satan then said, "For it is written, He shall give His angels charge concerning Thee:"

* "And in their hands they shall bear thee up, lest at any time thou dash thy foot against a stone." (Satan quoted Psalm 91:11-12)

* But Jesus knew that to do that would be putting God, His Father, to a test.

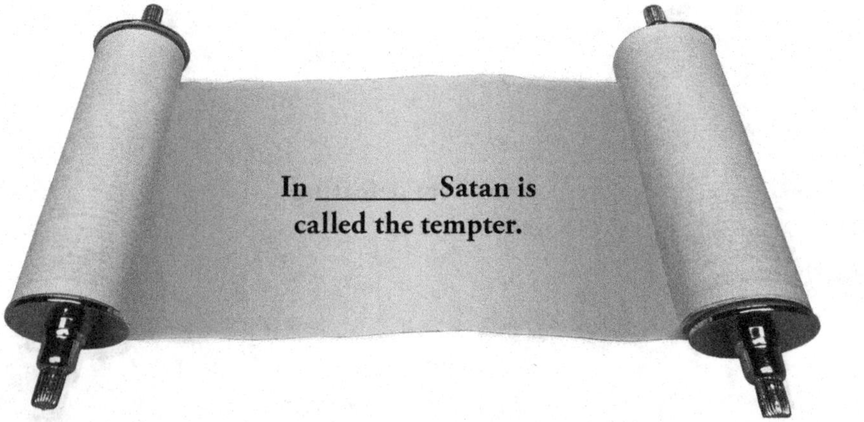
**In ________ Satan is**
**called the tempter.**

* Which was something Jesus was not going to do.

* So "Jesus defeated Satan again" by quoting scripture back at him, by saying "It is written…"

* "Jesus said unto him, "It is written again, Thou shall not tempt the Lord thy God." (Matthew 4:7)

* Jesus "quoted" scripture from "Deuteronomy 6:16."

* That says, "Ye shall not tempt the Lord thy God, as ye tempted Him in Massah."

* But Satan didn't give up, since that didn't work either, he figured he would try something else.
* Satan tried a "3rd time," this time Satan "took" Jesus to the top of a high mountain and showed Him all the kingdoms of the earth, and their glory. (Matthew 4:8)
* Satan told Jesus, "All these things I will give Thee, if Thou wilt fall down and worship me." (Matthew 4:9)
* But Jesus stood His ground and stayed strong in His faith and ordered Satan to leave.
* Then Jesus told Satan, "Get thee hence, (get out of here) Satan, for it is written, Thou shalt worship the Lord thy God, and Him only shalt thou serve." (Matthew 4:10)

Anna was ________ years
old when she saw Jesus.


* According to "Luke's Gospel" Satan still was going to try to tempt Jesus again at a later date.
* "And when the devil had ended all the temptations, he departed from Him "for a season." (Luke 4:13)
* "Matthew, Mark and Luke" use different names for Satan.
* In "Matthew" he is called "the tempter."
* In "Mark" he is called "Satan."

* In "Luke" he is called "the devil."

* The "temptation in the wilderness" is not mentioned in the book of "John."

* "Anna" was a holy woman; she was from the "Tribe of Asher."

* "Anna" got married when she was young, but her husband died after they had only been married "7 years."

* Anna never remarried; she just dedicated her life and herself to worshipping God.

* Anna lived a long life and she spent most of that time in Jerusalem, "praying and fasting" in the Temple.

* Anna was "84 years old" when she saw the baby Jesus, the promised "Messiah."

* Anna saw "Simeon" a religious man of Jerusalem, and "Mary and Joseph," all standing there with "Jesus."

* "Mary and Joseph" had brought the "baby Jesus" to the Temple "to be dedicated to God," according to "Jewish Law."

* Simeon was holding the baby Jesus, and was blessing God for letting him see the long awaited Messiah, the Son of God.

* Anna knew right away that Simeon was right.

* As soon as Anna entered the room, she said hello, and then began praising God.

* Anna began telling everyone that had been waiting on the promised "Messiah" that He was here.

* As soon as she left the Temple she began spreading the wonderful news about the Messiah.

* Anna is the only "prophetess" mentioned by name in the New Testament. (Luke 2:36)

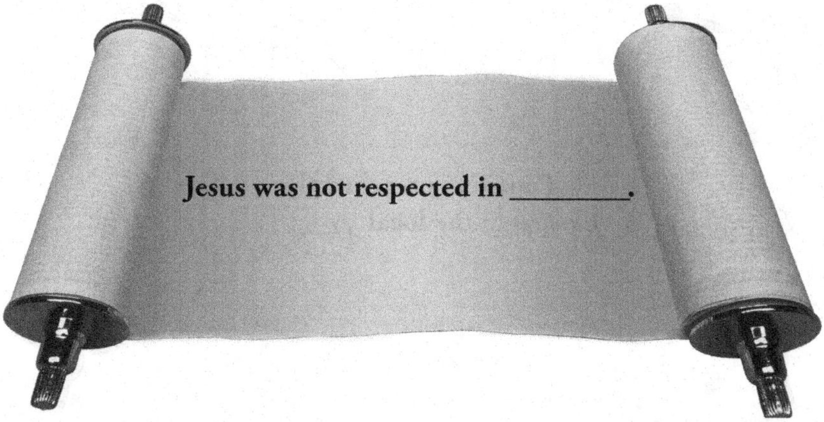
Jesus was not respected in ________.

* "John the Baptist" not only preached in the desert but he lived there as well.

* To hear him preach you had to go to the desert.

* "Jesus" on the other hand, went directly to the people.

* Most of the time Jesus would also go and teach the people in the "local synagogue" whenever He would come to a town.

* The Gospels talk about how Jesus not only "taught" in the synagogues, but "preached" the Gospel and "healed" people of all kinds of sickness and disease everywhere He went.

* Jesus' fame went throughout Syria and great multitudes came from Galilee, Decapolis, Jerusalem, Judaea and beyond Jordan just to see Him, hear Him and be healed by Him. (Matthew 4:24)

* Jesus was respected and welcomed in most cities.

* But in "Nazareth" His home town, He was not.

* The people doubted when Jesus stood and read from the "Book of Isaiah."

* They only saw "Jesus" as the "son of a carpenter."

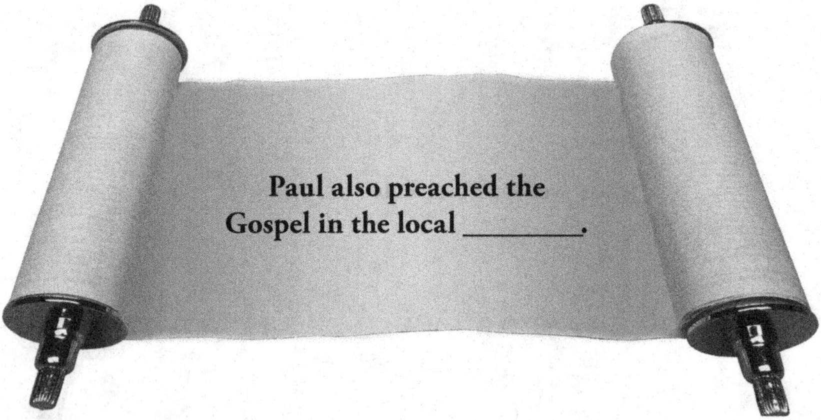
**Paul also preached the**
**Gospel in the local ________.**

* But at the synagogue in "Capernaum" the people were amazed by "Jesus' authority as a teacher."

* Jesus taught in synagogues throughout the land including the "Temple" in Jerusalem.

* Jesus' fame spread far beyond Galilee.

* "And they brought unto Him all sick people that were taken with divers diseases and torments,"

* "And those which were possessed with devils,"

* "And those which were lunatic,"

* "And those that had the palsy;"

* "And He healed them all." (Matthew 4:24)

* Everywhere Jesus went large crowds followed Him.

* This too was a large crowd, but Jesus healed them all, not some, but "all" of them.

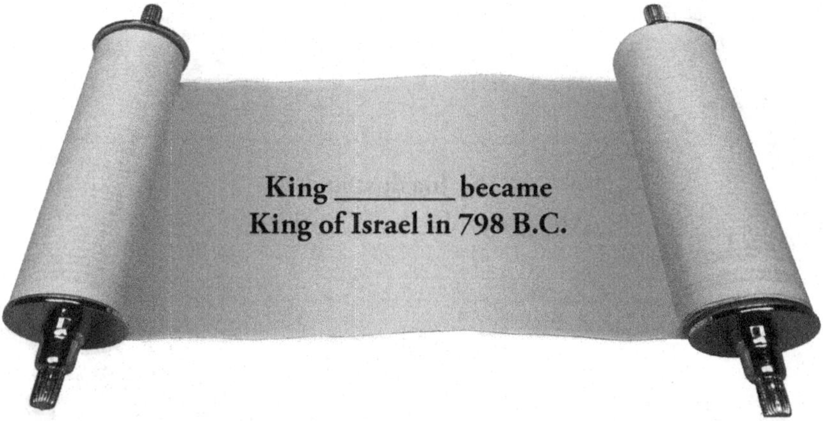
King ________ became
King of Israel in 798 B.C.

* Paul and his companions followed in the footsteps of Jesus as they traveled spreading the Gospel.

* By preaching the Gospel in the "local synagogues" in each city along the way.

* In the Bible God did many great things on mountains.

* On "Mount Sinai" God gave "Moses" the "Ten Commandments."

* On "Mount Carmel" God sent down "fire from Heaven" in answer to the "Prophet Elijah's" prayer.

* On the "Mount of Olives" is where Jesus spoke to His disciples about the "end of days" and "how He would return."

* King Joash cried when he went to visit the "Prophet Elisha" on his "death bed. (2 Kings 13:14)

* Here in 2 Kings 13:14 is the 1st time the "Prophet Elisha" is mentioned in scripture in approximately "43 years."

* The last time he was mentioned was the time he anointed "Jehu" King in 2 Kings 9:1.

* The "Prophet Elisha" was well respected for his prophetic powers and miracles that God had done through him for Israel.

King Joash struck
the ground ________ times.

* King Joash became King of Israel in "798 B.C.," but he was an "evil" king.

* King Joash cried over Elisha because he was afraid of what was going to happen to Israel when the "Prophet Elisha" died.

* King Joash believed that Israel's well-being was because of the "Prophet Elisha," not God.

* The "Prophet Elisha" told King Joash to get a bow and some arrows.

* Elisha told him to put his hands on the bow, and as he did, Elisha placed his hands on the King's hands.

* By doing this the Prophet Elisha placed the anointing of God on Joash's hands for the upcoming battles.

* Then the "Prophet Elisha" told King Joash" to shoot the arrows out the eastern window, and the King did so.

* Then Elisha told the King that this arrow of the Lord's represented "victory."

* So that when they encountered the Syrians in Aphek, that God was going to give them complete victory over there.

* Then Elisha told the King to take the rest of the arrows and strike the ground with them.

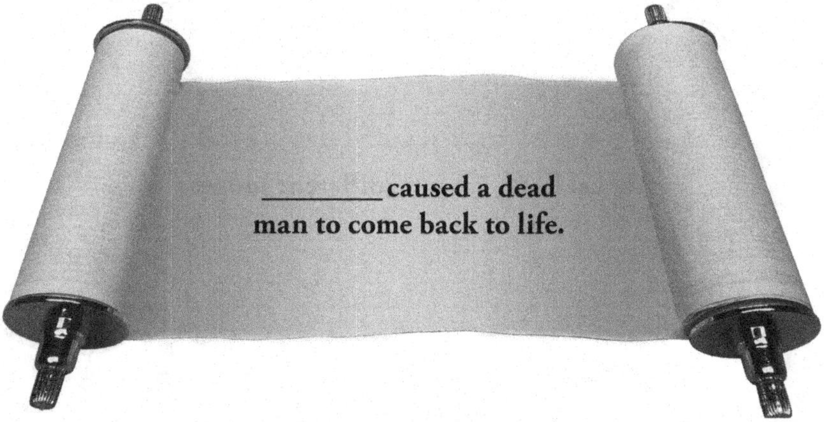

________ caused a dead
man to come back to life.


* But King Joash only struck the ground "3 times."

* When the "Prophet Elisha" saw this he got angry with the King.

* Elisha told King Joash that he should have struck the ground "5 or 6 times."

* Elisha told him, if you would have done it 5 or 6 times, then you would have beaten the Syrians until they were utterly destroyed.

* But, Elisha said, since you only did it 3 times, then you will only have victory over them 3 times.

* After that, the "Prophet Elisha" died.

* The "Prophet Elisha" was buried in a tomb near the Moabite border.

* King Joash waited for the Syrians powerful King Hazael to die, and then he took his army and attacked the Syrians.

* The Israelites defeated the Syrians only "3 times."

* But they never completely destroyed them, just as the "Prophet Elisha" had prophesied.

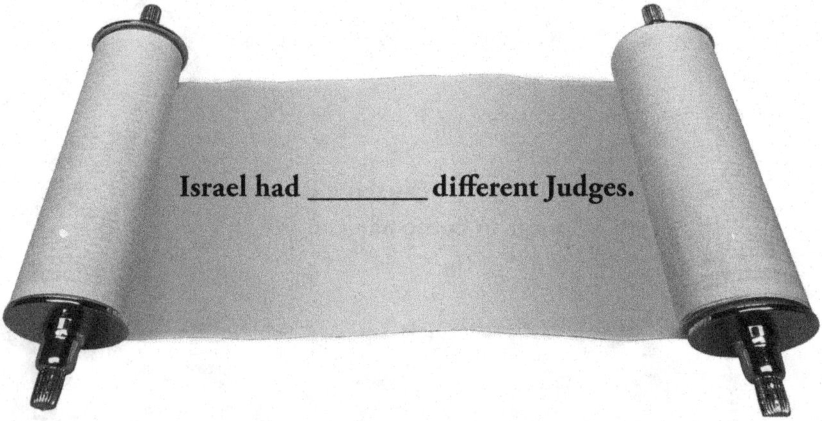
Israel had ________ different Judges.

* The anointing of God was really strong on the "Prophet Elisha."

* That one time the body of a dead man was thrown into the tomb where "Elisha's bones" were, and when the dead man landed against Elisha's bones, the dead man came back to life. (2 Kings 13:21)

* The first translation of the Bible into "English" was started by John Wycliffe.

* The translation was completed in "1388" by John Purvey.

* The "book of Judges" is a continuation of the conquests of the Promised Land that was started in the "book of Joshua."

* Scholars believe that the "Prophet Samuel" wrote the "book of Judges."

* During a period of approximately "325 years" Israel had "12" different Judges.

* During this time period there were "11" male Judges, and "1" female Judge.

* The book of Judges opens with where the Promised Land has already been divided up among the 12 Tribes of Israel.

* And Joshua has died at the age of "110," not long after entering the Promised Land.

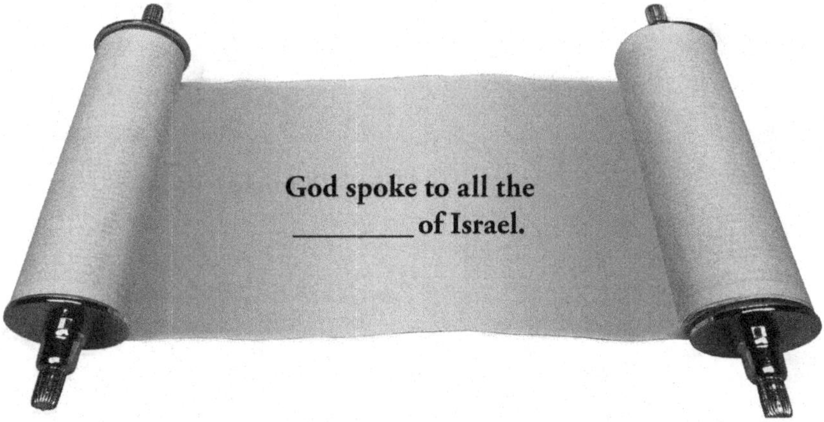
God spoke to all the
________ of Israel.

* So each tribe still had to conquer their own piece of land or territory that they were allotted by Joshua.

* The Lord had made a "covenant" with the people of Israel to help them drive out inhabitants of the Promised Land and give them victory over them.

* But, the Israelites were supposed to keep their part of the "covenant."

* They were supposed to "obey God,"

* "Worship only Him,"

* "Destroy all pagan altars,"
* "And they were not to make any covenants with the people living in the land,"
* "But they were to drive them all out."
* But, the Israelites disobeyed God.
* And because they disobeyed, the Lord "spoke to all" the people of Israel and said,

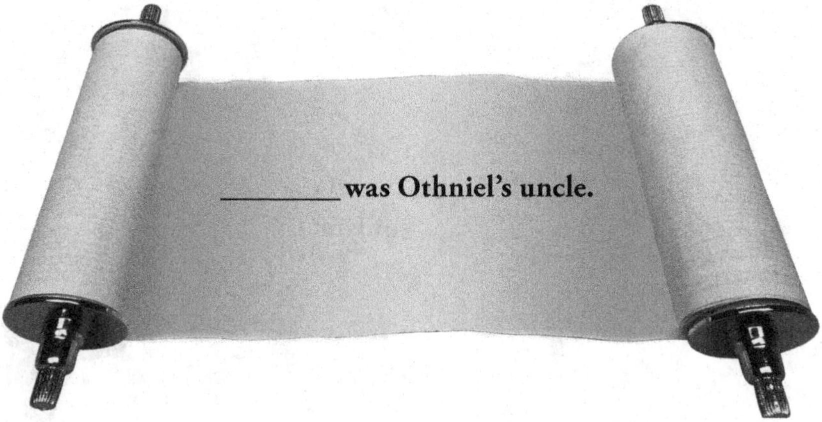


* "I will not drive them out from before you; but they shall be as thorns in your sides, and their gods shall be a snare (temptation) unto you." (Judges 2:3)
* When the Israelites heard this they all wept loudly, and they offered sacrifices to the Lord.
* They then called that place "Bochim," which means "weeping."
* So the Israelites served the Lord through all the days of Joshua, and until the elders that outlived Joshua had died.
* Then they turned away from God and began serving the false god Baalim, and other pagan gods, and began doing evil in the Lord's sight.

* So the Lord had to lift His Hand of protection and guidance off the Israelites.

* And He allowed the Israelites to be conquered by their enemies.

* But when the people of Israel would see the error of their ways, and cry out to God for help and forgiveness,

* Then the Lord would "always" raise up a Judge to rescue them from their enemies.

* The following is a list of the "12 Judges" and their stories that did just that, by the Hand and intervention of God.

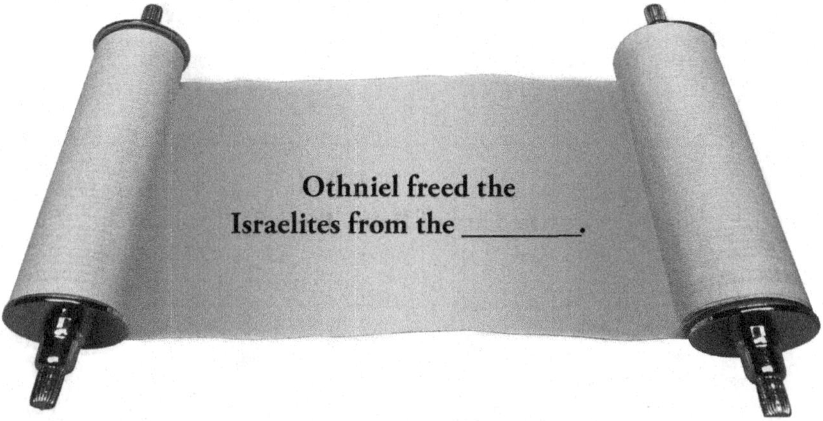
**Othniel freed the**
**Israelites from the ________.**

* The "1st Judge" over Israel was a man named "Othniel."

* Othniel was the Judge over Israel for "40 years." (Judges 3:11)

* Othniel's uncle was "Caleb," one of the Israelite spies that were sent to spy on the city of Jericho.

* Othniel was the son of Caleb's younger brother, Kenaz.

* Caleb was also Othniel's father-in-law.

* Othniel married Caleb's daughter, Acsah. (Judges 1:13)

* God used Othniel to bring the Israelites back to Him.

* God used Othniel to free the Israelites from "8 years" of oppression from the Canaanites.

* Othniel went to war against the Canaanite King Cushan-rishathaim of Aram, and God gave him victory.

* So the Israelites lived in peace for "40 years."

_________ is called
"the City of Palm Trees."

* But after Othniel died the Israelites turned away from God again.

* And because they turned away from Him, and did what was evil in His sight, God had to punish them again.

* So "the Lord" gave King Eglon of Moab control over Israel.

* So the Moabite King Eglon, along with the Ammonites and the Amalakites, attacked Israel. (Judges 3:12-13)

* And King Eglon took possession of "the City of Palm Trees."

* "The City of Palm Trees" is another name for the city of "Jericho."

* So the Israelites had to serve Eglon the King of Moab for "18 years."

* Then the Israelites cried out to God again for help and forgiveness.

* And again God raised up someone to rescue them.

* His name was "Ehud."

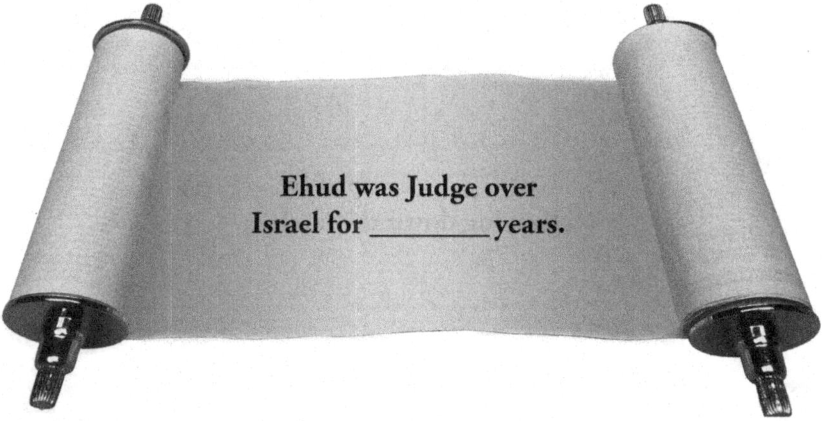
Ehud was Judge over
Israel for ________ years.

* He was the son of "Gera."

* Ehud was from the Tribe of Benjamin.

* Ehud was also left-handed.

* In Ehud's day being left-handed was considered a handicap.

* Many people from the "Tribe of Benjamin" were left-handed. (Judges 20:16)

* Ehud was Israel's "2nd Judge."

* Ehud was the Judge over Israel for "80 years."

* God used Ehud to free the Israelites from "18 years" of oppression from the Moabites.

* The Israelites sent Ehud to deliver a gift to the Moabite King Eglon.

* This gift may have been their tax money.

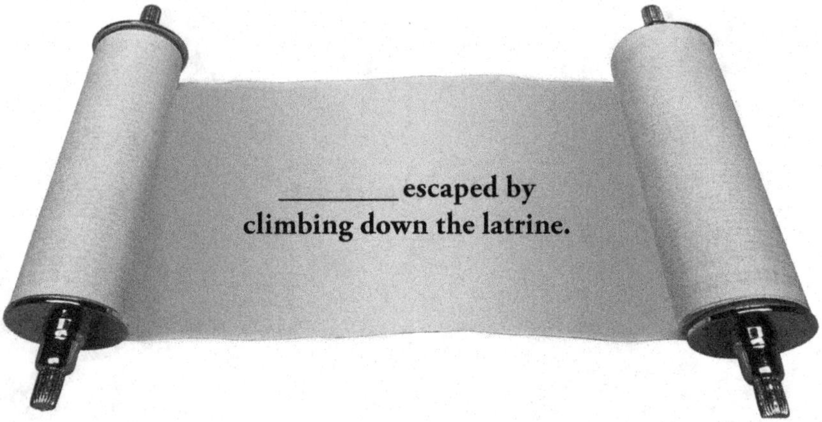
________ escaped by
climbing down the latrine.

* So Ehud made himself an "18 inch" dagger and strapped it to his right thigh underneath his clothes.

* And then he set off to take the gift to the Moabite King.

* After presenting the gift to the King he turned around and went back in to the King's room and told him that he had a message from God for him.

* So King Eglon made everyone clear the room so Ehud could give him the message.

* When the King stood up, Ehud took and reached over with his left hand and snatched the dagger from his right thigh.

* Then Ehud plunged the dagger into King Eglon's belly and killed him.

* Now the Moabite King Eglon was a very fat man.

* And the "18 inch" dagger went in his belly so deep that the handle disappeared underneath his fat.

* So Ehud could not draw the dagger out of the King's belly.

* Ehud locked the doors to the King's room and escaped by climbing down the latrine and then through the sewage access.

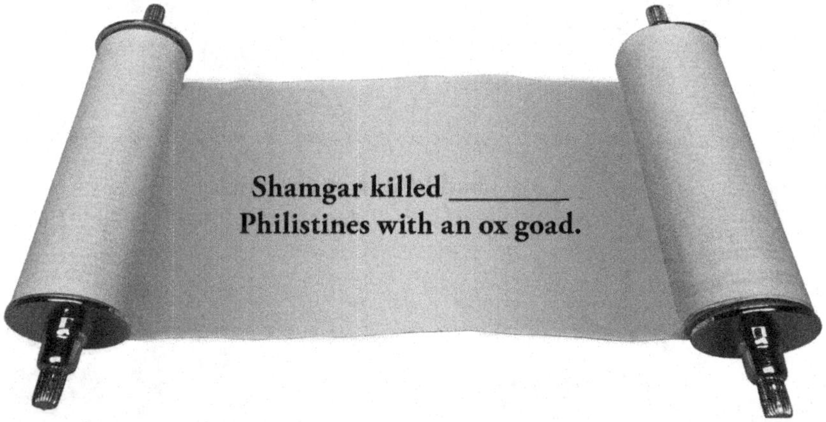
**Shamgar killed ________**
**Philistines with an ox goad.**

* When Ehud reached the hill country of Ephraim, he blew a "trumpet" calling the Israelites to join him in battle.

* Ehud told the Israelites, "Follow after me: for the Lord hath delivered your enemies, the Moabites, into your hand."

* The Israelites followed him and fought against the Moabites that day.

* The Israelites killed "10,000" Moabite warriors that day, not one of them escaped.

* God gave the Israelites victory over the Moabites, and He freed them once again from their enemies.

* Then the Israelites lived in peace for "80 years."

* After Ehud, the Israelites needed rescuing from the Philistines.

* So the Lord raised up a man named "Shamgar" to rescue them.

* Shamgar was Israel's "3rd Judge."

* The Bible doesn't say how long Shamgar was the Judge of Israel.

* Shamgar killed "600" Philistines using an "ox goad."

* An ox goad was a long stick.

* It has a small flat piece of iron on one side and a sharp point on the other.

* When plowing they would use the "sharp side" to drive the oxen.

* When they needed to get the mud off the plow they would use the "flat side."

* Archeologists have found ancient ox goads that were "8 feet" long.

* Ox goads are still used in the Middle East toady.

* After "Ehud's death" the Israelites turned away from God again.

* And because they turned away from Him and did what was evil in His sight, God had to punish them again.

* So "the Lord" allowed the Israelites to be oppressed by the Canaanites and their King Jabin of Hazor.

God raised up a ________
to rescue them this time.

* The commanding officer of King Jabin's army was a man called, Sisera.

* Sisera had "900 chariots."

* Sisera ruthlessly oppressed the Israelites for "20 years."

* Then the Israelites cried out to God again for help and forgiveness.

* Again, God raised up someone to rescue them.

* But this time God raised up a "woman" to rescue the Israelites from the Canaanites.

* God raised up a prophetess, named "Deborah" to rescue them.

* Deborah was Israel's "4th Judge."

* She was also the "only" female Judge of Israel.

* Deborah was the Judge over Israel for "40 years."

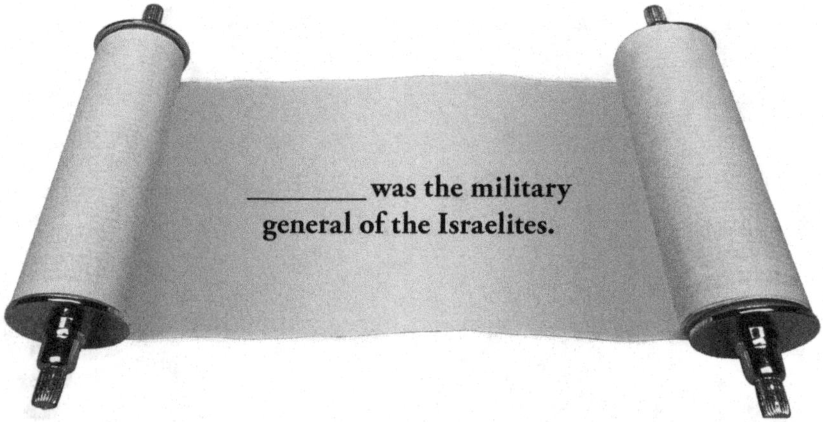
________ was the military
general of the Israelites.

* Deborah was also known for her prophetic power from God.

* She was also a song writer.

* Her husband's name was "Lappidoth."

* Deborah would hold court for the people of Israel under the "Palm Tree of Deborah."

* The "Palm Tree of Deborah" was located in the hill country of Ephraim.

* Ephraim was located between "Ramah and Bethel."

* The Israelites were supposed to destroy "all" the Canaanites out of the Promised Land.

* But, they failed to do so.

* If they would have obeyed God, the Israelites would not have been in this situation.

* The Canaanites rose up against the Israelites in their own land.

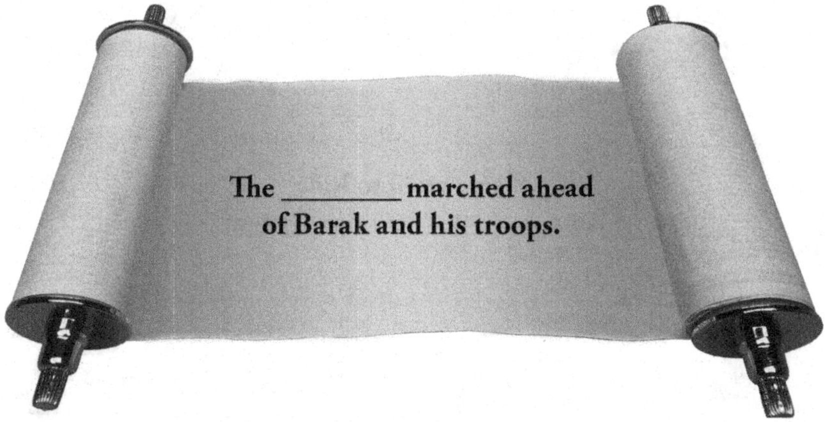

The ________ marched ahead
of Barak and his troops.


* This is the only time in the history of the Judges that Israel's enemies came from within their own land.

* God gave Deborah a battle plan.

* So she sent for "Barak" the military general of the Israelites.

* Deborah told Barak to assemble "10,000" warriors from "2 Tribes."

* The Tribes of "Naphtali and Zebulun."

* Deborah also told Barak to tell the troops to gather at Mount Tabor.

* She told Barak that she would lure Sisera, the commanding officer of the Canaanite army, and all his chariots and warriors to the Kishon River.

* Then Barak and his troops could defeat them there.

* But Barak would not go and gather the troops unless Deborah went with him.

* So Deborah agreed to go with him.

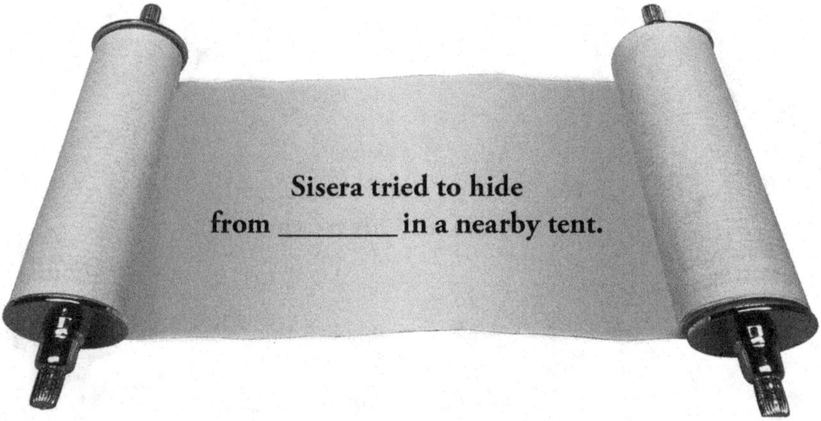

Sisera tried to hide
from ________ in a nearby tent.


* But she told him, since he had made that choice, then "the Lord's victory" over Sisera would be at the "hands of a woman."

* Once the troops had gathered at Mount Tabor, Deborah gave the charge for the battle to begin.

* "The Lord" marched ahead of Barak and his troops.

* And "the Lord" threw Sisera and all his warriors into a panic.

* And the Israelites defeated "all" of Sisera's warriors that day.

* But Sisera jumped down from his chariot and escaped on foot.

* Sisera went to a Kenite's tent nearby to hide from Barak.

* This tent belonged to a descendant of Moses' brother-in-law, Hobab, his name was Heber.

* Heber's family was on friendly terms with the Canaanite King Jabin.

* But, Heber's wife, Jael, was not.

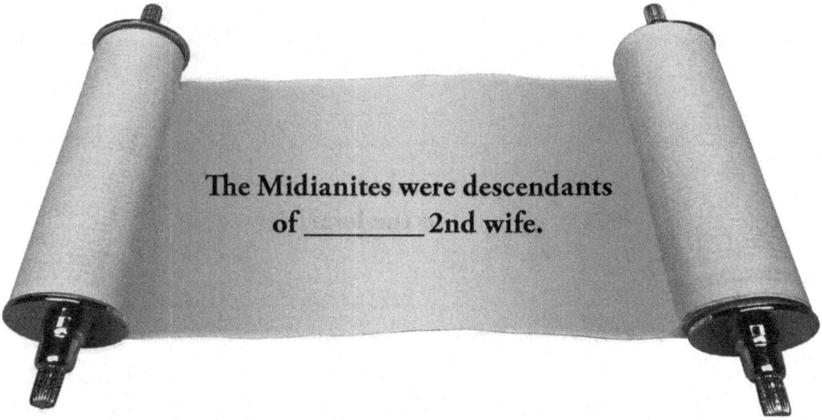
The Midianites were descendants
of ________ 2nd wife.

* So when Sisera arrived at Jael's tent she let him in.

* She gave him some milk to drink and covered him with a blanket so he could hide.

* Then she waited for Sisera to fall asleep.

* When he did, she crept over to him and took a hammer and a tent peg and drove it through his temple all the way to the ground.

* On that day Deborah and Barak sang a victory song.

* After that, there was peace in Israel for "40 years."

* "After the death of Deborah" the Israelites turned away from God again.

* So the Lord turned the Israelites over to the Midianites for "7 years."

* The Midianites were so mean and cruel that the Israelites fled to the mountains to hide.

* The Midianites took the Israelites' sheep, oxen and donkeys.

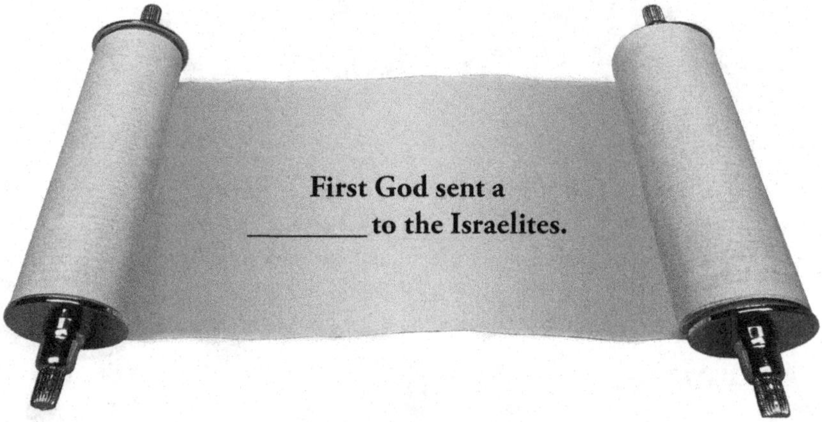
First God sent a
________ to the Israelites.

* They even brought their cattle and camels in and destroyed "all" the Israelites' grain, leaving them nothing to eat.

* The Israelites were literally starving to death.

* The Midianites were desert people.

* They were descendants of Keturah, "Abraham's 2nd wife."

* Because of this, the Midianite nation was always in conflict with Israel.

* When the Israelites were wondering in the wilderness, they battled against the Midianites and were supposed to "completely" destroy them.

* But once again, because they didn't, the Midianites were once again oppressing Israel.

* So the Israelites cried out to God again for His help and forgiveness.

* First, the Lord sent a "prophet" to the Israelites saying,

* "Thus saith the Lord God of Israel, I brought you up from Egypt, and brought you forth out of the house of bondage;"

The Angel waited
under the ________ tree.

* "And I delivered you out of the hand of the Egyptians,"

* "And out of the hand of all that oppressed you, and drave them out from before you, and gave you their land;"

* "And I said unto you, I am the Lord your God; fear not (do not worship) the gods of the Amorites, in whose land ye dwell:" but ye have not obeyed My voice." (Judges 6:8-10)

* Then once again, the Lord raised up someone to rescue them from their enemies, the Midianites.

* The Lord sent His Angel to "Gideon" to tell him that God had chosen him to rescue Israel.

* But Gideon argued with the Lord, because all he could see was his personal limitations. He was not thinking about how God provides all we need, we just have to be willing.
* The Lord told him that He would be with him and that he would defeat the Midianites like they were just one man.
* Gideon was not sure if that was really the Lord speaking to him or not.
* So he asked the Angel of the Lord, "If it is really You then stay here until I come back with my offering to You."
* The Lord told Gideon that He would stay there under the "oak tree" until he returned.

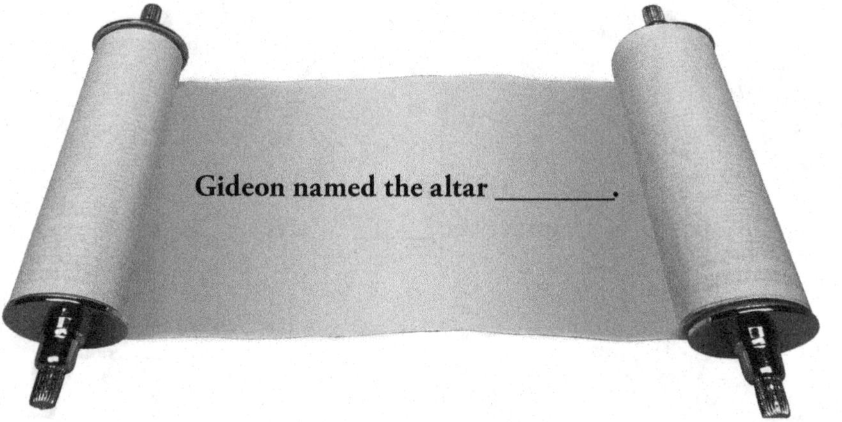


* Gideon went home and cooked a young goat, and some unleavened bread.
* Then he put the meat in a basket and the broth in a pot, and he took it back and presented it to the Angel of the Lord, along with the unleavened bread.
* The Angel told Gideon to place the meat and the bread on the rock.
* Then the Angel of the Lord told Gideon to take the broth and pour it over the meat and the bread, and so he did.
* Next, the Angel of the Lord touched the meat and the bread with the staff that he had in his hand.

* And "fire" came up from the rock and consumed "all" of the offering.

* Then the Angel of the Lord disappeared.

* When Gideon realized that he had seen an Angel of the Lord face to face, he built an altar to the Lord there.

* Gideon named the altar "Jehovah-shalom."

* Which means "The Lord is Peace."

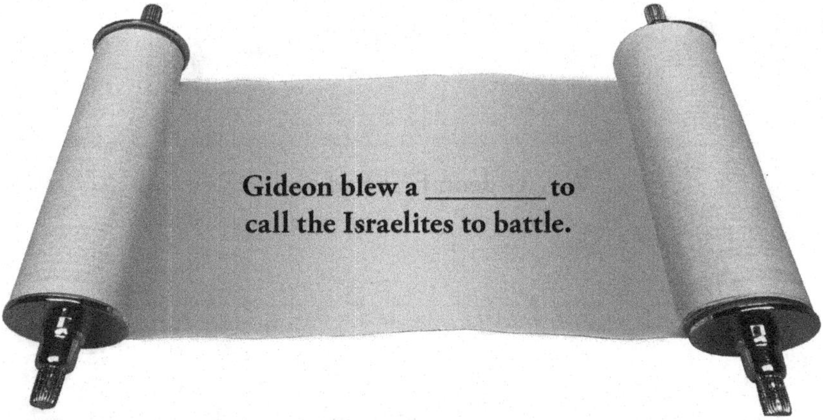

Gideon blew a ________ to
call the Israelites to battle.


* That altar is still in the city of "Ophrah" to this day.

* Gideon's father worshipped the Canaanite god "Baal."

* The first thing that God had Gideon do was, tear down his father's altar to "Baal," and to also cut down the pole that was beside it that represented the god "Asherah."

* So Gideon tore down his family's idols.

* When the townspeople found out who had done this, they wanted to "kill Gideon," but his father, Joash, came to his defense.

* Joash told them that if Baal is truly a god then let him destroy the one who did this.

* After that, Gideon was called "Jerubbaal," which means, "Let Baal defend himself" because Gideon had destroyed his altar.

* Not long after this, the armies of the Midianites, Amalekites and the people of the east joined together to attack Israel.

* So Gideon blew a "ram's horn" to call the Israelites to gather together for battle.

* People from the clan of Abiezer responded 1st to the call.

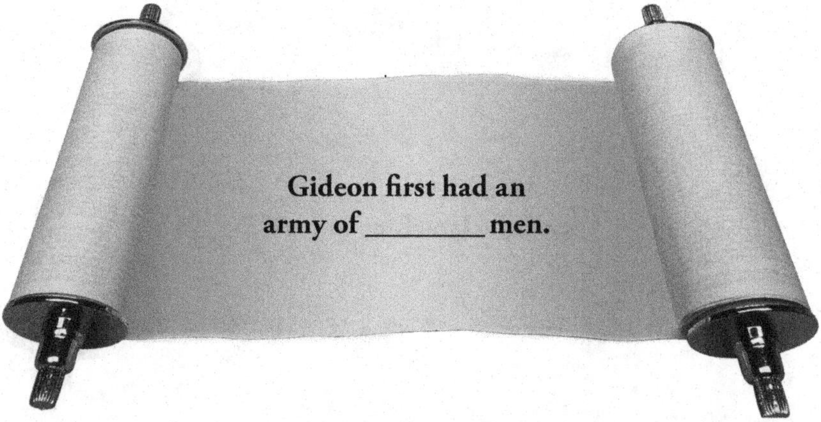


* Then the warriors from the Tribes of Manasseh, Asher, Zebulun and Naphtali all responded to Gideon's call.

* After the Israelite troops had gathered together, Gideon talked to the Lord.

* He told the Lord that he wanted to make sure that he heard right from Him.

* When God said that He was going to use him to rescue Israel.

* Gideon put "2 fleeces" out, "2 days" in a row, for God to confirm His Word to him.

* Gideon told the Lord, that he was going to put a fleece of wool on the floor.

* And if the dew was on the fleece only and the ground beside it was dry, then he would know that he heard correctly.

* And it was, the ground was dry and Gideon wrung about a bowl of water out of the fleece.

* Then Gideon approached God again and asked Him to please don't be angry with him, but could he please do the fleece one more time.

* But this time let the fleece be dry and the ground be wet with dew.

* And God did, the fleece was dry and the ground was wet with dew.

* So Gideon and his army of "32,000" men got up early and went to the spring of Harod.

* The Midianite army was camped north of there in the valley near the hill of Moreh.

* Then the Lord told Gideon that he had too many warriors.

* The Lord explained to him that if He was to let "32,000" Israelites fight and defeat the Midianites, then they would brag that they did it on their own.

* The Lord told Gideon to tell the men that whoever was afraid to fight could go home.
* So "22,000" men went home.
* And "10,000" were willing to stay and fight.
* But the Lord told Gideon that was still too many men.
* God told Gideon to bring the "10,000" men down to the spring and He would sort out who was going to go with him and who was not.

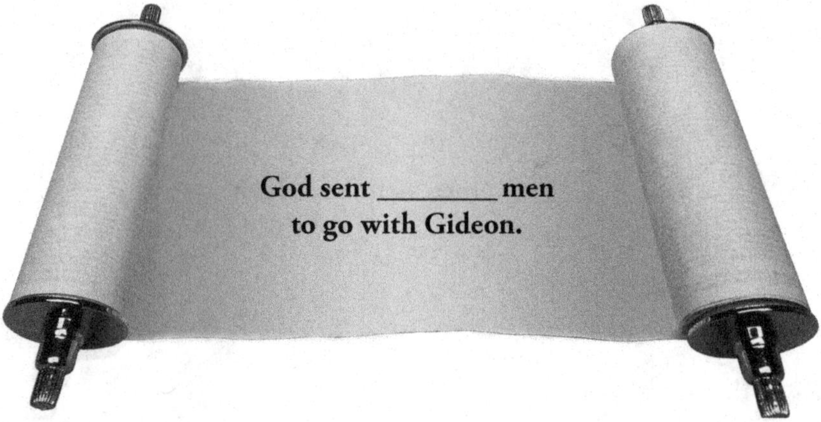
God sent ________ men
to go with Gideon.

* When they arrived at the spring, God told Gideon to divide all 10,000 men up into "2 groups."
* God said in "one group" put all the men that cup the water in their hands and lap it up with their tongues like dogs do.
* Then in the "second group" put the men that kneel down and put their face in the water to drink.
* There were only "300" men who drank the water by cupping it in their hands and lapping it up with their tongues like dogs do.
* There were "9,700" that knelt down to drink with their face in the water.

* Then the Lord said, "I will send the "300" men with you and give you victory over the Midianites.

* The Lord told Gideon to send the other "9,700" men home.

* Then in the middle of the night the Lord told Gideon to get up and attack the Midianites because He had given him victory over them.

* The Lord knew that Gideon was a little afraid so to encourage him he told him to send his servant Purah down to the Midianite camp and listen to what they were saying, then he wouldn't be afraid to fight.

* When they reached the outpost of the camp they were just in time to hear about a "dream" and the "interpretation" of that dream that one of the Midianites had.

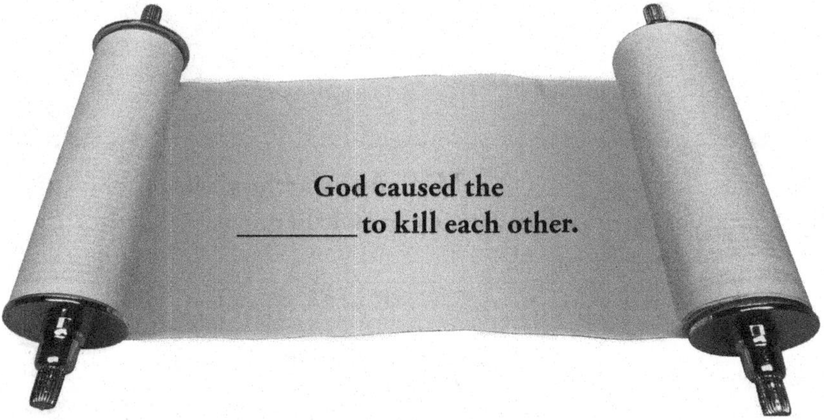
God caused the
________ to kill each other.

* One of the Midianites told his friend that his dream could only mean one thing.

* And that is, "That God has given Gideon the Israelite, victory over all the enemies united with Midian."

* When Gideon heard that he thanked God.

* Gideon went back to his camp and told his men to get up, that it was time to take the victory that God had given them over the Midianites.

* Then Gideon divided the "300" men up into "3 groups" of "100" each.

* Gideon gave all "300" of them a "ram's horn and a clay jar with a torch in it."

* When everyone was in position around the enemies' camp, they all blew their ram's horns and broke their clay jars.

* Then as they held their blazing torches in their left hand, and their ram's horns in their right hand, they all shouted.

* "The Sword of the Lord, and of Gideon!" (Judges 7:20)

* As the Israelites blew their horns, "the Lord caused" the Midianites to run around in a panic, shouting and killing each other with their swords.

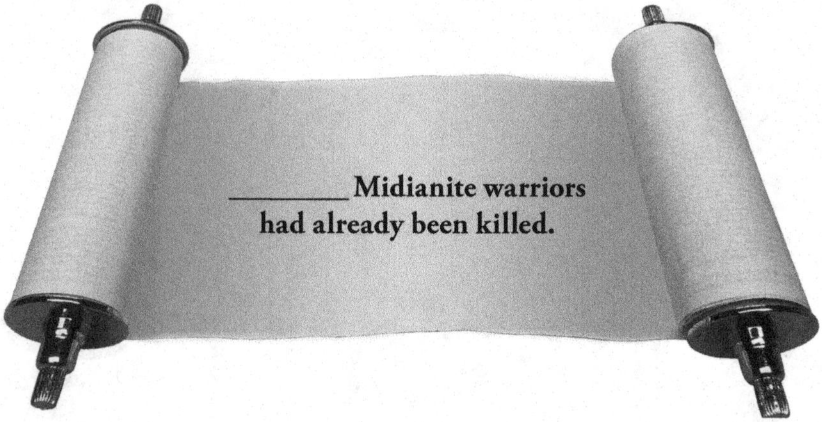
_______ Midianite warriors
had already been killed.

* Those that weren't killed fled, but Gideon's warriors went after them.

* The "2 generals" of the Midianite army were fleeing through the Israelite hill country of "Ephraim."

* Gideon called for the "men of Ephraim" to cut them off near the Jordan River.

* The "men of Ephraim" caught up with the "2 Midianite generals," Oreb and Zeeb.

* After they caught up with the 2 generals they killed them and cut their heads off and brought their heads to Gideon at the Jordan River.

* So Gideon and his "300 men" crossed the Jordan River still in pursuit of the rest of the Midianite army, even though they were hungry and exhausted.

* "120,000" Midianite warriors had already been killed.

* But there were still "15,000" left plus the "2 Midianite Kings."

* When Gideon and his men reached the town of Succoth, he asked the leaders there if they would please give his warriors some food.

* Gideon told them they were tired and hungry because they had been chasing the 2 Midianite Kings.

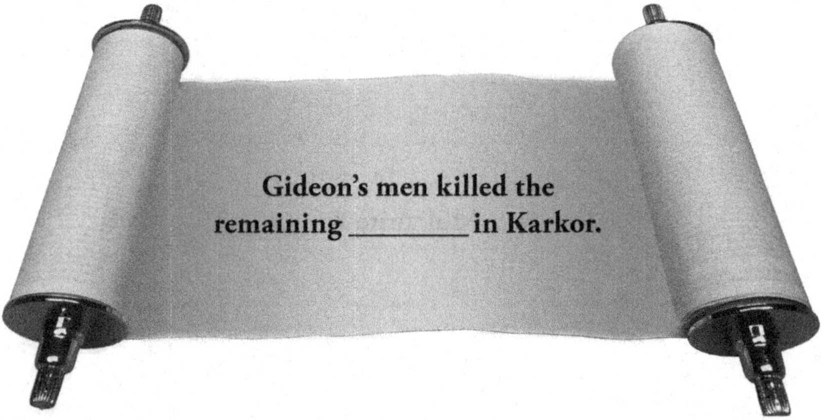
Gideon's men killed the
remaining ________ in Karkor.

* The town leaders told Gideon, "Catch them first then we will feed them."

* Gideon got very upset with their response.

* Gideon told them, "After the Lord gives me victory over these 2 Kings then I'm going to come back here, and tear your flesh with the thorns and briers of the wilderness."

* So Gideon and his men left from there and went to the town of Peniel and asked them for food.

* But again, the people of Peniel gave him the same answer.

* Gideon told the people of Peniel that when he returned in victory that he was going to tear down their tower."

* So Gideon and his 300 men left and caught up with the rest of the Midianite's 15,000 warriors in a city called "Karkor."

* Gideon and his men took them by surprise and captured the "2 Midianite Kings," Zebah and Zalmunna.

* From there Gideon was returning with them, when he stopped in a place called "Heres Pass."

* There he captured a young man from "Succoth" and made him write down all the names of the "77 rulers and leaders" of the town of Succoth.

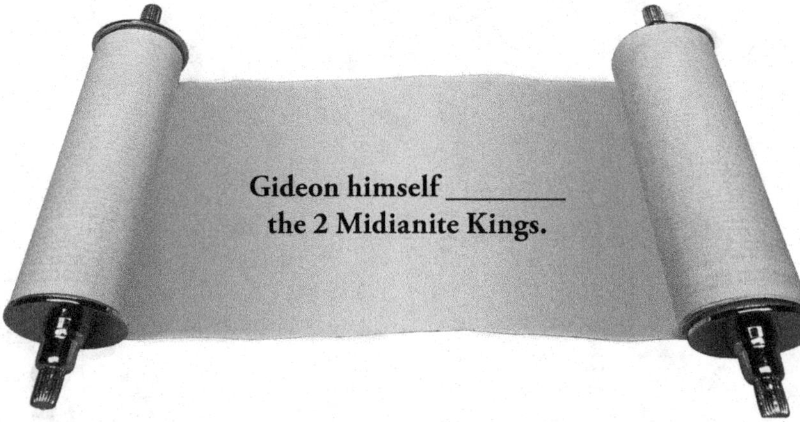
Gideon himself ________
the 2 Midianite Kings.

* Gideon then took the 2 Midianite Kings and returned to Succoth.

* Once there Gideon went to see the town leaders that had refused him and his men food earlier.

* Gideon told them, "Here are the 2 Kings that you told me to catch first, and then you would feed my exhausted and hungry warriors."

* Then Gideon "beat" all 77 leaders with thorns and briers from the wilderness.

* Gideon also knocked down the tower of Peniel.

* He then proceeded to "kill all the men" in the town of Peniel, as well.

* Then Gideon turned to the Midianite Kings and asked them a question.

* He asked them, "What were the men like that you killed at Tabor?"

* And they replied, "Like you, they all looked like they were a King's son."

* Gideon told them that those men they killed were his brothers.

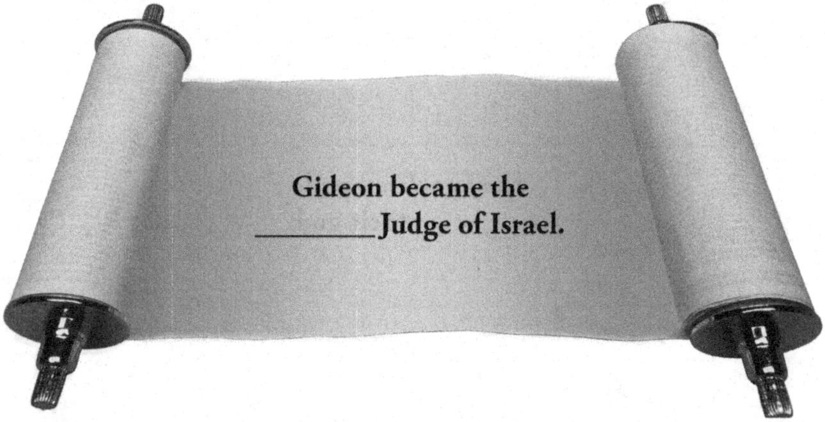
Gideon became the
________Judge of Israel.

* So Gideon turned to his oldest son, Jether, and told him to kill them.

* But Jether couldn't do it, he was afraid because he was just a boy.

* Then the 2 Kings, Zebah and Zalmunna said to Gideon, "Don't ask a boy to do a man's job! Do it yourself!"

* So Gideon killed them both and also took their royal ornaments that they had around their camels' necks.

* After this the Israelites were at peace for about "40 years."

* So God had raised a "farmer" named Gideon to rescue His people.

* God gave Gideon the wisdom to be a great military strategist.

* He became the "5th Judge" over Israel.

* Gideon was the Judge over Israel for "40 years."

* Gideon had "many wives."

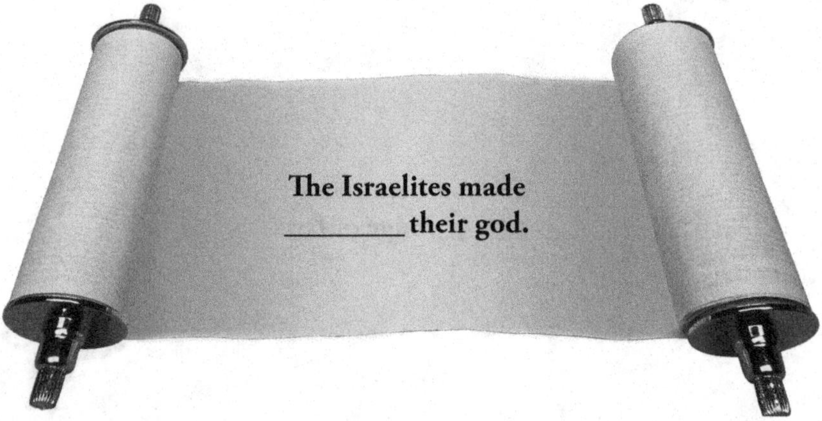
The Israelites made
________ their god.

* They gave him "70 sons."

* But Gideon also had "1 concubine" in the city of Shechem.

* She gave him "1 son."

* Gideon is also mentioned in the "Hall of Faith" in Hebrews chapter 11.

* As soon as Gideon died, the Israelites turned away from God again.

* The Israelites began worshipping other gods.

* They worshipped the images of Baal and they made Baal-berith their god.

* Baal-berith means "Baal (lord) of the covenant."

* Baal was the most worshipped god of the Canaanites, and is mentioned several times in the Bible.

* People usually shaped his image in the form of a "bull" and worshipped it.

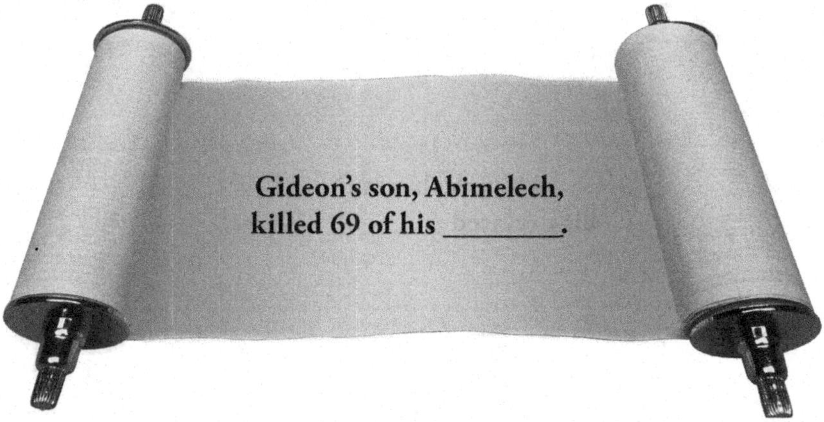
Gideon's son, Abimelech,
killed 69 of his ________.

* They believed that Baal symbolized strength and fertility.

* They also believed that Baal was the god of agriculture.

* The so called Canaanite god Asherah was supposedly Baal's female consort.

* They believed that she was the mother goddess of the sea.

* People usually shaped her image in the form of wooden poles that represented sacred trees, and worshipped them.

* Anytime the Canaanites experienced famine in their land they believed that Baal was angry with them and was punishing them by not allowing it to rain.

* Many Baal idols have been found in Israel by archeologists.

* After Gideon died, "his son Abimelech," by his concubine in Shechem, went to Shechem to visit his mother's brothers.

* Abimelech asked his mother's family and the town's people if they would rather be ruled by all of "Gideon's 70 sons" or by "1 man."

* And he said, "Remember, I am your flesh and blood."

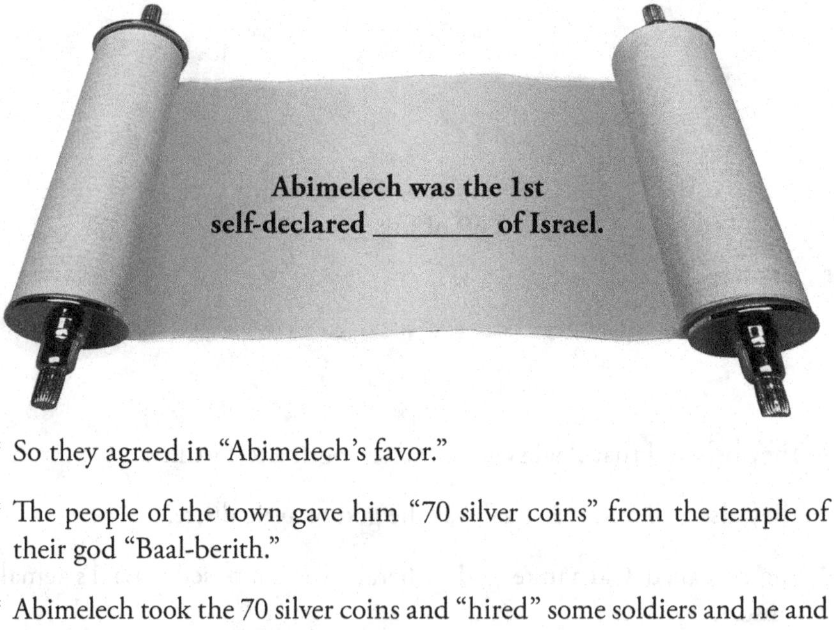
Abimelech was the 1st
self-declared ________ of Israel.

* So they agreed in "Abimelech's favor."

* The people of the town gave him "70 silver coins" from the temple of their god "Baal-berith."

* Abimelech took the 70 silver coins and "hired" some soldiers and he and the soldiers went to Gideon's house at Ophrah.

* Once there, they "killed 69 of Abimelech's half brothers."

* But "Jotham" the youngest brother escaped and hid.

* Abimelech was the "1st self-declared King" of Israel.

* Abimelech was an evil man.

* He not only killed 69 of his half-brothers, but he wiped out "entire cities" that refused to submit to him.

* After Abimelech had ruled over Israel for "3 years," God sent an "evil spirit" to stir up trouble between Abimelech and the people of Shechem.

* Then the people of Shechem revolted against Abimelech.

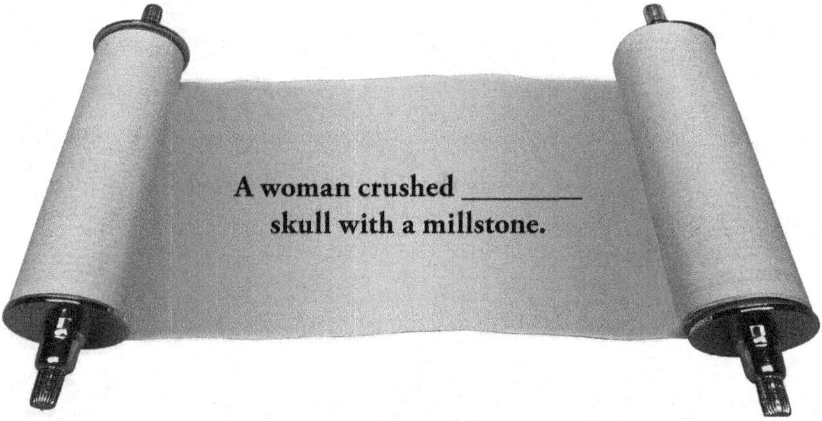
A woman crushed ________
skull with a millstone.

* Then Abimelech went on a killing rampage killing everyone and leveling their cities.

* When the people that lived in the tower of Shechem heard about all that he was doing, they ran and hid inside the temple of Baal-berith.

* But someone told Abimelech where they were, so he and his men took and set fire to the temple killing everyone inside.

* There were about a "1,000 men and women" who died in that fire that day.

* Then Abimelech went and attacked the city of Thebez and captured it.

* But, there was a tower in this city also and all the people ran to this tower and climbed to the roof top to escape from Abimelech and his men.

* Abimelech followed the people to the tower and was just about to set fire to it when a woman on the roof threw down a millstone right down on Abimelech's head and it crushed his skull.

* Abimelech knew he was dying, so he told his young armor bearer to take his sword and kill him, because he didn't want it to be said that he was killed by a woman.

* So the young armor bearer stabbed Abimelech with his sword and he died.

* So God punished Abimelech and the people of Shechem for all their evil.

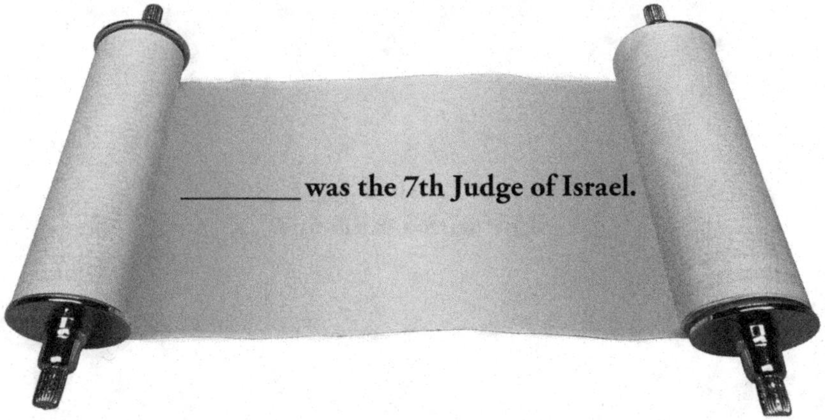
________ was the 7th Judge of Israel.

* After Abimelech's death, God raised up "Tola," the son of Puah and descendant of Dodo, to rescue Israel.

* "Tola" was the "6th Judge" of Israel.

* Tola was from the "Tribe of Issachar."

* But he lived in the town of Shamir in the hill country of "Ephraim."

* Tola was Judge over Israel for "23 years."

* After "Tola died," God raised up "Jair," a man from Gilead to be Israel's Judge.

* "Jair" was the "7th Judge" over Israel.

* Jair had "30" sons, who rode on "30" donkeys.

* Jair's "30" sons owned "30" towns in the land of Gilead.

* Still today these towns are called "the Towns of Jair."

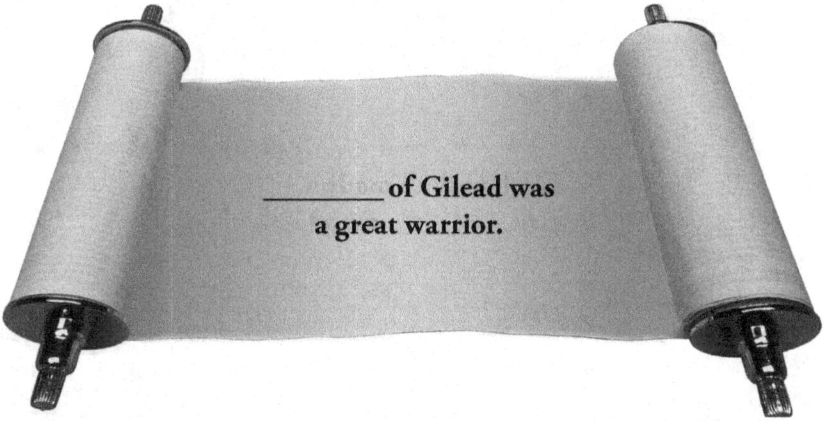
________ of Gilead was
a great warrior.

* Jair was Judge over Israel for "22 years."

* Jair died and was buried in Kamon.

* After Jair's death, the Israelites did evil in the Lord's sight again.

* They worshipped Baalim, Ashtaroth, and the gods of Syria, the gods of Zidon, the gods of Moab, the gods of the people of Ammon, and the gods of the Philistines. (Judges 10:6)

* And they abandoned the Lord and "didn't serve Him at all."

* And the anger of the Lord was hot against Israel because of this.

* So the Lord handed the Israelites over to the Philistines and the Ammonites.

* And they began oppressing the Israelites that very year.

* For "18 years" they not only oppressed all the Israelites east of the Jordan River, but they also crossed over to the west side of the Jordan River and attacked Judah, Benjamin and Ephraim, as well.

* The Ammonites and the Moabites were descendants of "Lot's 2 daughters," when they got their father drunk and then slept with him.

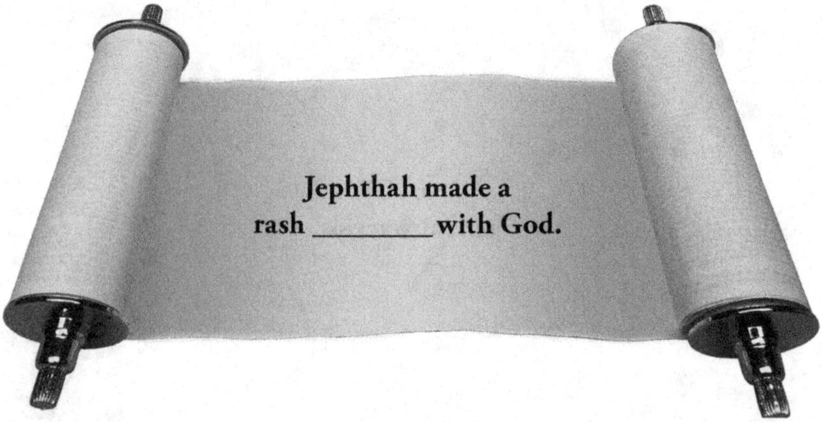
Jephthah made a
rash ________ with God.

* They were powerful nations at the time, so it was no easy task to defeat them.

* They treated the Israelites very harshly.

* Finally, 18 years later, the Israelites cried out to the Lord for help and forgiveness.

* So the Lord raised up "Jephthah" to rescue them.

* "Jephthah" of Gilead was a great warrior.

* Jephthah was also the son of "Gilead," but his mother was a "prostitute."

* He, as well as all the other Judges, were led by God's Holy Spirit.

* Jephthah is also listed in the "Hall of Faith" in Hebrews chapter 11.

* He was also a brilliant military strategist who negotiated before fighting.

* Jephthah made a "rash vow" with God.

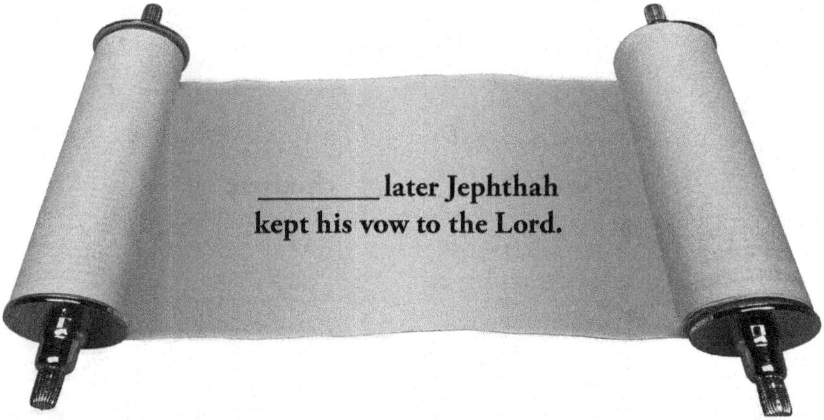

________ later Jephthah
kept his vow to the Lord.


* Probably thinking it would be one of his animals, Jephthah told God that if He would give him victory over the Ammonites, that he would "sacrifice" as a burnt offering to the Lord the 1st thing that came running out of his house to greet him when he returned victoriously.

* "The Lord helped" Jephthah defeat the Ammonites.

* But when Jephthah returned home, the 1st thing that came running out to greet him was his "only child," his daughter.

* As was the custom she ran out to meet him playing a tambourine and dancing for joy, because of her father's victory over the Ammonites.

* Jephthah was very grieved when he saw that it was her.

* So he told his daughter about the vow that he had made with the Lord, and how he couldn't take it back.

* But Jephthah's daughter was a very special girl and she loved the Lord also.

* She told her father that he must do to her what he had promised the Lord he would, because God did give him victory over the Ammonites.

* "But," she said, "Because I will die a virgin and never have children, let me go up and roam in the hills and cry with my friends for 2 months."

* So Jephthah agreed and let her go away for 2 months.

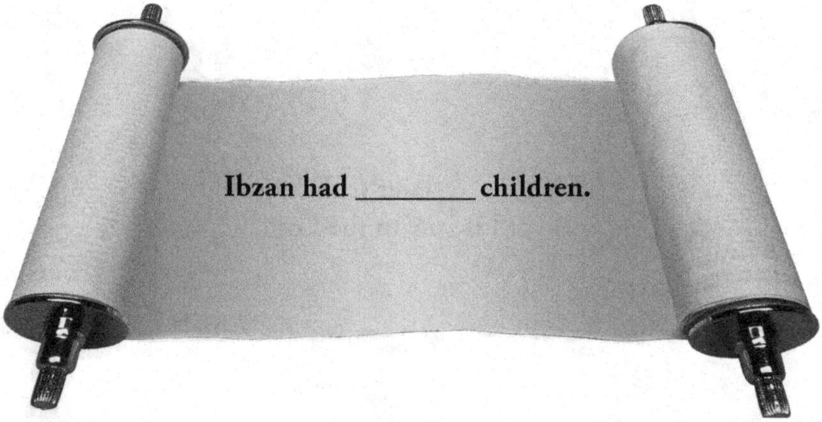


* When she returned home, Jephthah kept his vow and she died a virgin.

* Since then it has become a custom in Israel that young Israelite women are suppose to go away for "4 days each year" to lament the fate of Jephthah's daughter.

* Jephthah was the "8th Judge" over Israel.

* Jephthah was Judge over Israel for "6 years."

* He died and was buried in one of the towns of Gilead. (Judges 12:7)

* After Jephthah died "Ibzan" became Israel's Judge.

* "Ibzan" was the "9th Judge" over Israel.

* Ibzan was Judge over Israel for "7 years."

* He lived in Bethlehem.

* He had "30" sons and "30" daughters.

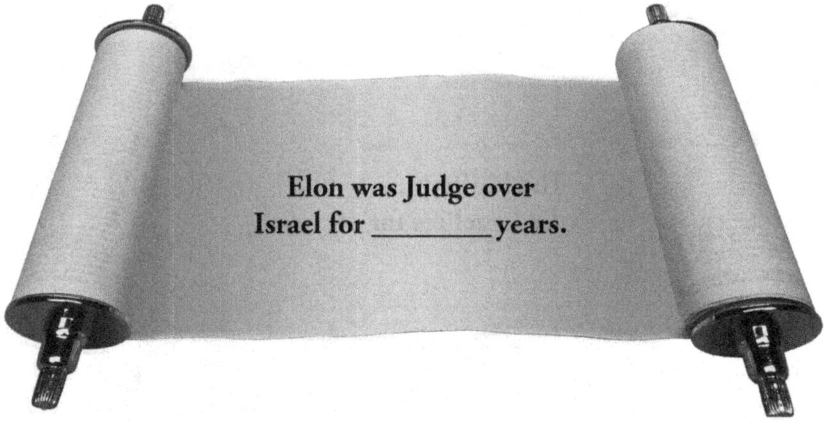
Elon was Judge over
Israel for ________ years.

* Ibzan had his daughters marry men "outside" his clan.

* He also brought in "30 women" from "outside" his clan to marry his sons.

* Ibzan died and was buried in Bethlehem.

* After Ibzan, "Elon" from Zebulun became the Judge over Israel.

* Elon was the "10th Judge" over Israel.

* Elon was Judge over Israel for "10 years."

* When he died he was buried at Aijalo in Zebulun.

* After Elon, "Abdon" from Pirathon, became Israel's Judge.

* Abdon was the "11th Judge" over Israel.

* He was Judge over Israel for "8 years."

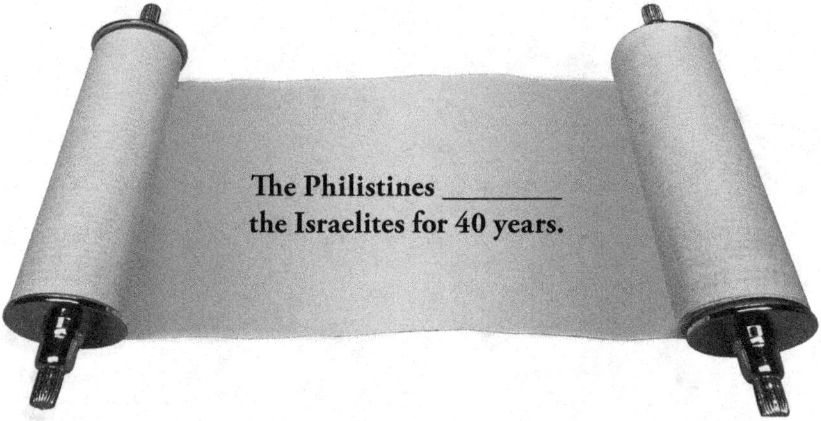
The Philistines ________
the Israelites for 40 years.

* Abdon had "40" sons and "30" grandsons, each of whom rode and owned his own donkey, so he was a very wealthy man.

* He died and was buried at Pirathon in Ephraim in the hill country of the Amalekites.

* There is little else known about the "3 Judges," Ibzan, Elon or Abdon, or their accomplishments.

* There may have been peace in Israel for "31 years" from the time of Jephthah through Abdon, because there were no battles that were mentioned in the Bible. The Bible does not say.

* The large number of children and donkeys are an indication of the wealth of these men.

* After Abdon died the Israelites turned away from God again. (Judges 13:1)

* So "the Lord" handed the Israelites over to the Philistines for "40 years."

* But then God raised up "Samson" to rescue them.

* Samson was a Judge over Israel for "20 years."

* He was the "12th Judge" over Israel.

Samson killed 30 men
and took their ________.

* Samson was ordained "before he was even conceived," to be the one who delivered the Israelites from the oppression of the Philistines.

* Samson was so strong that he once killed a lion with his "bare hands."

* He grew up in the city of "Zorah."

* But one day, when he was in the city of "Timnah," Samson took a liking to a "Philistine girl" there so much that he wanted to "marry" her.

* As Samson's father was making final arrangements for the marriage, Samson threw a party and invited "30 young men" from the city, and he gave them a riddle to solve.

* Samson told them that he would give them "30 plain robes" and "30 fancy robes" if they could solve the riddle.

* Samson also said, "But, if you can't solve the riddle then you have to give me "30 plain robes" and "30 fancy ones."

* But since these young men couldn't solve the riddle on their own they decided to cheat.

* They threatened the life of "Samson's wife," to make her ask Samson for the answer to the riddle.

* Then the young men gave the answer to Samson.

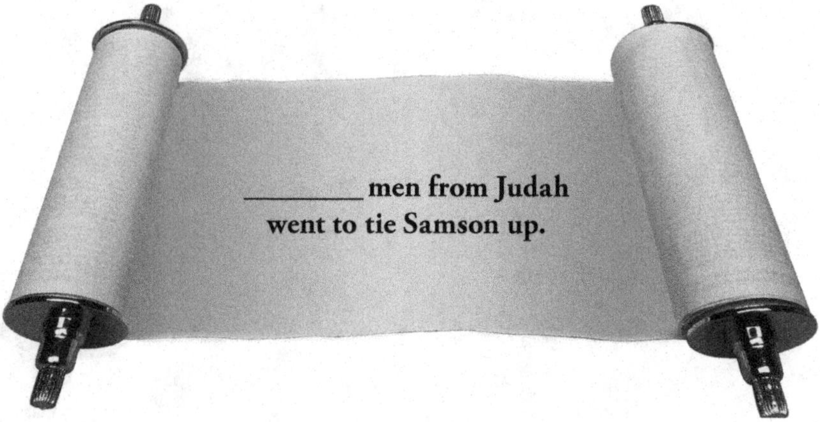

_______ men from Judah
went to tie Samson up.


* Since Samson lost the bet, even though these young men tricked him, he had to give them the robes.

* So Samson went to the city of Ashkelon and killed "30 Philistine men" and took their robes and gave them to those young men.

* Samson was so angry about everything that had happened that he went back home to live with his mother and father for awhile.

* And while he was gone, Samson's father-in-law gave Samson's wife to be married to his best man.

* Later on, when Samson came back to be with his wife and found out that she was now married to his best man, he became furious.

* So he went out and caught "300 foxes."

* Then he divided them up into "150 pairs," and tied each pair together with a "torch between their tails."

* Then Samson lit the torches, and let the foxes run through the fields of the Philistines.

* Samson burned all their grain, grapevines and olive trees.

* When the Philistines found out that Samson did it and why he did it, they took his wife and her father and "burned them to death."

**God made ________ come**
**out of a hole in the ground.**


* Now this really upset Samson even more, so he attacked the Philistines and killed many of them.

* Then Samson went to live in a cave in the rock of "Etham."

* While Samson was in the cave, the Philistines retaliated by setting up their camp in the "Israelite" town of "Judah."

* Then the Philistines raided and attacked the town of "Lehi," as well.

* Because of this "3000 men" from Judah went to get Samson and tie him up and turn him over to the Philistines.

* Samson "let" the men of Judah tie him up with "2 new ropes" and "allowed" them to take him to the town of Lehi where the Philistines were.

* As the Philistines came shouting in victory, Samson "snapped the ropes" that were on his arms like they weren't nothing and got free.

* He then reached down and picked up a donkey's jawbone and killed a "1,000" Philistines with it.

* This place became known as "Ramathlehi," translated it means "Jawbone Hill."

* After his battle with the Philistines, Samson was very thirsty.

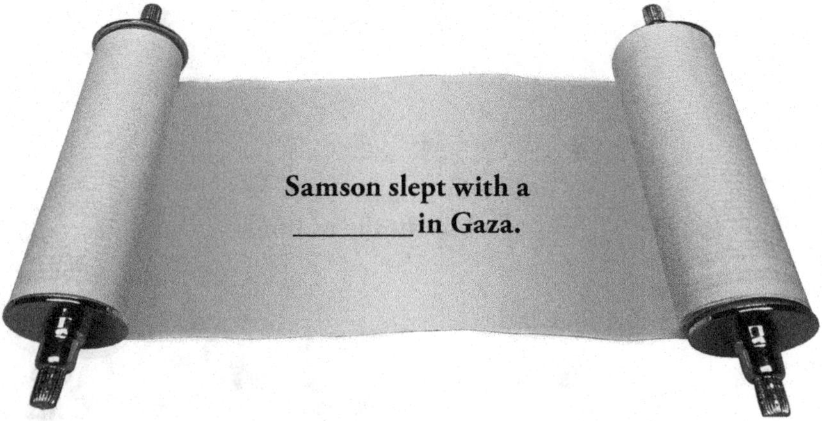
**Samson slept with a**
**________ in Gaza.**

* So Samson cried out to the Lord for water.

* And God heard him, and the Lord made water come out of a hole in the ground, in Lehi.

* Samson named this place, "Enhakkore," translated it means, "The Spring of the one who cried out."

* This spring is still in Lehi today.

* The Philistines had "5 different rulers," in "5 different cities."

* Their cities were Ashdad, Ashkelon, Ekron, Gath and Gaza.

* One day Samson went to the Philistine city of "Gaza" and he saw a prostitute there and he slept with her.

* The Philistines heard that Samson was in town so they devised a plan to try and kill him.

* They decided that they would wait for him at the city gate and when it got "daylight" they would kill him there.

* But Samson got up at "midnight" and went to the city gate and pulled it up, the 2 posts, the bar and all.

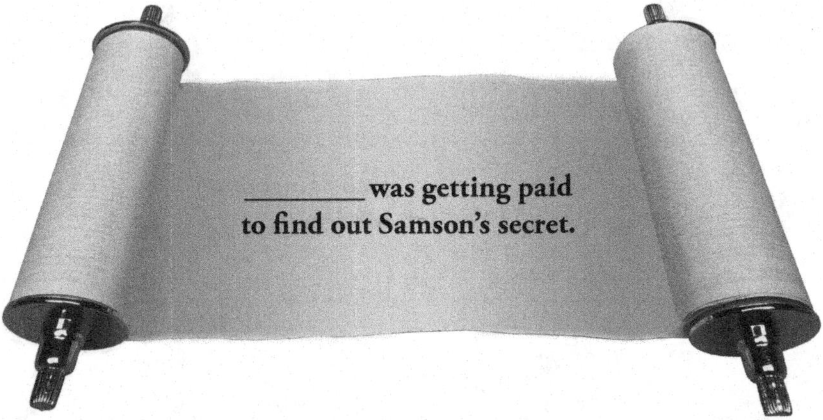

________ was getting paid
to find out Samson's secret.


* Then he carried this iron gate on his shoulders to the top of the hill, across from the city of Hebron.

* Samson was a member of the "Nazirite" sect.

* A "Nazirite" was someone who was set apart for God's service.

* And as a "symbol" of this service they vowed to never cut their hair.

* Samson was a mighty warrior.

* But when he fell in love with a beautiful "Philistine" woman named "Delilah" he eventually let his guard down.

* Samson's enemies the "Philistines" used "Delilah" to get to Samson.

* By offering her large amounts of money to find out the secret of his strength so they could destroy him.

* One day when Samson came to visit Delilah, she asked him where does his strength come from.

* She also asked him what someone could use on him to tie him up with that he couldn't get out of.

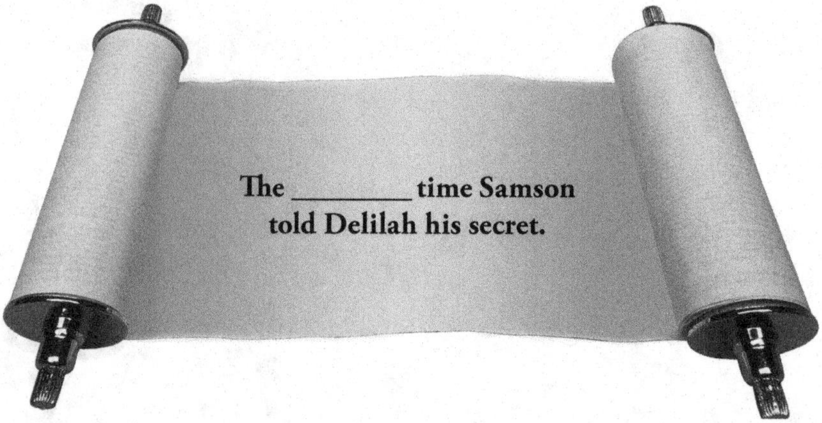
The ________ time Samson
told Delilah his secret.

* 1st time – Samson tells her that if someone took "7 new bowstrings" that had never been dried and tied him up with them then he would be like any other man.

* So Delilah got "7 new bowstrings" and tied him up.

* But Samson easily broke them and got free.

* 2nd time – Samson told her if someone tied him up with "new ropes" that had never been used then he would be as weak as any other man.

* So Delilah got some "new ropes" and tied him up but again he easily broke them and got free.

* 3rd time – Samson told her if she took the "7 braids of his hair and wove it into a loom" then he would be as weak as any other man.

* So Delilah "wove his hair into the loom" but again he easily yanked his hair free.

* Then Delilah pouted and used that old terrible line, "If you loved me."

* She basically told him, "How can you say you love me when you will not even confide in me and tell me your secret?"

* She continued with, "You've already made fun of me "3 times.""

The Philistines gouged
________ eyes out.

* Delilah nagged Samson every day, until he finally couldn't stand it any longer.

* Samson finally gave in and told Delilah the secret to his strength.

* Samson told her that his hair had never been cut.

* Because from birth he was dedicated to God as a Nazirite.

* 4th time – Samson told her if someone was to "shave his head" then he would become as weak as any other man.

* So while Samson was sleeping Delilah had a man come in and shave his head.

* After that, Samson's "strength and the Lord," had left.

* When Samson allowed himself to be put in a situation where his hair got cut, he broke that vow with God.

* When he broke that vow, he lost the "gift of extraordinary strength" that God had given him.

* So then Delilah called for Samson's enemies, the Philistines, and they came and captured him.

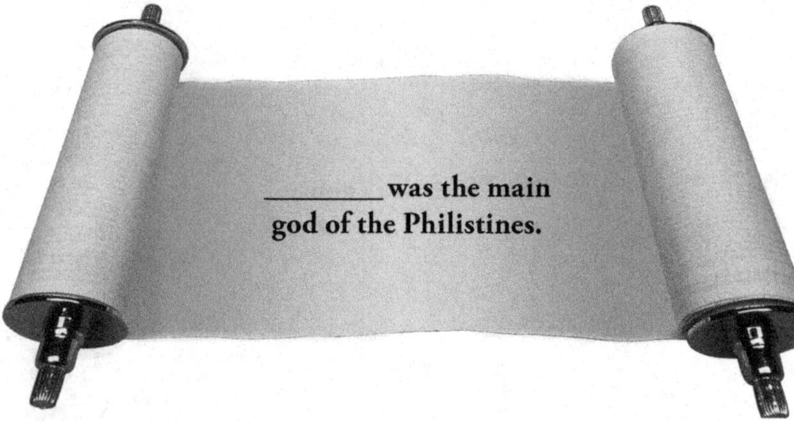
________ was the main
god of the Philistines.

* The first thing the Philistines did when they captured Samson was "gouge both his eyes out."

* Then the Philistines took Samson to a city called "Gaza."

* The Philistine city of Gaza was one of their "5" capital cities.

* The city of Gaza was also well known for its abundance of wells.

* It was an important stop on the trade route between Egypt to the south, and Aram to the north.

* Gaza is also where Samson had earlier used his strength to uproot the city gates when the Philistines were plotting to try and kill him.

* The Philistines took Samson to Gaza and bound him in chains made out of brass.

* And while in chains they forced him to grind grain in the prison there.

* But while in prison Samson's hair began to grow back.

* To celebrate the "capture of Samson" the Philistines held a great festival.

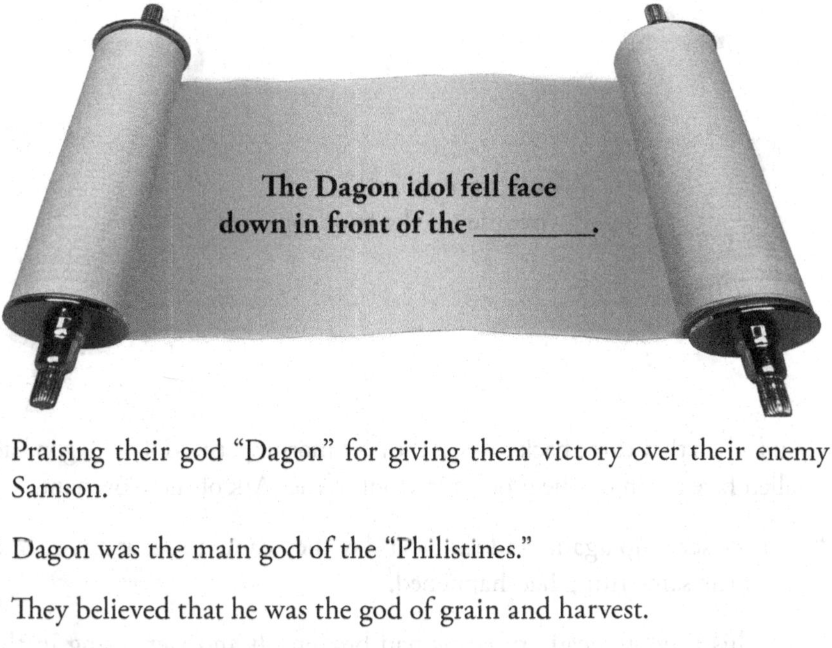

The Dagon idol fell face
down in front of the ________.


* Praising their god "Dagon" for giving them victory over their enemy Samson.

* Dagon was the main god of the "Philistines."

* They believed that he was the god of grain and harvest.

* The Philistines offered "human sacrifices" to their god Dagon.

* The many temples they built for him were also places for entertainment.

* Such as the humiliation and torture of prisoners.

* Multitudes of people would come and fill the temple.

* They all came to watch prisoners get tortured and sometimes killed.

* If there was no room in the courtyard of the temple, then they would gather on the flat roof top of the temple.

* Later on in the Bible in 1 Samuel 5:1-7, when the "Philistines" captured the "Ark of the Covenant," they placed it in one of their temples beside the idol of Dagon.

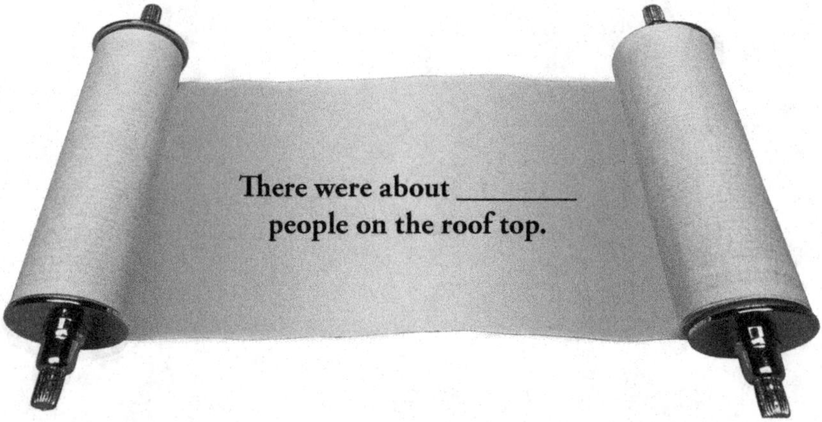
There were about ________
people on the roof top.

* And when they came back to see it the next morning, the idol of Dagon had fallen face down on the ground in front of the "Ark of the Covenant."

* So they set it up again, and the next day they came to see it again, and again the same thing had happened.

* But this time its head and arms had broken off and were lying in the doorway.

* That is why to this day, anyone entering the temple of Dagon, including its priests, will not step on the threshold of the doorway leading into the temple. (1 Samuel 5:5)

* The Philistines were so proud of themselves for capturing their enemy Samson.

* So they wanted to show him off to everyone who was attending the festival at the temple of Dagon.

* As soon as the people saw "Samson" they started shouting for them to bring Samson out so he could entertain them.

* So they brought him out and put him in the center of the temple in between the "2 pillars" that were supporting the roof.

* Since Samson was "blind" one of the guards had to lead him out there by the hand.

* So Samson told the man that he wanted him to take his hands and place them against the "2 pillars" because he wanted to rest against them.

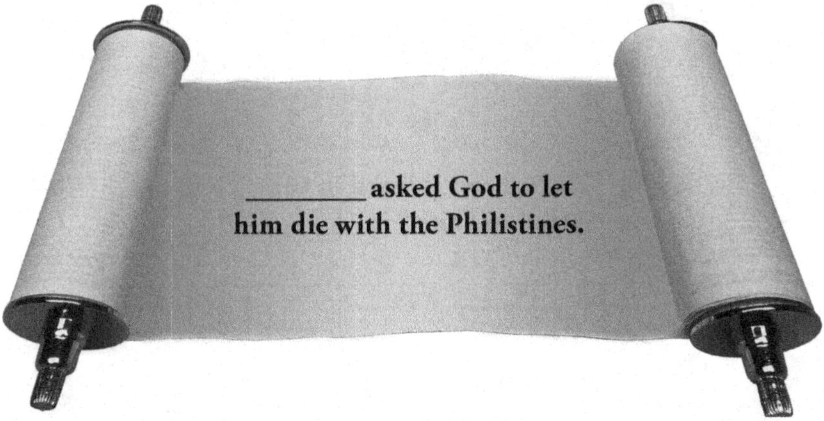

________ asked God to let him die with the Philistines.


* Then the man took and placed Samson's hands, one on each pillar.

* Now the temple was full of men and women, and all the Philistine leaders were there as well.

* There were approximately "3,000" men and women on the roof alone, all watching and making fun of Samson.

* "And Samson called unto the Lord, and said,"

* "O Lord God, remember me, I pray thee,"

* "And strengthen me, I pray thee, only this once, O God,"

* "That I may be at once avenged of the Philistines for my two eyes."

* Then Samson put his hands on the 2 pillars that were supporting the roof.

* "And Samson said, Let me die with the Philistines."

* Then Samson began to push against the 2 pillars with all his might.

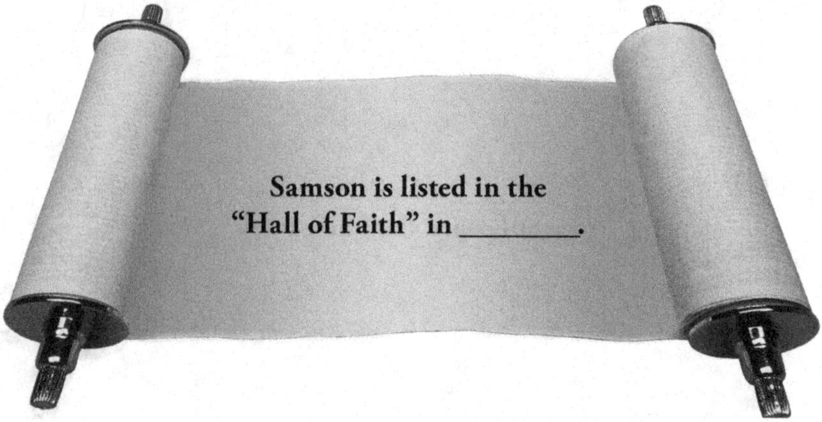
Samson is listed in the
"Hall of Faith" in ________.

* Then the roof and the entire pagon temple came crumbling down.

* It killed "all" the Philistine leaders and "all" the people, including Samson.

* Samson killed way over 3,000 people that day, because there were approximately 3,000 on the roof alone.

* Samson killed more people at his death, than he had during his lifetime.

* Then "Samson's brothers" and some of his relatives came and got his body to bury it.

* They took Samson's body back home to "Zorah."

* Samson was buried in between "Zorah and Eshtaol" where his father was buried.

* God proved that He still loved Samson.

* He loved him in spite of his past mistakes.

* God still answered Samson's prayer.

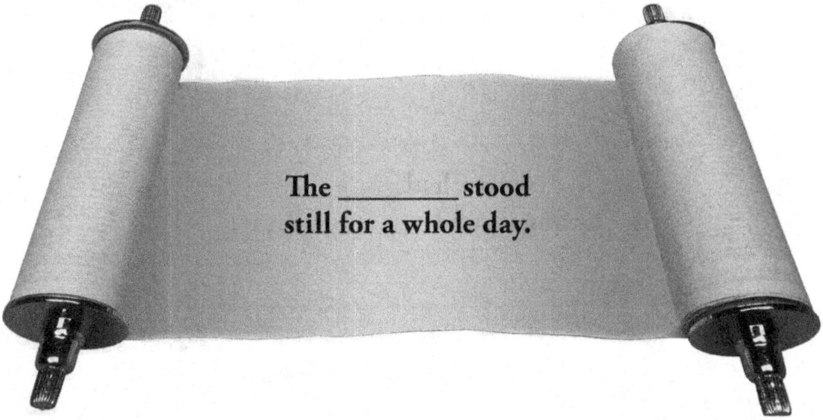
The ________ stood
still for a whole day.

* God still used him to destroy the pagan temple, its worshippers and all the Philistine leaders.

* Samson is listed in the "Hall of Faith" in Hebrews chapter 11.

* Scholars believe that the "1st American" edition of the Bible may have been "published" sometime before the year "1752."

* As of the year "1964" the entire Bible or parts of it has been translated into over "1200 different languages or dialects.

* The Bible was divided into "chapters" by Stephen Langton about "1228 A.D."

* The Old Testament was divided into "verses" by R. Nathan in "1448 A.D."

* The New Testament was divided into "verses" by Robert Stephanus in "1551 A.D."

* The entire Bible divided up into "chapters and verses" first appeared in the Geneva Bible of "1560."

* "Battle won" because "man stretched out his hand" is in Exodus 17:11.

* "Man" who had "bed 13½ feet long and 6 feet wide" is in Deuteronomy 3:11.

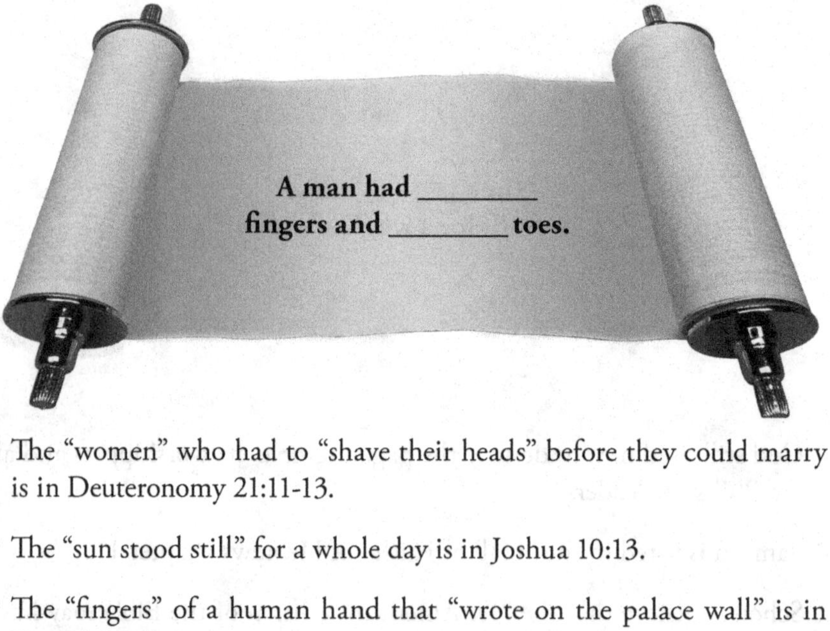
A man had ________
fingers and ________ toes.

* The "women" who had to "shave their heads" before they could marry is in Deuteronomy 21:11-13.

* The "sun stood still" for a whole day is in Joshua 10:13.

* The "fingers" of a human hand that "wrote on the palace wall" is in Daniel 5:5-6.

* "Man" that "ran faster" than a horse drawn chariot is in 1 Kings 18:46.

* "3 men" placed alive in a "flaming furnace" but were not harmed is in Daniel 3:19-27.

* "Man" whose "hair weighed 6 2/3 pounds" when it was cut annually is in 2 Samuel 14:26.

* Where a "ferry boat" was "used" is in 2 Samuel 19:18.

* "Man" who had "12 fingers and 12 toes" is in 2 Samuel 21:20.

* "Man" had "700 wives" and "300 concubines" is in 1 Kings 11:3.

* "Woman" who "boiled and ate her son" is in 2 Kings 6:29.

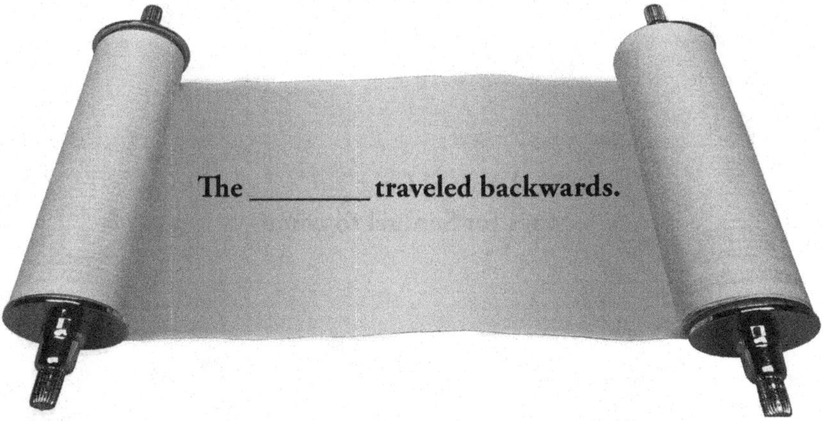
The ________ traveled backwards.

* "Father" who had "88 children" is in 2 Chronicles 11:21.

* "No taste" in the "white" of an egg is in Job 6:6.

* "Man" thrown into "lions' den" overnight but was not harmed by the lions is in Daniel 6:16-22.

* "Army" of "185,000" destroyed in "one night" by one Angel is in Isaiah 37:36.

* A "man" whose "life" was increased by "15 years" because he "prayed" is in Isaiah 38:1-5.

* The "sun traveled backwards" in Isaiah 38:8.

* "Man" was "transported supernaturally" from one city to another by God's Holy Spirit is in Acts 8:39-40.

* "Graveyard" full of dead "bones resurrected" is in Ezekiel 3:7.

* "Man" who "ate locusts" for food is in Matthew 3:4.

* "Saul" was the "1st King" of Israel.

Saul waited for ________
days for Samuel to come.

* He was "30 years old" when he became King.

* Saul was King of Israel for "42 years."

* Saul was a very impatient, quick tempered man.

* He deliberately disobeyed God several times.

* And by doing that it cost him the Lord's support, protection and guidance.

* One instance of disobedience was in a city called "Gilgal."

* In preparation for a battle Saul had his troops gather together with him in Gilgal to offer a "burnt offering" to the Lord.

* And he knew that he was supposed to wait on "Samuel" a prophet and priest, to come and perform the sacrifice.

* Saul waited for "7 days," but the Prophet Samuel still didn't come, and his troops began to drift away.

* Saul was afraid if he didn't do something quickly then there would be no one left to fight the battle.

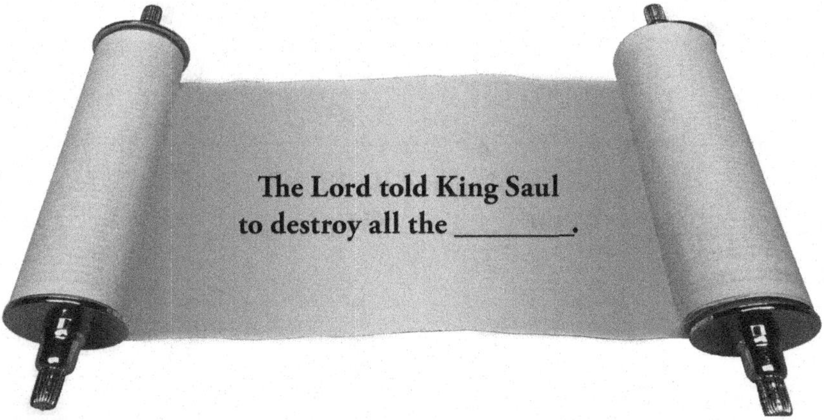

The Lord told King Saul
to destroy all the ________.


* So Saul decided to offer the sacrifice himself. (1 Samuel 13:9)

* Saul knew that only a priest was allowed to offer sacrifices, but out of desperation he did it anyway.

* Just as Saul was finishing up with the burnt offering, the Prophet Samuel arrived.

* The Prophet Samuel scolded King Saul for his disobedience.

* Samuel told Saul that because of his disobedience God was not going to let Saul's sons succeed him as rulers of Israel.

* And that God had already chosen someone to replace him, a man that was after God's own heart.

* Later on, the Prophet Samuel brought King Saul another message from the Lord.

* Samuel said, "Thus saith the Lord of hosts, I remember that which Amalek did to Israel,"

* "How he laid wait for him in the way, when he came up from Egypt."

* "Now go and smite Amalek, and "utterly destroy all" that they have, and spare them not;"

Saul spared the life of
the ________ King Agag.


* "But slay both man and woman, infant and suckling, ox and sheep, camel and ass."

* The Lord wanted King Saul to destroy "all" the Amalekites.

* The Amalekites were a band of terrorists that lived by attacking other nations and carrying off all their wealth and families.

* When the Israelites finally made it to the Promised Land, the Amalekites were the first ones to attack them.

* And they continued to attack them every chance they got.

* So the Lord said that it was now time to destroy Israel's longtime enemy.

* So King Saul went and attacked the Amalekites and killed them all but one.

* Saul spared the life of the "Amalekite King Agag."

* He also kept the best of the livestock and only killed those that were worthless.

* "Then the Lord said to Samuel, I am sorry that I ever made Saul King, for he has not been loyal to Me and has again refused to obey Me."

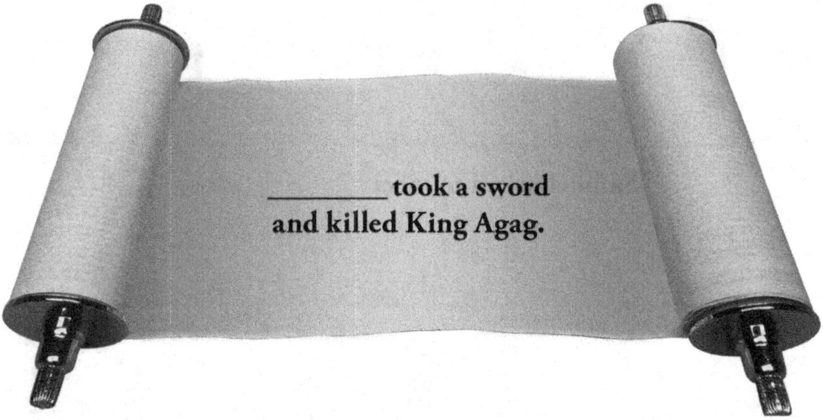
________ took a sword
and killed King Agag.

* Samuel was very hurt and upset that Saul had disobeyed God again.

* Samuel went looking for Saul early the next morning to tell him what the Lord had said.

* When Saul heard the Words of the Lord from the Prophet Samuel, he begged for forgiveness.

* And as Samuel turned to leave, Saul tried to grab Samuel and when he did he tore his cloak.

* A little while later, Samuel told them to bring the Amalekite King Agag to him.

* Then the Prophet Samuel took a sword and cut King Agag to pieces before the Lord at Gilgal.

* And even though Saul remained King for awhile longer, his fate was sealed.

* The Lord decided that "Saul" was no longer worthy of ruling Israel, because of his constant disobedience.

* So the Lord selected someone else to be "Saul's successor."

* Someone who loved the Lord and would be obedient in ruling the nation of Israel in a way that was pleasing in God's eyes.

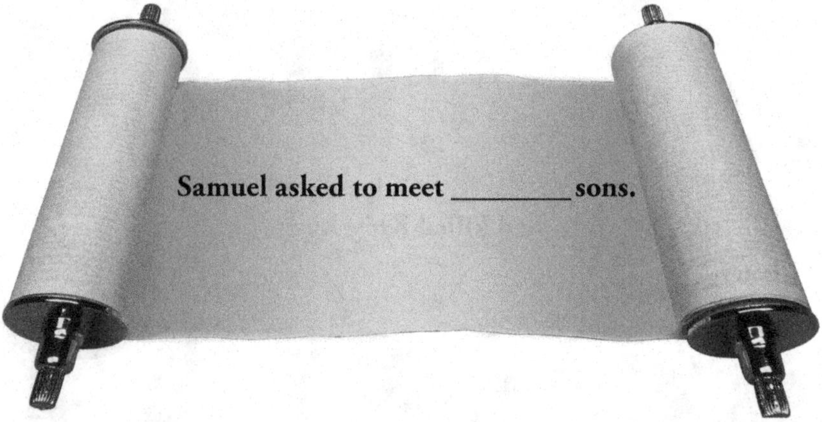
**Samuel asked to meet ________ sons.**

* So the Lord told the "Prophet Samuel" to go to Bethlehem and find a man named Jesse, because it is one of his sons that God has chosen to be the new King of Israel.

* So the Prophet Samuel asked the Lord, "How can I do that?"

* Samuel was concerned for his life and he expressed that concern to the Lord.

* He told the Lord, if "King Saul" found out about what he was going to Bethlehem for then Saul would kill him.

* The Lord told him to take a heifer with him, and say that he had come to Bethlehem to make a sacrifice to the Lord.

* The Lord also told Samuel to invite Jesse to the sacrifice.

* The Lord also told him that He would show him which one of Jesse's sons to "anoint" as the new King.

* The Prophet Samuel did as the Lord commanded him to do and he performed the "purification rite" for Jesse and his sons.

* Then Samuel asked to meet Jesse's sons.

* So Jesse presented "7" of his sons one by one before the Prophet Samuel.

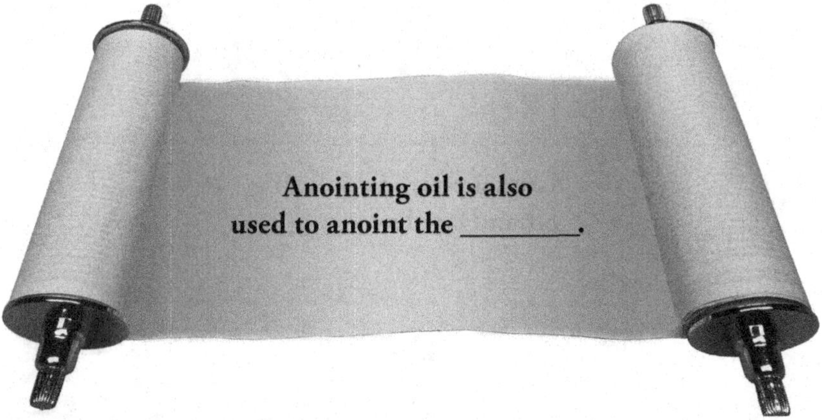
Anointing oil is also
used to anoint the ________.

* But each time Samuel said no, "This is not the one that the Lord has chosen."

* Because the Lord had told Samuel that the Lord chooses a person by their "heart" not their outward appearance.

* Samuel asked Jesse if this was all the sons that he had.

* Jesse replied, "No, I have one more, my youngest son."

* But he is out in the fields taking care of the sheep.

* Samuel told Jesse to send for him at once, we will not sit down to eat until he arrives.

* So Jesse sent for his youngest son, who was called "David."

* Now David was just a teenager, but he was ruddy and handsome, and his eyes were pleasant to look at.

* As soon as David walked into the room, God told the Prophet Samuel,"

* "Rise up and anoint him; for this is the one." (1 Samuel 16:12)

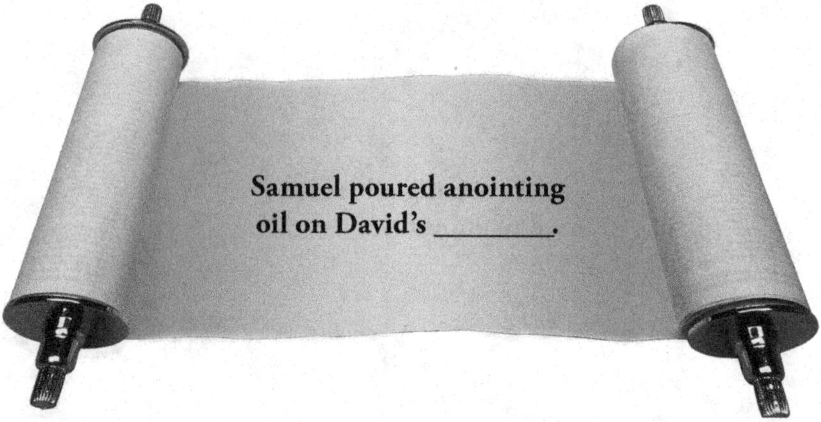
Samuel poured anointing oil on David's ________.

* It was customary before a priest or ruler was placed in office they were to be anointed with oil first.

* "Anointing oil" is a special blend of spices and olive oil, etc. that has been prayed over and blessed before using it.

* Anointing oil is not only used for anointing priests and rulers to their positions, but it is also used to anoint the "sick," as in James 5:14-15.

* "Is any sick among you?"

* "Let him call" for the elders of the church;"

* "And let them pray over him,"

* "Anointing him with oil in the name of the Lord."

* "And the prayer of faith shall save the sick,"

* "And the Lord shall raise him up;"

* "And if he have committed sins,"

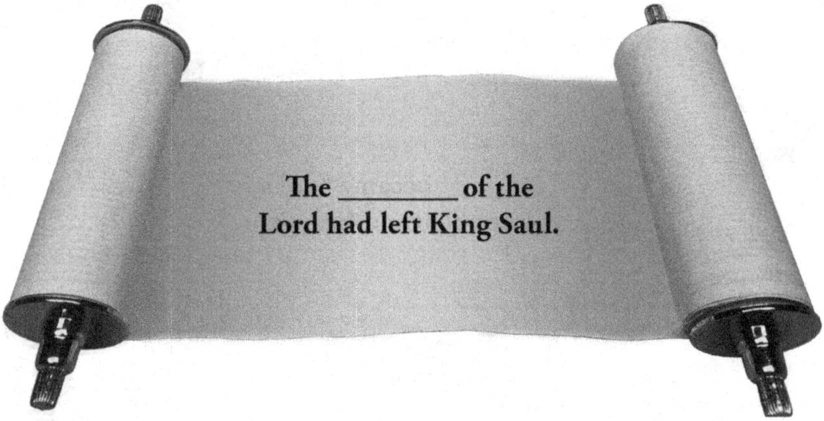
The ________ of the
Lord had left King Saul.

* "They shall be forgiven him." (James 5:14-15)

* If anyone used the "holy anointing oil" for an ordinary purpose, they would be banned from the community.

* So the Prophet Samuel stood up and poured the oil on David's head, in secret, with only his father and brothers present.

* And the Spirit of the Lord came upon David from that day forward.

* The ritual of the Prophet Samuel pouring oil on David's head was symbolic.

* It symbolized how "God was pouring out His favor and anointing upon" the young teenager.

* But in turn, David was to obey the Jewish Law and God.

* Even though David was anointed King of Israel by God and the Prophet Samuel, he still had to wait a few more years before he could take his seat on the throne.

* Because of King Saul's disobedience the Lord's favor was no longer upon him.

* And the Spirit of the Lord had left him.

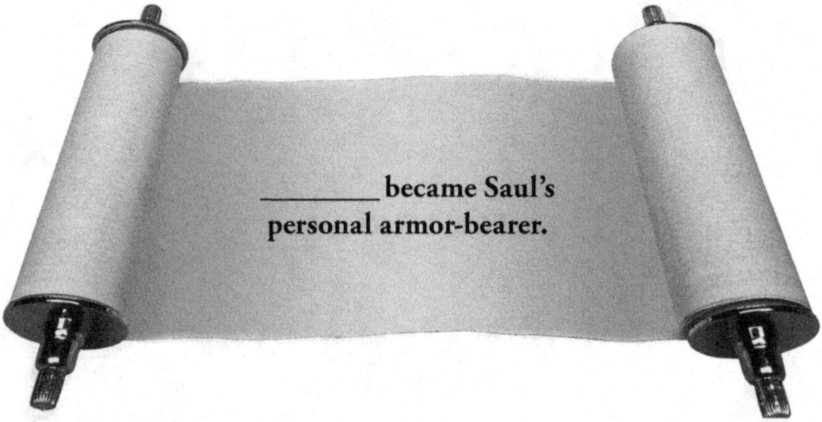
________ became Saul's
personal armor-bearer.

* And "the Lord sent a tormenting spirit" that "filled" Saul with depression and fear. (1 Samuel 16:14)

* On the battlefield, Saul was a mighty warrior.

* But he could not control his terrible mood swings.

* Saul's mood would go from pitiful despair to raging violence.

* Saul's servants suggested that he let them find a good musician that could play the harp for him whenever the "tormenting spirit" was bothering him.

* Because the music on the harp would sooth him and then he would be alright again.

* The servants did not realize they were following God's plan.

* And they sent for a young shepherd boy named David, who had been secretly anointed to take Saul's place as the next King of Israel.

* David was well known in Bethlehem for his talent for playing the harp.

* "And it came to pass, when the "evil spirit" from God was upon Saul, that David took a harp, and played with his hand:"

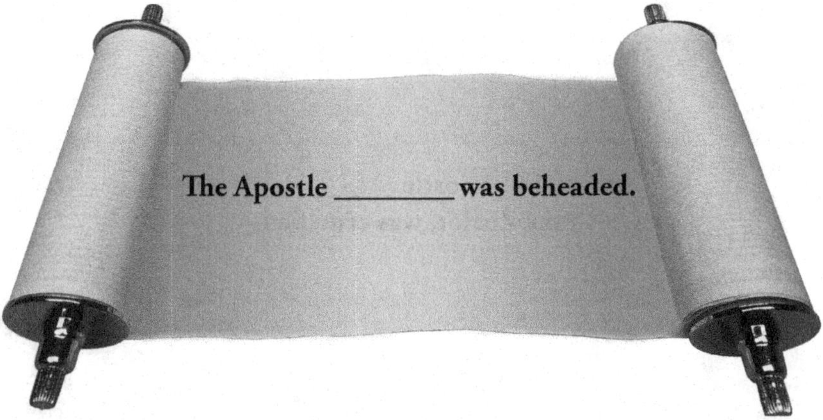
The Apostle ________ was beheaded.

* "So Saul was refreshed, and was well, and the evil spirit departed from him." (1 Samuel 16:23)

* King Saul like David very much, so he put him on his staff and made him his personal armor-bearer.

* Whenever the tormenting spirit came to bother Saul, David was always there to help sooth him.

* For awhile King Saul sincerely loved and trusted the young David.

* But eventually King Saul became jealous of him and wanted to kill him.

* But God always protected David.

* After the death of King Saul, was when David took his place on the throne as the King of Israel.

* David became the "most powerful" King in the history of Israel.

* The Apostle "Andrew," the brother of Peter, was crucified on an "X-shaped cross."

* The Apostle "James" was "beheaded" by Herod in 44 A.D. (Acts 1, 2)

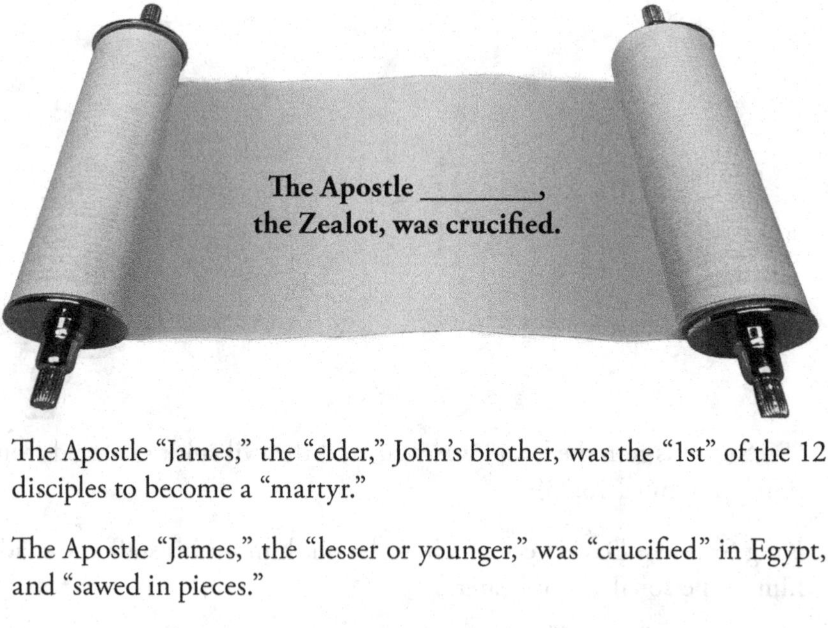
The Apostle ________,
the Zealot, was crucified.

* The Apostle "James," the "elder," John's brother, was the "1st" of the 12 disciples to become a "martyr."

* The Apostle "James," the "lesser or younger," was "crucified" in Egypt, and "sawed in pieces."

* The Apostle "John," son of Zebedee, died of "natural causes."

* The Apostle "Judas Iscariot" "hanged" himself.

* The Apostle "Jude" was killed with "arrows" at Ararat.

* The Apostle "Matthew" died a "martyr" in Ethiopia.

* The Apostle "Peter" was "crucified upside down" on the cross.

* The Apostle "Philip" was "hanged."

* The Apostle "Simon," the Zealot, was "crucified."

* The Apostle "Thomas," was killed with a "spear" in India.

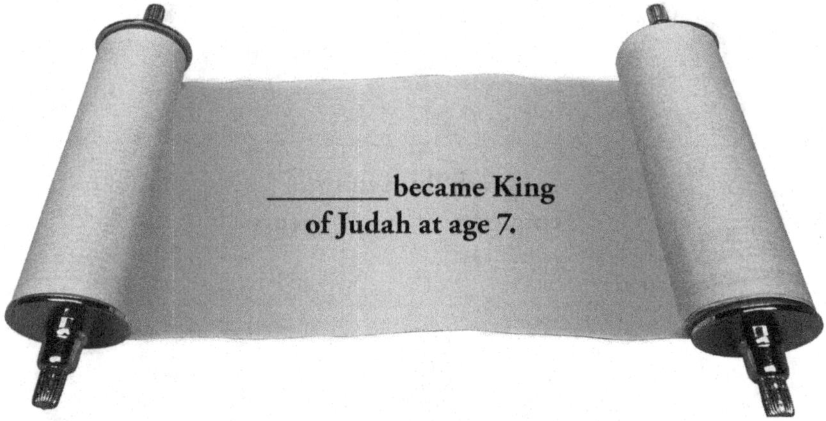

________ became King
of Judah at age 7.

* The Apostle "Bartholomew" died as a martyr for the Lord in India.

* Bartholomew was "flayed alive" with knives.

* There are different names in the Bible for "Mount Sinai" and they are the following:

* Mount Horeb, the Mountain and the Mountain of God.

* The actual location of "Mount Sinai" isn't known for sure.

* But they do believe it is in Egypt at the border of Israel near the Sinai Peninsula.

* Moses received the Ten Commandments from God on "Mount Sinai."

* Elijah hid on "Mount Sinai" after he was threatened by Jezebel.

* While on "Mount Sinai" is where the Prophet Elijah encountered God in the sound of silence. (1 Kings 19:11-12)

* The Israelites agreed to obey God in return for His protection and guidance while camped at the bottom of "Mount Sinai." (Ex. 19:11)

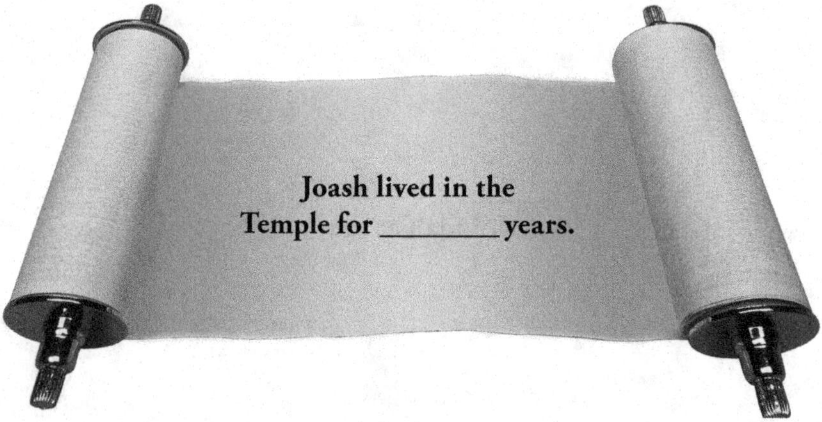
Joash lived in the
Temple for ________ years.

* "Joash" was crowned King of Judah when he was only "7 years old."

* Queen Athaliah was the ruler of Judah before "Joash" was.

* Queen Athaliah was "Joash's grandmother," but all the people of Judah feared and hated her.

* She was a harsh ruler and she worshipped pagan gods.

* She was a very evil woman.

* Queen Athaliah was so evil and desperate to stay in power that she had all the males that had royal blood murdered, including her own sons and grandsons.

* But "1 grandson," Joash, was able to escape with help from his Aunt Jehosheba.

* Joash was just an infant, so his Aunt took and hid him in the Lord's Temple.

* Jehosheba's husband, Jehoiada, was the priest of the Lord's Temple.

* So Joash lived in the Temple with his nurse and was taught the ways of the Lord by his Uncle the priest, for "6 years."

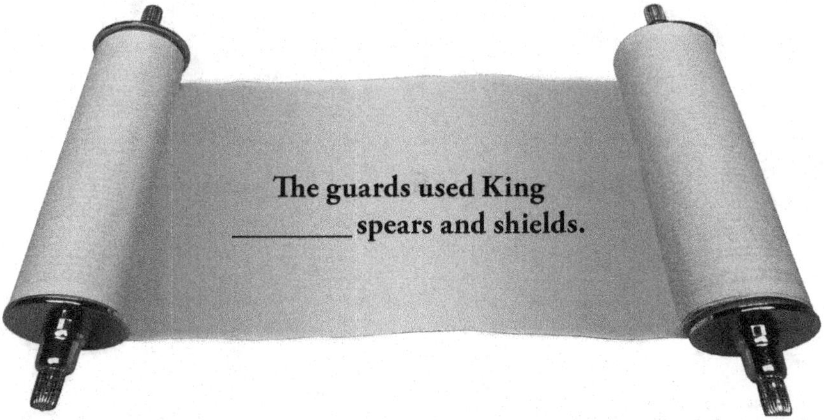
The guards used King
________ spears and shields.

* When Joash was "7 years old" his Uncle the priest came up with a plan to overthrow his grandmother Queen Athaliah and make Joash King.

* Jehoiada, Joash's Uncle, met with all the Temple guards and the captains of the army.

* He made a pact with them, and made them pledge their loyalty to Joash.

* Then he showed them Joash to prove to them that he was not dead.

* Then Jehoiada proceeded to set everything in place as to when, where and how "Joash's crowning" was going to take place.

* He set it all up to take place in the courtyard of the Lord's Temple on the "Sabbath" at the changing of the guards.

* He called for all the guards.

* All those that were on duty on the Sabbath, and those that were not.

* He told them all to come to the Temple and guard and protect the young Joash.

* Jehoiada the priest supplied them all with King David's spears and shields that were stored in the Temple.

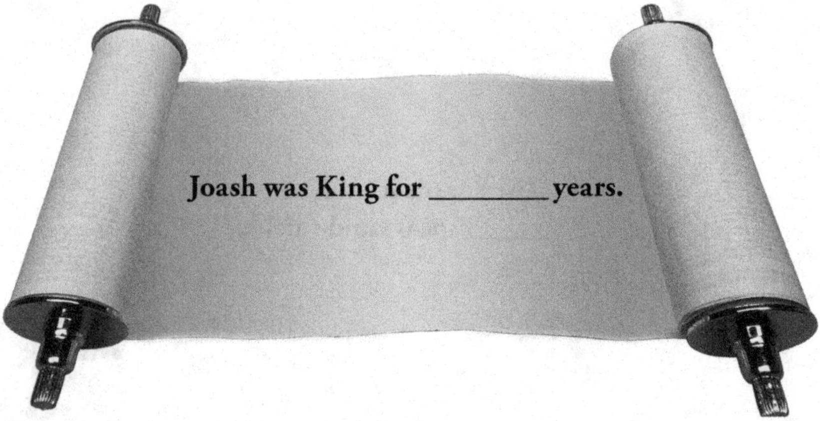
Joash was King for ________ years.

* Jehoiada told the guards if any unauthorized person tries to enter the Temple they were to be killed.

* Once all the guards were in place Jehoiada brought the young Joash out and placed the royal crown on his head.

* Jehoiada gave Joash a copy of God's Covenant and proclaimed him King and anointed him with oil.

* Trumpets blew and all the guards and people rejoiced and clapped their hands, shouting "God save the King."

* When the evil Queen Athaliah heard all the noise she rushed to the Temple to see what was going on.

* When she saw that they had made Joash King she tore her clothes and shouted, "Treason, Treason!"

* But Jehoiada told the guards to seize her and take her away from the Temple and kill her.

* He also told them that if anyone tries to rescue her kill them too.

* So the guards took her to the place where the horses enter the palace grounds and killed her there.

* Then Priest Jehoiada made a covenant between "God, King Joash and all the people" to worship only God.

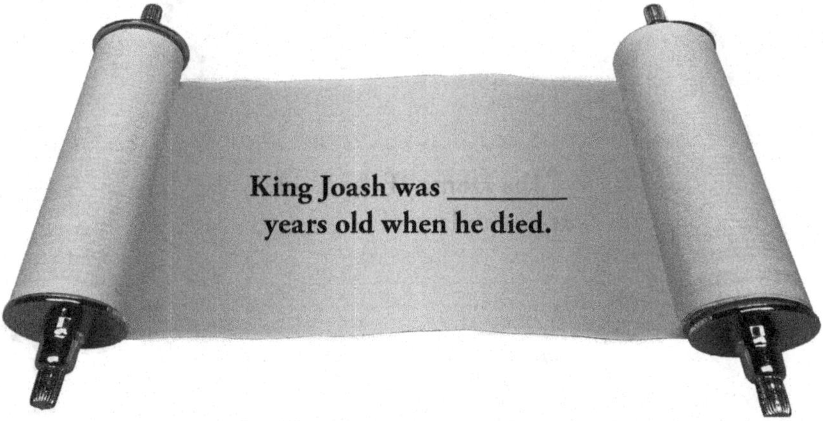
King Joash was ________
years old when he died.

* Then "all the people" went over to the temple of Baal and tore it down.

* They destroyed all the idols and altars, and they even killed Baal's priest, Mattan, in front of the broken altars.

* Then the guards and all the people escorted the young King Joash to the palace.

* The "7 year old" King Joash took his seat on the throne and began his "40 year" reign.

* One day in his "40th year" of reign he was assassinated by his officers at Beth-millo, on the road to Silla.

* King Joash was "47 years old" when he died.

* The "Muslim Shrine" also known as the "Dome of the Rock," in Jerusalem is one of the most magnificent buildings in the world.

* It is considered today as one of modern Jerusalem's most beautiful buildings.

* The "Dome of the Rock" is a shrine for the religion of "Islam."

* The monument is "8 sided" and stands "108 feet" tall with a shiny "gold dome" on top of it, that is "78 feet" across.

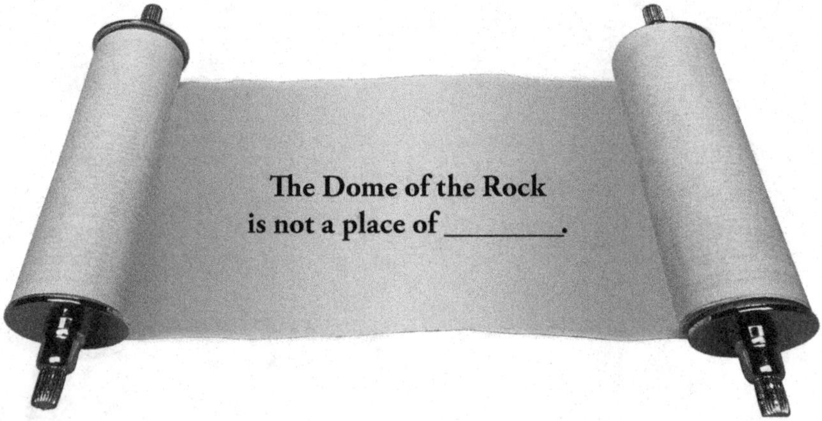
**The Dome of the Rock**
**is not a place of ________.**

* The inside is beautifully decorated with "marble pillars and columns, ornamental wood and mosaic tiles."

* It's stained glass windows let natural light flow through.

* Inside the monument there is a huge "Rock" that is the "Rock" on which "Abraham" prepared to offer his son "Isaac" to the Lord on.

* It was "over this rock" that Solomon built the Temple about "1,650" years earlier.

* The Romans destroyed Solomon's Temple in "70 A.D."

* The "Dome of the Rock" was built between "685 A.D. and 691 A.D." by the Muslims.

* It was originally constructed as a shrine for "Muslims" who wanted to make a pilgrimage to Jerusalem.

* The Dome of the Rock was mistakenly thought to be the Jewish Temple by Muslims and Christians of the Middle Ages.

* But the "Jews" as well as "Muslims" see it as a sacred site.

* The "Islamic" religion was founded in the early "7th century" by a man named "Muhammad."

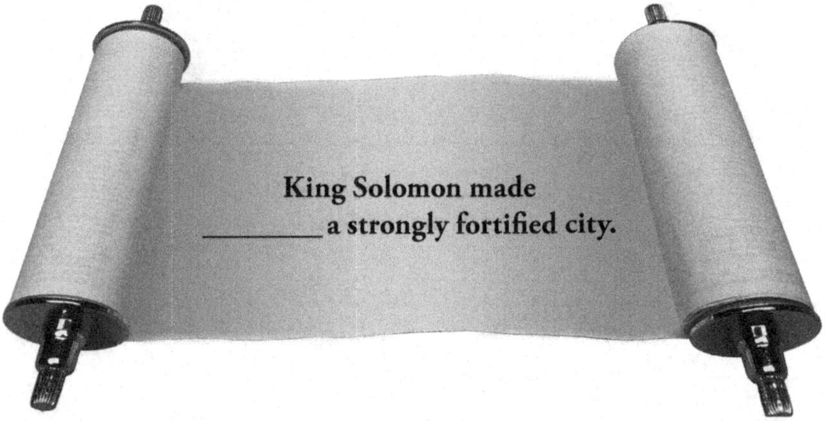
King Solomon made
________ a strongly fortified city.

* The Muslims believe that on this "Rock" is where "Muhammad" was taken up to heaven by the Angel Gabriel.

* Where they believe Muhammad saw how righteous people are rewarded with eternal life.

* Because of this, Muslims consider this "Rock" the foundation of the world and call it the "Stone of Paradise."

* They believe that Muhammad's foot step left a "notch" in the "Rock" as he climbed toward heaven.

* The Dome of the Rock is "not a Mosque" or "a place of worship."

* It is only considered a "shrine" and a "holy place."

* The city of "Megiddo" lies in ruins today.

* But it used to be the scene where many battles took place.

* Archeologists have discovered "20 layers" of ruins at Megiddo.

* Which means in the past "5,000 years" there has been approximately "20 different cities" that have been built on that site.

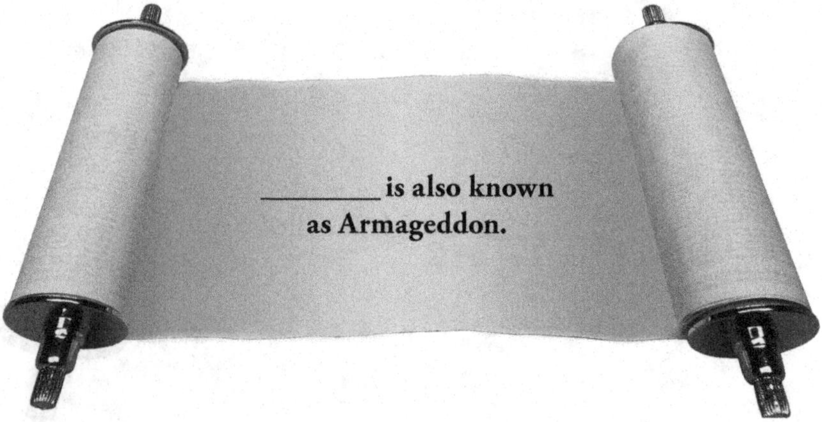
________ is also known
as Armageddon.

* Joshua and the Israelites defeated the King of Megiddo when they entered the Promised Land.

* Megiddo used to be a major city in ancient Israel.

* Megiddo was located along the "great highway" which was from Egypt to Mesopotamia, and it always had a great supply of fresh water.

* Because of this, King Solomon chose Megiddo to be one of the cities that he strongly fortified to protect its resources.

* King Solomon enclosed it with massive stonewalls with a great entrance gate.

* Then after Solomon, "King Ahab" built an amazing network of stables there that could hold "500" horses and "100" chariots.

* Because Megiddo was such an important city many empires fought for control over it.

* And many rulers died there because of those battles.

* King Jehu of Israel and his men shot King Ahaziah of Judah with an arrow while on his chariot, he made it as far as Megiddo and he died there. (2 Kings 9:27)

* King Josiah in "609 B.C." while in a battle with the "Pharaoah Nico" of Egypt also lost his life near Megiddo.

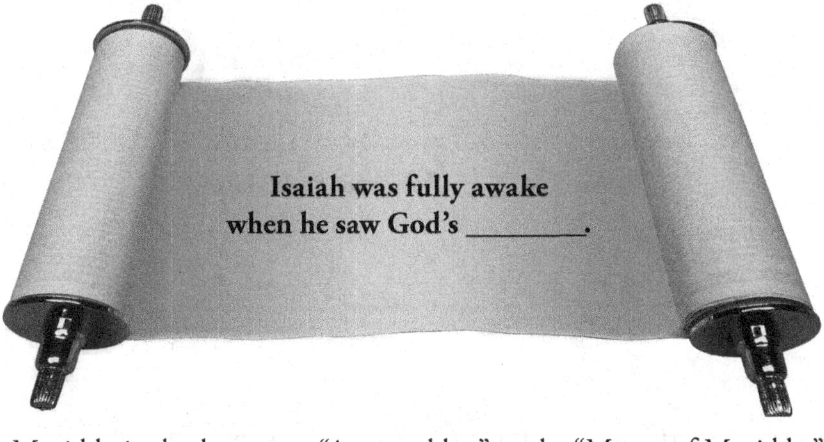
Isaiah was fully awake
when he saw God's ________.

* Megiddo is also known as "Armageddon" or the "Mount of Megiddo."

* Even in Revelation 16:16, it talks about how in the end times the "final battle" will take place at this historical site called "Megiddo."

* "Isaiah" is considered "one of the greatest prophets" in the Old Testament.

* One day in the year "740 B.C.," Isaiah went to the Temple to worship the Lord and while there an amazing thing happened. (Isaiah 6:1-13)

* He received a spectacular vision of "God on His Throne."

* The difference between a "dream" and a "vision" is when God gives you a dream, you are asleep; when He gives you a vision you are awake.

* So Isaiah was fully awake when he saw this.

* Isaiah saw, "The Lord sitting upon a Throne,"

* "High and lifted up,"

* "And His train (Robe) filled the Temple."

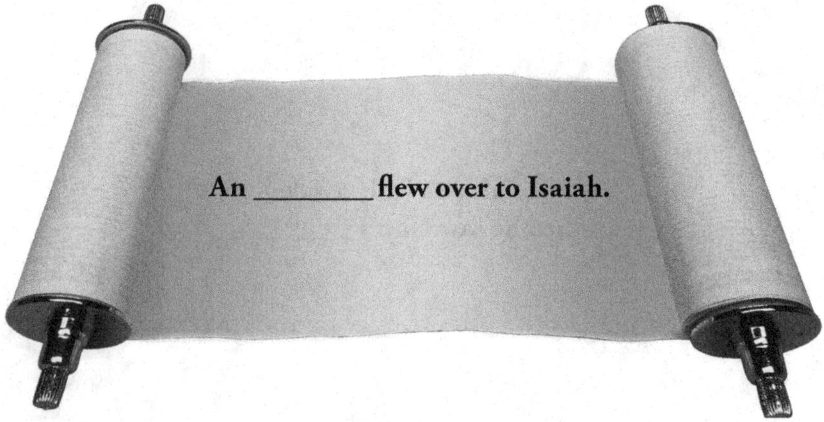


* "Above it (Throne) stood the seraphims (Angels):"

* "Each one (Angels) had six wings;"

* "With twain (Wings) he covered his face,"

* "With twain (Wings) he covered his feet,"

* "And with twain (Wings) he did fly."

* "And one cried (Sang) unto another, and said,"

* "Holy, holy, holy is the Lord of hosts (Almighty):"

* "The whole earth is full of His glory."

* "And the posts of the door moved (the walls shook) at the voice of (Angels) that cried (Sang),"

* "And the house (Sanctuary) was filled with smoke."

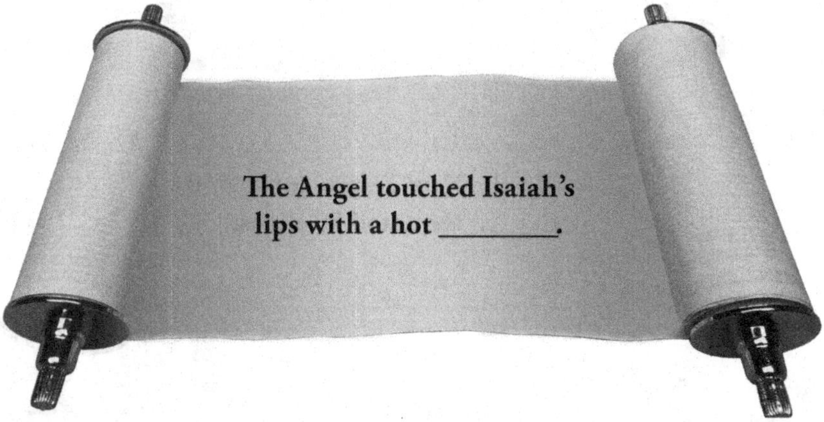

The Angel touched Isaiah's
lips with a hot ________.


* Then Isaiah said, "Woe is me! for I am undone; because I am a man of unclean lips, and I dwell in the midst of a people of unclean lips: for mine eyes have seen the King, the Lord of host."

* When Isaiah saw God's holiness and His Angels he realized that he was a sinful man and because of that, unworthy to be God's spokesman, and that he could not measure up to God's holiness.

* But, "Then flew one of the seraphim (Angels) unto me (Isaiah),"

* "Having a live (Hot) coal in his hand,"

* "Which he (Angel) had taken with the tongs from off the altar:"

* "And he (Angel) laid it upon my (Isaiah) mouth, and said,"

* "Lo, this (Hot Coal) hath touched (Representing Cleansing and Purifying) thy (Isaiah) lips;"

* "And thine (Isaiah) iniquity (Guilt) is taken away (Removed), and thy (Isaiah) sins purged (Forgiven and Wiped Away)."

* Isaiah had to go through a painful cleansing process before he could fulfill the "Call" that God placed on him.

* We too have to go through a cleansing process by the Fire of God's Holy Spirit.

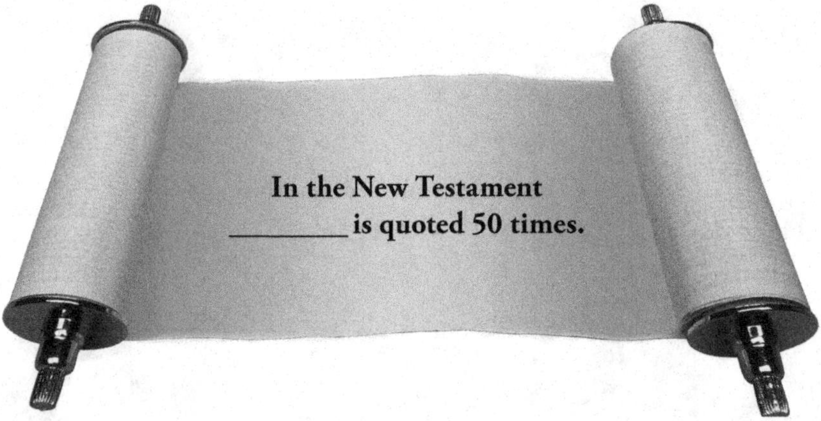
In the New Testament
________ is quoted 50 times.

* And also receive the forgiveness of our sins by His Son, Jesus Christ.

* So we can also fulfill the task that God has "Called" each one of us to do.

* Then Isaiah heard the "voice" of the Lord, saying,"

* "Whom shall I send, and who will go for us?"

* Isaiah said, "Here am I; send me." (Isaiah 6:8)

* So God made Isaiah His prophet.

* Then the Lord gave Isaiah a message to deliver to His people.

* The Lord wanted Isaiah to tell the Israelites to "listen to God's Word" even though He knew "they wouldn't understand it."

* Isaiah asked the Lord how long was he suppose to preach this message.

* God told him until all the Israelites cities were destroyed and only a handful of people survived.

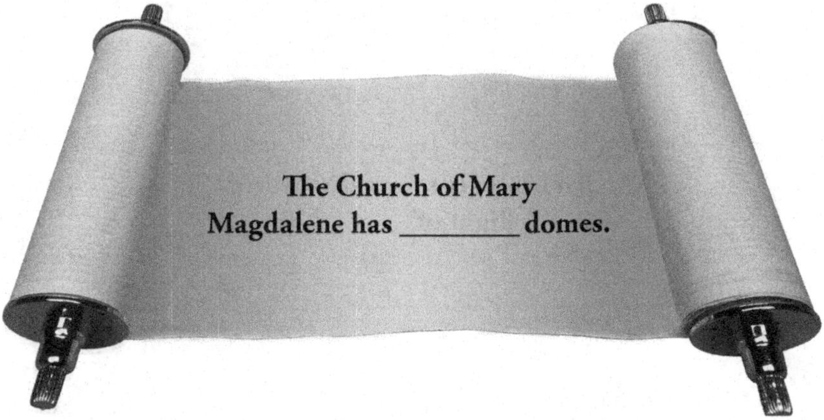
The Church of Mary
Magdalene has ________ domes.

* God had given the people several warnings to stop sinning, but they ignored Him.

* So God was going to give them one more chance to change before disaster struck.

* Although God knew the nation itself would not repent, He knew some individuals would.

* In the New Testament Isaiah is quoted at least 50 times.

* Isaiah delivered messages of "Judgment and Hope."

* Isaiah was consistent even though there was little positive response from his listeners.

* Isaiah's ministry spanned the reigns of several Kings of Judah.

* Through Isaiah's teachings we see that God is "pure, holy, just and loving."

* The Church of "Mary Magdalene" is a beautiful Russian style church and monastery.

* The church is located on the slopes of the "Mount of Olives" that overlooks the ancient Jerusalem.

Archeologists have discovered
a flight of ________.

* The architectural design of the Church is the style that was common in the "17th century" in "Moscow."

* The exterior of the building has "7 golden domes" that seem to glow in the dark at night.

* Czar Alexander III, from Russia, built the Church of Mary Magdalene.

* He built it in loving memory of his mother, the Empress Maria Alexandrovna.

* In the year "1888" he dedicated the Church to his mother's patron saint, "Mary Magdalene."

* Mary Magdalene was not only healed by Jesus, but she also became one of His most faithful followers.

* The interior of the church contains paintings by "2" famous "19th century" Russian artists.

* There is also a wooden screen on the inside of the church that is decorated with paintings of Jesus, Mary His Mother and other godly Christians.

* Outside the church, archeologists have discovered part of an "ancient flight of stairs."

* These steps may have been part of the "537 steps" that led from "the top of the Mount of Olives to the Valley of Jehoshaphat."

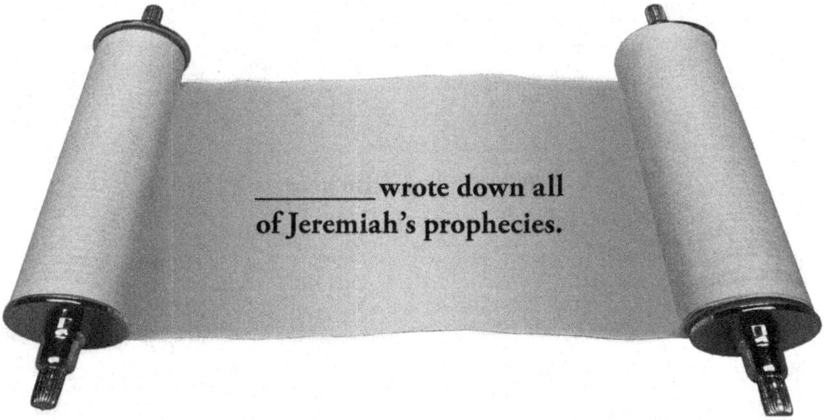
________ wrote down all
of Jeremiah's prophecies.

* Which is where the Prophet Joel said the "Last Judgment" would take place." (Joel 3:2)

* A standard item usually seen in eastern churches is a decorative screen called an "iconostasis."

* This decorative screen is used to separate the area around the altar from the rest of the church.

* The artwork on the screen plays an essential part in the way people pray in eastern churches.

* This artwork is called, "icons."

* In "605 B.C." the Lord told the "Prophet Jeremiah" to write down everything that He had told him over the years.

* The people of Judah had been sinning and the Lord had already sent messages through the Prophet Jeremiah.

* He warned them to turn from their evil ways or disaster was going to befall them, but they wouldn't listen.

* So the Lord told Jeremiah to put all those messages in writing hoping if the people would see it in writing maybe they would repent before it was too late.

* The Prophet Jeremiah sent for "Baruch," his scribe, and dictated to him all the prophecies that the Lord had given him. (Jeremiah 36:4)

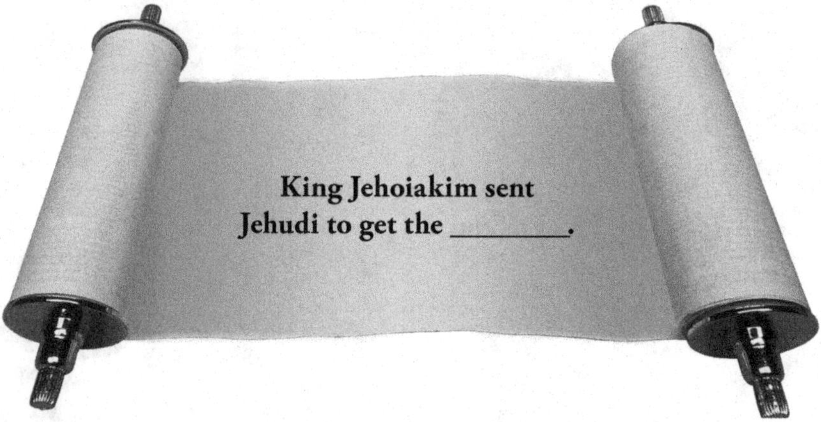
King Jehoiakim sent
Jehudi to get the ________.

* And Baruch wrote all of the "Prophet Jeremiah's" prophecies down on a scroll.

* Jeremiah was unable to go to the Temple.

* So he told Baruch to take the scroll to the Temple and read it out loud to all the people there.

* Jeremiah told him to take it to the Temple on the next day of "fasting."

* Because there would be more people there, from all over Judah.

* So Baruch took the scroll to the Temple and stood near the "New Gate" entrance and read it aloud.

* When the King's officials heard about what Baruch was reading to the people, they sent for him.

* They brought Baruch to the palace and had him read it to them.

* When Baruch finished reading the message from the Lord, they all became very frightened.

* They decided that the King should also know what it says.

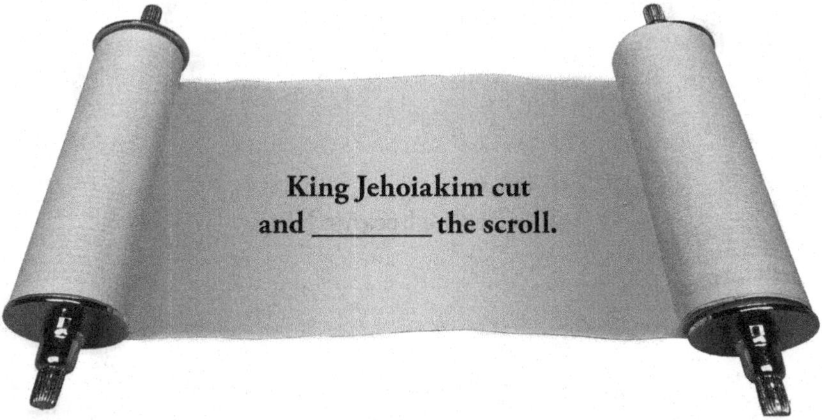
King Jehoiakim cut
and ________ the scroll.

* The officials told Baruch that him and the Prophet Jeremiah should go into hiding and not tell anyone where they are.

* The officials took the scroll and put it in the secretary's room to keep it safe and then went and told the King.

* King Jehoiakim sent "Jehudi" to get the scroll.

* The officials stood around the King as Jehudi read the scroll to him.

* King Jehoiakim was sitting in a winterized part of the palace in front of a fire to keep warm as he was listening to the message.

* King Jehoiakim kept quiet during the reading of the scroll.

* But after Jehudi would read 3 or 4 columns, the King would cut that section off with his pen knife and throw it in the fire.

* With all those people standing around and watching and listening, "only 3 people," Elnathan, Deliaiah and Gemariah, begged the King not to burn it, but he wouldn't listen.

* The King continued until he had burned and destroyed the entire scroll.

* Then King Jehoiakim ordered the arrest of "Baruch and Jeremiah."

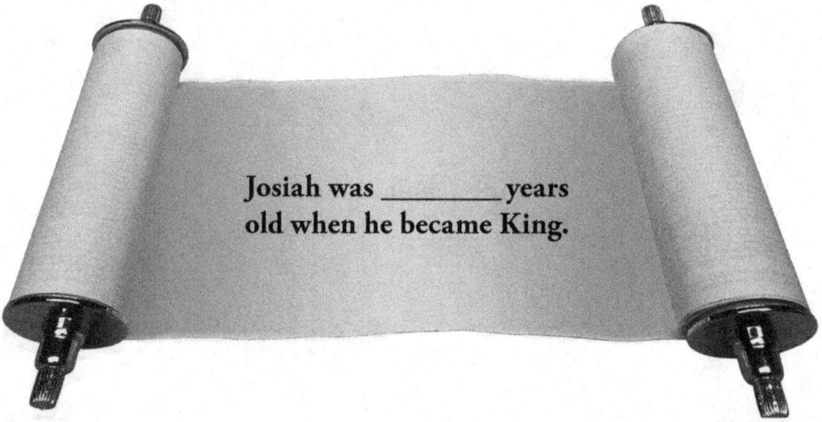

Josiah was ________ years
old when he became King.


* But they were nowhere to be found because "the Lord had hidden them." (Jeremiah 36:26)

* After the King burned the scroll, the Lord told Jeremiah to write it again.

* But the Lord added more to it this time, because of the King's actions and reactions to the first scroll.

* Jeremiah is remembered as the "weeping Prophet."

* Because it broke his heart when people would turn away from God and refuse to turn back, because he knew the suffering that they would have to go through.

* "Josiah" was the "16th King of Judah," the southern Kingdom.

* He reigned in Jerusalem for "31 years." (2 Kings 22)

* Josiah became King of Judah when he was "8 years old."

* By the time he became King, most all the people in Judah had turned away from God.

* And the beautiful Solomon's Temple laid in ruins.

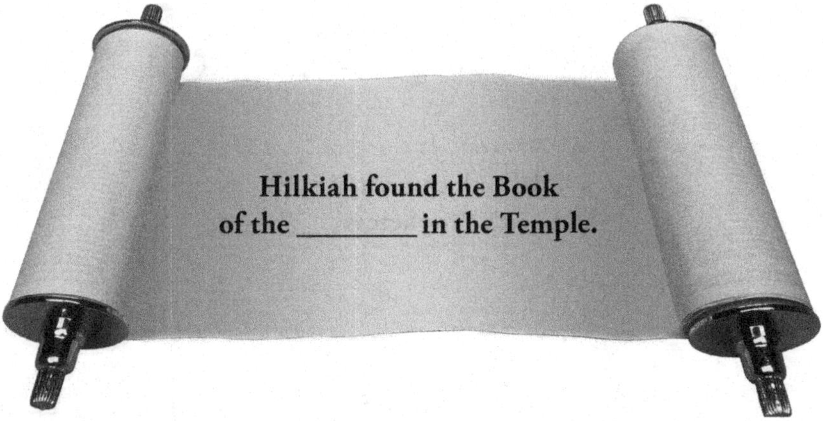

Hilkiah found the Book
of the ________ in the Temple.


* But Josiah loved the Lord with all his heart and soul.

* When Josiah was "26 years old" and was in the "18th year" of his reign as King, he decided to have the "Lord's Temple" restored.

* King Josiah had the High Priest Hilkiah count the money from the Temple Treasury.

* This was the tithe that had been collected over the years from the people "as they entered" the Temple.

* Josiah used it to pay for the restoration of the Temple.

* One day as the High Priest Hilkiah was working in the Temple he made an awesome discovery.

* As he was going through the collection boxes to gather the money for the workers he discovered an old "scroll."

* Hilkiah had found the "Book of the Law" in the Lord's Temple.

* This Book of the Law may have been the whole first 5 books of the Bible or just the book of Deuteronomy.

* The High Priest Hilkiah gave the money to the workers who were restoring the Temple.

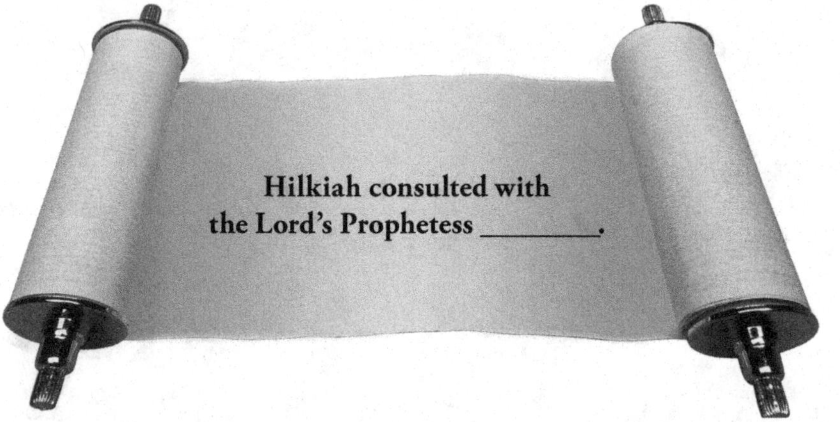
Hilkiah consulted with
the Lord's Prophetess ________.

* And he gave the "scroll" to the court secretary to take to the King.

* So Shaphan, the court secretary, read the scroll to King Josiah.

* When King Josiah heard the Words of the Lord written in the scroll, he tore his clothes in despair.

* He heard in the scroll of God's warnings to the Israelites on how He intended to punish them for their sins and disobedience.

* Josiah was very upset and saddened because he knew that the people had not been doing what the scroll said they must do.

* Josiah told Hilkiah the High Priest and 4 other men to go to the Temple and speak to the Lord about the Words written in the scroll.

* So they all went to a newer section of Jerusalem to consult with a Prophetess of the Lord's, named "Huldah."

* She told them to tell Josiah that the Lord said he would be saved from all the disaster that He was going to bring to this city.

* Because he had humbled himself and wept in front of Him in repentance.

* But the Israelite nation would still have to face God's punishment, but not until after Josiah has died.

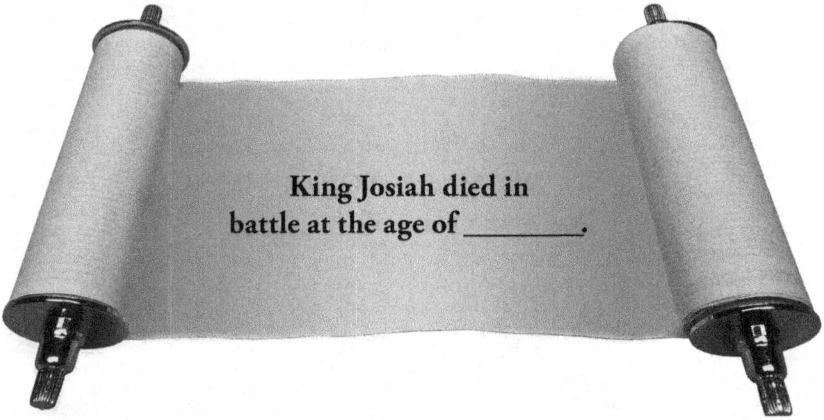
King Josiah died in
battle at the age of ________.

* Then King Josiah gathered all the leaders, priests, prophets and all the people in Judah and Jerusalem at the Temple and there he read the entire Book of the Law to them.

* Josiah and all the people made a pledge that they would all obey all the Laws of God.

* The Lord was finally worshipped again in Jerusalem.

* King Josiah traveled across the kingdom, tearing down, burning and utterly destroying all the pagan objects he could find.

* King Josiah is remembered as a royal defender of the faith, and Judah's most obedient King in obeying the Lord.

* He is "2nd" only to King David.

* King Josiah died in battle at the age of "39 years" old.

* The "Mount of Olives" is located across the Kidron Valley, east of Jerusalem.

* The Mount of Olives is a "mile long" ridge that runs north and south of the Old Jerusalem.

* The Mount of Olives got its name because of the "olive trees" that have grown there since ancient times.

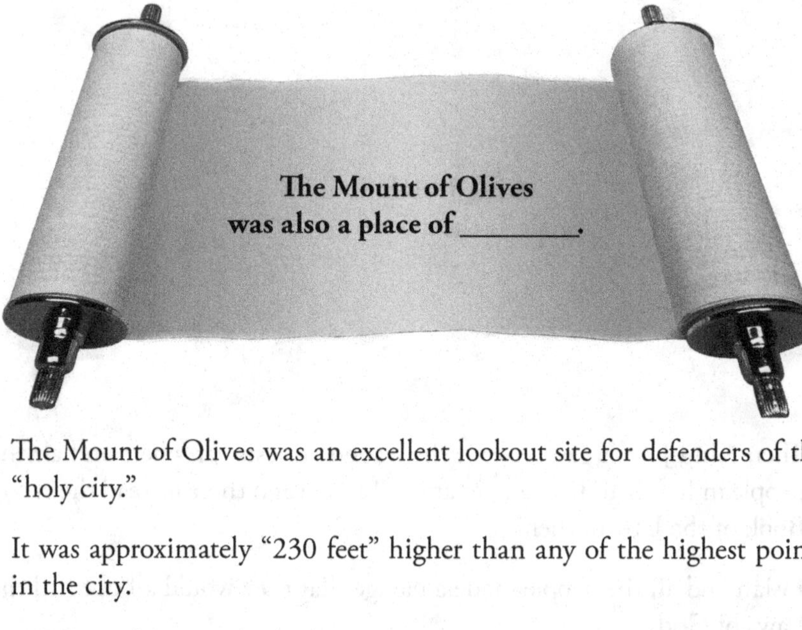

**The Mount of Olives**
**was also a place of ________.**


* The Mount of Olives was an excellent lookout site for defenders of the "holy city."

* It was approximately "230 feet" higher than any of the highest points in the city.

* In times of danger the lookout person that was on top of the mountain ridge would light a "signal fire" to warn the people because he knew it could be seen for miles.

* It was against Jewish Law to bury the dead inside the city, so tombs were located just outside the city gates.

* Usually these tombs were located in the narrow Kidron Valley and on the lower slopes of the Mount of Olives.

* The Mount of Olives was also considered a place of "refuge."

* Often travelers who could not find a place to stay in the city would usually go and spend the night on the Mount of Olives.

* On the Mount of Olives is where Jesus was arrested.

* He was arrested while He was praying in the "Garden of Gethsemane" there.

* The Bible doesn't specify the place where Jesus ascended to Heaven from after His resurrection, but it may have been the Mount of Olives.

Book of ________
mentions a donkey's colt.

* Many Christians believe that when Jesus returns that it will be on the Mount of Olives.

* The town of "Bethany" is located on the lower eastern slopes of the Mount Olives.

* "Bethany" is where Jesus raised Lazarus from the dead.

* Today, the Mount of Olives is home to many Christian churches.

* A week before Jesus was arrested, He rode into Jerusalem and was welcomed by the crowds. (Matthew 21:1-11)

* Great multitudes of people greeted Jesus shouting "Hosanna, to the Son of David;"
* "Blessed is He that cometh in the name of the Lord; Hosanna in the highest."
* The Book of Matthew mentions a "donkey's colt."
* This particular event is mentioned in all 4 Gospels, but Matthew is the only one that mentions Jesus riding on a donkey's colt.
* Which "fulfills" the prophecy in Zechariah 9:9, which says,

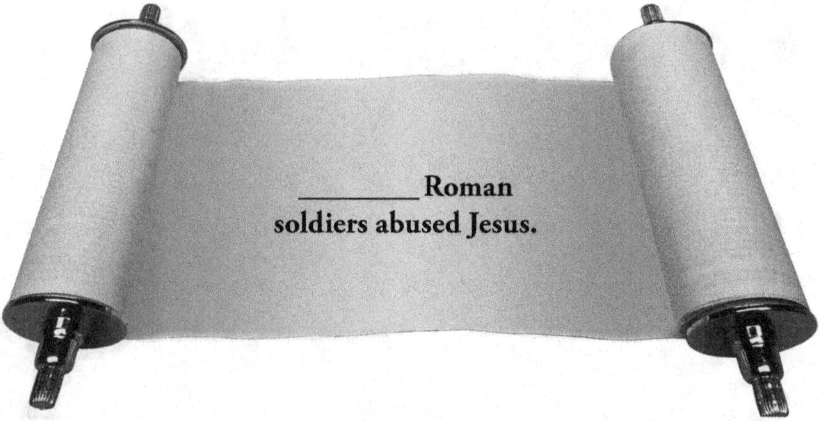
________Roman
soldiers abused Jesus.

* "Rejoice greatly, O daughter of Zion: shout, O daughter of Jerusalem:"
* "Behold, thy King cometh unto thee: He is just and having Salvation; lowly, and riding upon an ass, and upon a colt the foal of an ass."
* Jesus got angry because people were buying and selling things in the Temple.
* So He overturned the tables and threw everyone out, which really upset the priests.
* During Jesus' ministry, He cleared the Temple twice; this was the "2nd time."

* The "1st time" Jesus cleared the Temple was "3 years" earlier.

* This too "fulfilled prophecy," "For the zeal of Thine house hath eaten Me up." (Psalm 69:9)

* After Jesus was arrested, He was put on trial, but Pilate and Herod could not find anything that Jesus was guilty of, but Pilate wanted to please the crowd so he sentenced Jesus to be crucified.

* Pilate ordered Jesus to be beaten as well, with a lead-tipped whip, and then he turned Him over to the Roman soldiers to be crucified.

* Then over "200 Roman soldiers" took Jesus and stripped Him and put a scarlet robe on Him.

* Then they put a crown of thorns on Jesus' head.

* They put a stick in His right hand like a royal scepter.

* They mocked Him and spit on Him.

* Then they beat Him again with the stick they had given Him.

* Then the Roman soldiers led Jesus to Golgotha to be crucified.

* For at least "3 hours," from noon until 3 o'clock, the whole land was covered in darkness.

* Even though Jesus had never sinned, He felt the spiritual death, the separation from God that sin causes, in order to reconcile us with God.

* Then when Jesus died on the Cross, the "Veil" in the Temple tore from "top to bottom."

* There was an "earthquake."

* And "rocks split in two."

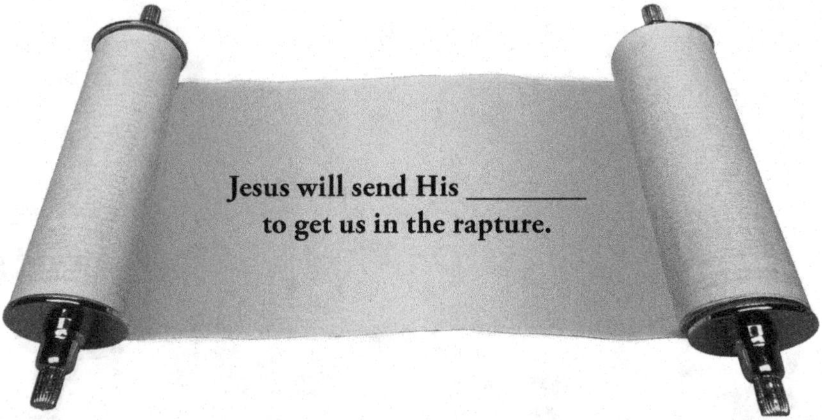

Jesus will send His ________
to get us in the rapture.


* "Tombs" were "opened."

* And "many godly people" that were dead and buried "rose from the grave" and were "walking around."

* Jesus laid in the "Garden Tomb."

* And "after 3 days He rose again,"

* And is "still alive over 2000 years later!"

* Jesus tells of how He will return to gather His people and take them to their home in Heaven with Him, in the rapture.

* No one but God, the Father, knows when Jesus will return.

* The "sign of Jesus' return" will "appear in the heavens."

* "Jesus will stand on the clouds of heaven" with power and great glory.

* The "Archangel will give a mighty trumpet blast."

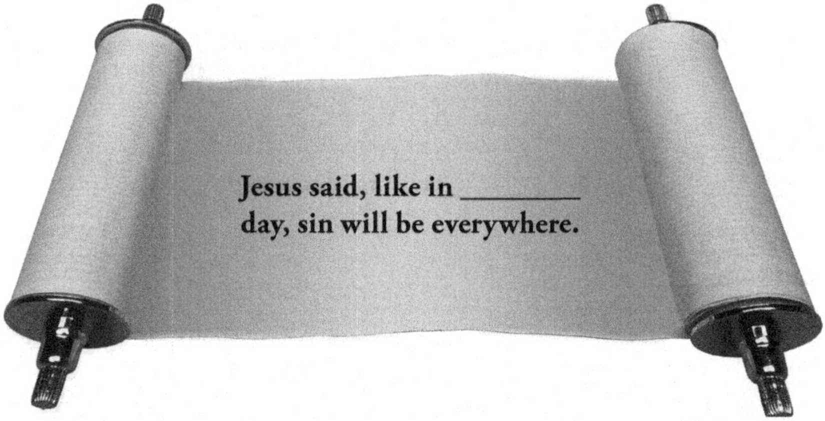
Jesus said, like in ________
day, sin will be everywhere.

* And "Jesus will send His Angels to earth to get His people" and bring them to Heaven to be with Him.

* In Matthew 24, Jesus listed the "signs of the end of the world" that we should look for.

* Jesus said there would be "many false Messiahs."

* Jesus said there would be "many false prophets," that would lead many people astray.

* Jesus said there would be "wars."

* And "rumors of war."

* Jesus said that "nation would rise against nation," and "kingdom against kingdom."

* Jesus said there would be "famines."

* There would be "pestilences."

* And there would be "earthquakes in many parts of the world."

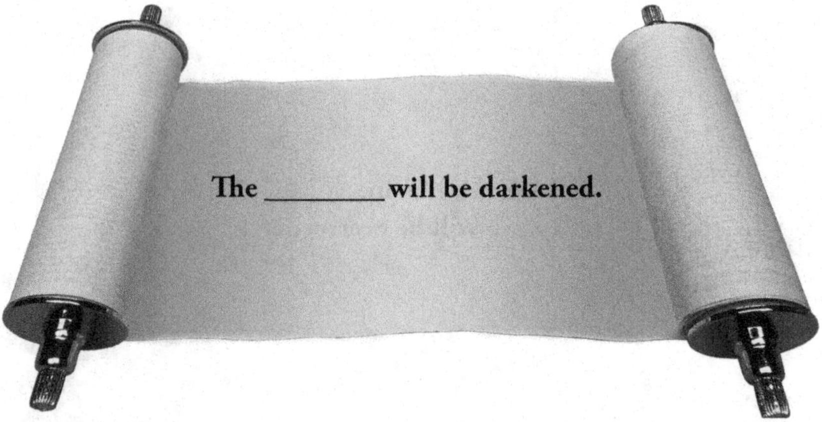


* Jesus said "His people will be arrested."

* His people will be "persecuted."

* His people will be "killed."

* And His people will be "hated all over the world, because they follow Him."

* Jesus said, "like in Noah's day, sin will be everywhere."

* Jesus said "when you see the sacrilegious object that causes desecration standing in the Holy Place of God's Temple," you know the end is very near.

* Jesus is talking about when the "Anti-Christ" puts an image of himself in there and orders everyone to worship it. (2 Thessalonians 2:4)

* Jesus said "immediately after the tribulation of those days:"

* The "sun will be darkened."

* The "moon will not give her light."

People will be ________
to their parents.

* The "stars shall fall from heaven."

* And the "powers of the heavens shall be shaken."

* Then you will "see the sign" of the Lord's return. (Matthew 24)

* God's Word also tells us in 1 Timothy 3:1-9, how people will act in the last days.

* People "will love only themselves and their money."

* They will be "boastful and proud."

* They will "scoff God."

* They will be "disobedient to their parents."

* They will be "ungrateful."

* They will "consider nothing sacred."

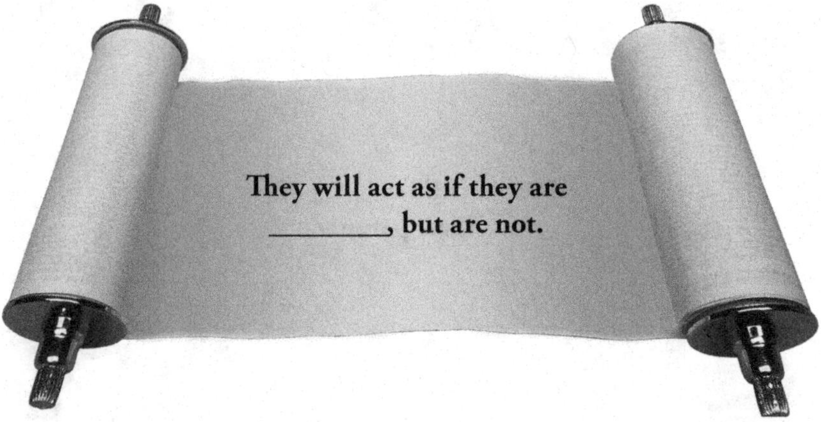

They will act as if they are
________, but are not.


* They will be "unloving and unforgiving."

* They will "slander others."

* They will have "no self-control."

* They will be "cruel."

* They will have "no interest in what is good."

* They will "betray their friends."

* They will be "reckless."

* They will be "puffed up with pride."

* They will "love pleasure rather than God."

* They will "act as if they are religious," but they will "reject the power that could make them godly.

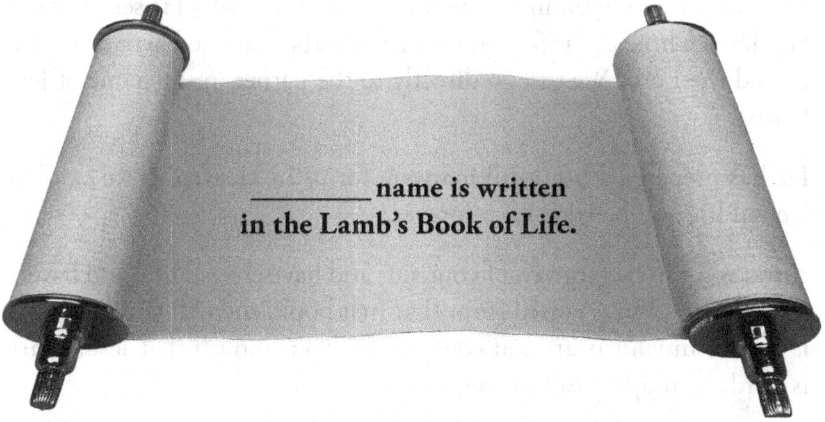
_________ name is written
in the Lamb's Book of Life.

* In the book of Revelation, the Lord tells us about different "books" that He keeps in Heaven.

* "And I saw the dead, small and great, stand before God; and the "books" were opened: and "another" book was opened, which is the Book of Life:"

* "And the dead were judged out of those things which were written in the books, according to their works." (Rev. 20:12)

* In the first set of books are all the things that each of us have done, good or bad, in our lifetime.

* These are not just the physical things like, murder, stealing, etc., but also the words that we have spoken. We will be judged on what we have said and done.

* In Matthew 12:36-37, the Lord says, "But I say unto you, That every idle word that men shall speak, they shall give account thereof in the day of Judgment."

* "For by thy words thou shall be justified and by thy words thou shalt be condemned."

* The second book is the Book of Life; in it are all the names of the people who have accepted Jesus Christ as their Lord and Savior.

* Jesus came to rescue us from that first book, so we wouldn't have to receive the punishment we deserve from what is written there, He loved us enough to take that punishment for us.

* Just like a loving Father, God wants us to come back to Him because He misses us not spending time with Him. That's why He sent His only Son Jesus Christ to die for our sins, so now there are no barriers between us and the Lord. We can go directly to the Father in the name of Jesus Christ.

* He has prepared a beautiful mansion for us in Heaven so we can have eternal life and be with Him forever.

* If you want to be forgiven of your sins and have eternal life, and have all those "bad" things erased from that first book, then all you have to do is believe in your heart and confess with your mouth that Jesus Christ is Lord, by praying this prayer,

* Dear Jesus, I believe you are the true Son of God and that you died for my sins, and that You rose again so that I will have eternal life. Please come into my heart and forgive me of my sins and create in me a clean heart and be my Lord and Savior. In Jesus' name I pray Amen.

* If you have prayed the prayer of Salvation and have accepted Jesus as your Lord and Savior then "your name" is written in the "Lamb's Book of Life."

* You now have a clean start and everything that you did in the past is forgiven and wiped clean, and you will now live in Heaven with the Lord forever and ever.

# Scroll Answers

1) 930 2) The Priest's Manual 3) Stop 4) oil 5) 127 6) 180 7) breaking out 8) red 9) sea snails 10) 3 11) undergarment 12) Tabernacle 13) wine 14) burials 15) High Priest Caiaphas 16) mud 17) 5,000 18) 2 19) oil 20) embalm 21) Jacob 22) Peter 23) Salt 24) 3 months 25) criticized 26) leprosy 27) 12 years 28) roof 29) 350 30) ax head 31) High Priest 32) 6,000 33) Pharisees 34) Sadducees 35) 1189 36) 773,692 37) grandmother 38) 2 feet 39) goat 40) Exodus 19:13 & 16 41) 125 pounds 42) 650 B.C. 43) 150 miles 44) Roman 45) salt and olive oil 46) 6 months or more 47) Augustus Caesar 48) Olympic Games 49) limestone 50) 80,000 51) scholars 52) front 53) tentmaker 54) mother 55) Camel 56) purity 57) Business 58) pens 59) wine 60) wine 61) week 62) Babylonians 63) 12 64) Dinah 65) Levi 66) front 67) left side 68) 3 69) front 70) guarded 71) God 72) ephod 73) Benjamin 74) Naphtali 75) Rachel 76) Holy Place 77) Holy of Holies 78) outside 79) 400 years 80) Incense 81) 586 B.C. 82) synagogues 83) clean 84) trample 85) veiled 86) years 87) newly planted 88) Babylonians, Assyrians 89) tax collectors 90) lyre 91) terraces 92) Terracing 93) 600 94) 119 95) cool of the day 96) solar 97) sorcerer 98) Mangers 99) marketplace 100) marketplace 101) purchases 102) Holy Spirit 103) Holy Spirit 104) Jesus 105) Holy Spirit 106) 100 107) Lord 108) year 109) 3rd 110) Japheth 111) 45,000 112) Jews 113) 3 114) Mordecai 115) 5th 116) Jewelry 117) 479 118) god 119) Mordecai 120) God's 121) 12 122) Purim 123) liquor 124) celebration 125) Mustard 126) medicinal 127) hardship 128) 20 miles 129) David 130) Galilee 131) linen 132) Linen 133) sycamore 134) apple 135) pomegranate 136) eternal life 137) Michal 138) Numbers 139) 12 140) worship 141) serpent 142) banner 143) warrior 144) Flags 145) Worship 146) flag 147) flesh and blood 148) Flags 149) Dancing 150)

Dance 151) David 152) 44 153) torches 154) lifting 155) rejoiced 156) sign 157) 4 158) Lazarus 159) 12 160) Haman's 161) beat 162) star 163) 9 times 164) inaccurate 165) donkey 166) donkeys 167) 3 168) 50,000 169) Quails 170) 2 million 171) oxen 172) 8 173) repentance 174) 450 175) Samson 176) lambs 177) Lamb 178) Grasshoppers 179) 2 weeks 180) Goats 181) 8 182) dove 183) dove 185) Cedars 186) cedar 187) purity 188) pillars 189) 11,000 190) dogwood 191) dogwood 192) pine tree 193) dye 194) fasting 195) stones 196) Deuteronomy 8:3 197) written 198) Matthew 199) 84 200) prophetess 201) Nazareth 202) synagogues 203) Joash 204) 3 205) Elisha's bones 206) 12 207) people 208) Caleb 209) Canaanites 210) Jericho 211) 80 212) Ehud 213) 600 214) Sisera 215) woman 216) Barak 217) Lord 218) Barak 219) Abraham's 220) prophet 221) oak 222) Jehovah-shalom 223) ram's horn 224) 32,000 225) 22,000 226) 300 227) Midianites 228) 120,000 229) 15,000 men 230) killed 231) 5th 232) Baal-berith 233) half brothers 234) King 235) Abimelech's 236) Jair 237) Jephthah 238) vow 239) 2 months 240) 60 241) 10 242) oppressed 243) robes 244) 3,000 245) water 246) prostitute 247) Delilah 248) 4th 249) Samson's 250) Dagon 251) Ark of the Covenant 252) 3,000 253) Samson 254) Hebrews 255) sun 256) 12, 12 257) sun 258) 7 259) Amalekites 260) Amalekites 261) Samuel 262) Jesse's 263) sick 264) head 265) Spirit 266) David 267) James 268) Simon 269) Joash 270) 6 271) David's 272) 40 273) 47 274) worship 275) Megiddo 276) Megiddo 277) Throne 278) Angel 279) coal 280) Isaiah 281) 7 282) stairs 283) Baruch 284) scroll 285) burned 286) 8 287) Law 288) Huldah 289) 39 290) refuge 291) Matthew 292) 200 293) Tombs 294) Angels 295) Noah's 296) sun 297) disobedient 298) religious 299) Your Name